Boethius

Twayne's World Authors Series

George D. Economou, Editor of Latin Literature
Long Island University

TWAS 672

Boethius

By Edmund Reiss

Duke University

Twayne Publishers • Boston

Boethius

Edmund Reiss

Copyright © 1982 by G. K. Hall & Company
All Rights Reserved
Published by Twayne Publishers
A Division of G. K. Hall & Company
70 Lincoln Street
Boston, Massachusetts 02111

Book Production by John Amburg
Book Design by Barbara Anderson

Printed on permanent/durable acid-free
paper and bound in The United States
of America.

Library of Congress Cataloging in Publication Data

Reiss, Edmund.
  Boethius.

  (Twayne's world authors series ; TWAS 672)
  Bibliography: p. 192
  1. Boethius, d. 524.   I. Title.   II. Series.
B659.Z7R44   1982   189   82–11784
ISBN 0–8057–6519–0

D. W. Robertson, Jr.

Magnum saepe certamen cum stultitiae temeritate certavimus
(De consolatione Philosophiae, I:pr. 3)

Contents

About the Author

Edmund Reiss was born in Brooklyn, New York, in 1934. He received the Ph.D. degree from Harvard University and has held professorships at Duke University, Pennsylvania State University, and Western Reserve University, as well as visiting professorships at Harvard University and Columbia University. Along with publishing more than forty-five articles in learned journals on medieval and American literature, he is the editor of two volumes of Mark Twain's writings and the author of *William Dunbar* (1979), *The Art of the Middle English Lyric* (1972), *Elements of Literary Analysis* (1967), and *Sir Thomas Malory* (1966). He is particularly interested in the history of ideas and in the classical and patristic backgrounds of literature, and is on the Board of Directors of the International Center for the Study of Christian Origins.

Preface

As the "last of the Romans and first of the Scholastics," Anicius Manlius Severinus Boethius straddles two worlds. More than anyone else he both epitomizes the achievements of classical civilization and provides a bridge between Antiquity and the Middle Ages. No matter whether one focuses on Boethius's thought or his expression, one can hardly help but recognize both his innate worth and his value to the developing modern world. But because what he offers is so rich and varied, one can scarcely hope to make an accurate assessment of his impact on Western culture.

Indeed, it is difficult to overestimate Boethius's significance, for few individuals have done so much so well, or been so instrumental in shaping the course of civilization. Rarely has any single author been so significant in framing the thought and expression of an age—or, in Boethius's case, of several ages—and so influential in so many different fields of study. In mastering the arts and sciences of his time while going beyond his age in his thought and vision, Boethius anticipates Leonardo da Vinci; and in combining the world of the scholar and poet with that of the public administrator, and in making valuable contributions in both realms, he foreshadows John Milton.

Boethius's contributions to Western civilization stem from his mastery of Greek—along with Latin—thought, and his program for transmitting Hellenic wisdom to the West. Had Boethius been able to carry out his ultimate plan of comparing and reconciling Plato and Aristotle, he would have changed the course of subsequent philosophy even more than he did. In fact, trying to imagine what Western thought would have been like had Boethius been successful with this synthesis is like trying to imagine what Western civilization would have been like had the Persians defeated the Greeks at the Battle of Marathon. As it is, Boethius's work was essential to the medieval understanding of Neoplatonism and represented all that the West knew of Aristotle for centuries. As philosopher and theologian, Boethius created the terms that represented in the main the vocabulary of Scholastic discussion, and his work on the question of universals provided a starting point for the controversy concerning realism and nominalism that dominated medieval thought. Moreover, it may be said that as his philosophical writings set the course of later Western philosophy, and as his theological works demonstrated how the method and language of logic could be meaningfully applied to matters of Christian doctrine, so his treatises on the Liberal Arts provided a foundation for medieval and modern education.

Noteworthy as all of these accomplishments of Boethius are, they must pale beside that of the *Consolation of Philosophy,* which is not only Boethius's masterpiece but one of the most significant books ever written. In its Latin original and its several translations into virtually every European language, it represented a best seller in the Western world for more than a thousand years. Along with providing the definitive word for the next millennium on such perplexing matters as the role of fortune in this world and man's free will in relation to God's foreknowledge, it also affected subsequent literature so much that its influence is virtually impossible to measure. Its blend of verse and prose, its use of allegorical personification, and its method of dialogue and debate determined much of the character of medieval and Renaissance literature. And finding a writer between the eighth and the eighteenth century untouched by the *Consolation* is like finding a man of letters of the time not influenced by the Bible.

For all of his acknowledged importance in the development of Western thought and literature, however, Boethius is at present hardly a household name in either Europe or America. It is difficult to think of any other literary figure who has plummeted from such heights of prestige to such depths of oblivion. Whereas from the Middle Ages to the nineteenth century every educated person in the Western world knew Boethius's name, now he is virtually unknown to all except advanced students of classical and medieval thought and literature. Because of this neglect, which has come about only in the twentieth century, it is necessary to insist on a greatness that would otherwise seem obvious. Still, Boethius is too important—and too interesting—to be known only by the few who have had occasion to come to him through their study of something else.

The principal barrier facing anyone wishing to study Boethius is not so much the remoteness of his age or the difficulty of his language—real as these hurdles are—but the need for expertise in mathematics, music, logic, rhetoric, theology, metaphysics, and poetry; and few modern scholars possess Boethius's breadth and depth of knowlédge. Though readers of Boethius may find common ground in the *Consolation of Philosophy,* those interested in the thought and poetry, for instance, are not likely to make the effort to study the scientific and logical treatises. Understandable as this may be, the result is the present fragmented state of Boethian studies where historians, students of literature, logicians, theologians, musicologists, and medievalists concentrate on writings pertinent to their individual fields and have little to say to those working in the other areas. While the bibliography of scholarly writings on Boethius is large, few articles or books are concerned with his total literary output. For instance, the last full-length study in English of Boethius—published forty years ago—includes only two pages on the scientific writings and three pages on the logical works.

Although as a student of literature I cannot pretend to have the expertise or the interest necessary for explicating Boethius's more technical and arcane treatises, I can at least try to make clear what each of these works is doing and relate them to each other in such a way that modern readers may acquire a sense of their meaning and accomplishment. And I can certainly suggest some of the many reassessments of Boethius and his work that have come about in the last forty years. My purpose is to introduce Boethius to the student and the general reader and to reaffirm his achievements and importance. While my particular interests are in understanding the interrelationship of the different writings and in examining how the *Consolation of Philosophy,* detached from the legend of Boethius the martyr, functions as a finely wrought piece of literature, I have tried to say something—and in some cases something new—about each work.

Chapter 1 concerns Boethius's early life and scientific writings; Chapter 2, his logical treatises; and Chapter 3, his theological tractates. Chapter 4 examines his later life and its relationship to the *Consolation of Philosophy;* Chapter 5, the argument of the *Consolation;* and Chapter 6, Boethius's patterning of his material in this work. Finally, Chapter 7 looks briefly at Boethius's legacy and its importance to the Western world.

I wish to thank the Research Council of Duke University for providing financial support for this study, and, as usual, I am particularly indebted to Louise Reiss and to Beverly Taylor for their careful readings of my manuscript and for a multitude of critical comments that made this book much clearer than it otherwise would have been.

Edmund Reiss

Duke University

Chronology

476 Visigoth Odovacar deposes Romulus, the last Roman emperor.

ca. 480 Birth of Boethius; also births of Cassiodorus and St. Benedict.

484 Acacian Schism, rupture between Eastern and Western Empires.

485 Death of Proclus.

ca. 488 Boethius orphaned, becomes ward of Senator Symmachus.

493 Ostrogoth Theodoric deposes Odovacar and rules Italy.

500 Theodoric visits Rome, perhaps meets Boethius, who soon afterward enters the employment of the king.

510 Boethius becomes sole Consul of Rome; begins Book 2 of his commentary on Aristotle's *Categories*.

ca. 512 Boethius writes *Contra Eutychen et Nestorium*.

519 End of Acacian Schism.

ca. 521 Boethius writes *De Trinitate* and *Utrum Pater*.

522 Boethius's two sons become joint Consuls of Rome.

523 Boethius named Master of the Offices by Theodoric.

524 Imprisonment of Boethius and writing of *De consolatione philosophiae*.

524–526 Deaths of Boethius and Symmachus.

526 Death of Theodoric.

Chapter One

The Master of the Arts

A World in Limbo

The Rome of Boethius's time was hardly the Rome of the Caesars or of the great Latin writers of antiquity. The classical world was past and the medieval world had not yet begun. The Rome that was the heart of the Roman empire was but a memory, and the Rome that was the center of Western Christianity was still to be.

After remaining inviolate for eight hundred years, Rome had been sacked by Alaric and the Visigoths in 410; and throughout the fifth century the city in particular and Italy in general suffered one indignity after another. Still, the decline and fall of the Western Empire was not at all a cataclysm but a gradual process lasting two centuries; and at the center of fifth-century Europe were the invading Germanic tribes. The history of this century is by and large the record of their internecine conflicts and their wars with barbarians more destructive than they. While Italy remained the prize for the conqueror, the Romans themselves had little to say about what was happening in their land or in the rest of Europe. Although the emperors in the East kept a controlling hand over the Empire, functioning as heads of both Church and State, in the West during this century the emperors were for the most part puppets. Neither the once-powerful Senate nor the once-proud people of Rome were able to resist the barbarians. And after 476, when the Visigothic chieftain Odovacar deposed Romulus, last of a series of feeble Roman emperors, the fortunes of Rome ebbed still lower.

Even though Odovacar chose not to become emperor, preferring instead to eliminate the title and to rule as Patricius, his decision resulted in Rome's further losing its prestige and identity. Ruled over by a king who functioned as a viceroy of sorts for the Eastern Emperor, Italy became a satellite state of the Eastern Empire. And when Odovacar was in turn deposed by the Ostrogoth Theodoric in 493, the situation remained by and large the same for Rome. The fact that Theodoric, like Odovacar before him, ruled well redounded to his and the Goths' credit, not to that of the Romans.

At the same time, incongruous as it may seem, Theodoric was responsible for improving remarkably the fortunes of Rome and of Western culture, at least for a while. This man of violence and treachery, who began his reign by assassinating his ostensible partner Odovacar as well as Odovacar's brother, wife, and son, was hardly a likely candidate to revive Roman prestige and culture. Moreover, besides being a barbarian—and, according to tradition, an illiterate[1]—Theodoric, like all the Goths of the time, was an Arian Christian who, in emphasizing the divinity of God the Father, denied eternity and equal divinity to the Son. That such a man, a heretic from the point of view of the orthodox Christians of Italy, could control Rome, the very center of orthodox Christianity, was even more improbable. But Theodoric brought peace and prosperity to the land for thirty-three years and effected a rebirth of thought and letters in early sixth-century Italy.[2]

What allowed Theodoric to be successful in spite of the incongruities of his situation was, first, his sense of the practical, vividly seen in the several alliances he made. He himself married the sister of Clovis, King of the Franks; his sister married the King of the Vandals; one of his daughters married the King of the Visigoths; another daughter married the heir of the King of the Burgundians; and his niece married the King of the Thuringians. After the death of his son-in-law, the King of the Visigoths, Theodoric ruled Spain and Visigothic Gaul in the name of his young grandson. In fact, by the time of Theodoric's death in 526, all the lands that had comprised the Western Empire of the Romans—except for Africa, Britain, and part of Gaul—were once again under the control of a single ruler, though now not a Roman emperor but the unlikely King of the Ostrogoths.

Along with this pragmatic sense, Theodoric had great admiration for Roman accomplishments—and this is the second reason for his success as ruler. Not only did he restore ancient Roman buildings and repair old walls, aqueducts, and drains, but he also employed the Roman administrative institutions that remained. Continuing the prudent plan of governing begun by Odovacar, Theodoric did not try to unify Goths and Romans, but instead gave each a role and responsibility in society. By making the defense of Italy the responsibility of the Goths and the administration of it that of the Romans, he was able to overcome the difficulties of ruling simultaneously two quite different peoples as well as to solve the problem of establishing his own identity— how he could be at one and the same time a Gothic king and a Roman governor. Moreover, though he functioned ostensibly as a viceroy for the Emperor in Constantinople, he came to rule Italy as practically an independent sovereign.[3]

Theodoric's acceptance of Rome extended to its religion. Tolerating all faiths, including Judaism, the Arian king wisely detached himself from theological disputes within the orthodox Catholic Church and even placed several orthodox Romans in high positions in his government. The result of these practices was that at the turn of the sixth century Ostrogothic Italy represented the hallmark of culture among the Germanic nations and held a commanding position in Western Europe. Although contemporary accounts of ambassadors at Theodoric's court being awed by its magnificence and by the wisdom of the king himself may be dismissed as hyperbole, there is no denying that under Theodoric the condition of Italy improved greatly, with a return of what the *Anonymous Valesii* makes clear is happiness, peace, order, security, and prosperity.[4] And while he did not restore the grandeur that was ancient Rome, Theodoric did effect a significant revival of learning and culture.

Throughout the fifth century in Italy classical culture had declined so much that by the end of the century it was at its lowest point. Related to this decline—if not a major source of

it—was the loss of the ability to read Greek. Rather than blame
this loss on the advent of the barbarians, it may be more accurate
to say that the loss was a product of the political decadence and
intellectual stagnation of the Roman world, which allowed the
barbarian invasions to be possible.[5] While the loss of a foreign
language might seem to be a trivial matter, the loss of Greek in
the West in the fifth and sixth centuries meant that "the concept
of culture itself was compromised."[6] Although classical and early
Christian Rome had functioned as the transmitter of Greek culture, its own contribution to learning was minimal. What might
be termed the wisdom of the ancient world, as well as the major
thought of the early Christian Church, existed mainly in Greek.
For all the works of Cicero, Seneca, Jerome, and Augustine, as
well as those of other classical and patristic Latin *auctoritates,* what
was available in the arts, sciences, philosophy, and theology in
Latin was but a fraction of that available in Greek. At a time
when few translations existed, an ignorance of Greek meant a real
loss of knowledge and, indeed, of culture itself. Not only was
the great literary and philosophical heritage of classical Greece
fast becoming lost to the Latin West, but the Roman Church
was increasingly at a lack in understanding and participating in
the theological debates that proliferated during the fifth and sixth
centuries.

The revival of learning induced by the reign of Theodoric at
the turn of the sixth century was entirely unexpected. Although
this revival has been referred to as a "splendid outburst of Greek
literature" and even as "the triumph of Hellenism in Italy," it
may be more accurately termed the last gasp of a dying classi-
cism.[7] But credit for the fact that in Italy, more than anywhere
else in the West, this moment was long drawn out may be given
to Theodoric, who in many respects actually did rule "for the
good of Rome," as the stamp—*Bono Romae*—on the bricks he
used to restore Roman monuments affirmed.[8]

Still, while acknowledging the role of Theodoric as a moving
force in this revival, we must also recognize that the Ostrogothic
king could have accomplished little without the help of Romans
whom he recruited, and that other great men of the time had

nothing to do with the king or with public office. Of these latter the outstanding example is St. Benedict, founder of Western monasticism and author of the *Rule,* an essential guide to the contemplative life throughout the Middle Ages and a work that may have been subsequently printed in more languages than any other book except the Bible. Like Benedict, even so important a figure in Theodoric's government as Cassiodorus, whose official letters provide the best record of his reign, is most significant for his nonpublic works. Cassiodorus's major contribution to history is his *Institutes,* reflecting the educational program he initiated at the end of his long life after he had withdrawn from public activity to the monastic life. While Cassiodorus may be taken to demonstrate the reciprocal nature of the relationship between Theodoric and those whose works actually brought about the revival of classical culture, an even better example is to be found in Boethius. This contemporary of both Cassiodorus and Benedict was probably the Roman most celebrated by Theodoric and certainly the figure most responsible for establishing the cultural reputation of the age.[9]

The Young Scholar

The association of Anicius Manlius Severinus Boethius with the Ostrogothic king may seem, on the surface at least, both extremely unlikely and another of the incongruities marking Theodoric's reign. Boethius, born about 480,[10] soon after Odovacar had begun his rule, was from first to last an aristocrat. His full name reflects his noble ancestry and his connection with some of the oldest and most illustrious patrician families of the Western Empire. The *gens Anicia* included in the fifth century alone numerous Consuls, two Emperors—Petronius Maximus, who ruled in 455, and Olyrius, who ruled in 472—and one Pope, Felix III, who served from 483 to 492.[11] Similarly, the *gens Manlia* may be traced back to the earliest days of Rome; and the name Severinus may indicate a relationship to the illustrious Severi family, which likewise included Emperors of Rome.[12]

Boethius's heritage also reveals a tradition of public service. His father, Aurelius Manlius Boethius, had served under Odov-

acar as Prefect of the City of Rome (twice), as Praetorian Prefect—
in effect, vice regent of the king—and, in 487, as Consul. Apparently soon after holding the Consularship, the elder Boethius
died, and his young son was entrusted as ward to a member of
the same great Aurelian family, Quintus Aurelius Memmius Symmachus. This Symmachus was the great-grandson and namesake
of the illustrious Quintus Aurelius Symmachus, who had flourished in the late fourth century as both a man of letters and a
champion of paganism and who was admired even by his oppo-
nents for his learning and his virtues. The Symmachus who was
Boethius's guardian not only inherited his ancestor's worthiness,
but he was also one of the most distinguished and important
senators of the time and also a key member of the most exclusive
circle of the Roman nobility. [13]

Although no account of Boethius's early years has come down
to us, his guardian Symmachus apparently exerted an immense
influence on him. Besides becoming Boethius's lifelong friend
and his father-in-law, after Boethius married his daughter Rus-
ticiana, Symmachus from the first may have determined Boethius's education and, by extension, the course of his life. [14]
Although Boethius may very well have begun his education before
the death of his father, the guidance of Symmachus probably
determined its particular nature and extent.

How and where Boethius received the education that made
him expert in Greek and knowledgeable in the sciences and philosophy available in this language are questions still being posed.
Although because of the scarcity of extant records no definite
answer is now possible, the questions themselves are worth asking
if for no other reason than that they allow us to appreciate the
unusualness of Boethius's accomplishment. Even though a classical education was still the privilege of the Roman aristocracy
in the fifth century, this education was uniquely literary, con-
centrating in grammar and rhetoric, not in science or philosophy,
and offering little more than the rudiments of Greek. [15] Whereas
at the time Greek studies were still possible in the Latin world
in Gaul and North Africa—only to decline there in the early
sixth century—in late fifth-century Italy the serious student,

much less the master, of Greek and its culture was a rarity. Though the Papal court claimed a few specialists, necessary in its dealings with the East; though the Scythian monk Dionysius Exiguus resided in Rome during Boethius's lifetime, translating Greek hagiography and theology; and though Cassiodorus, who may have studied with Dionysius after learning Greek at his home in the south of Italy, was in the service of Theodoric, teachers of Greek in Rome at this time were increasingly uncommon. Moreover, such teachers were neither well rewarded nor well regarded. Because the Gothic aristocracy wished to give their children a traditional Germanic education, they did not support Roman schools; and apparently Theodoric himself ruled that Goths could not enroll in Roman schools. This intellectual environment offered little encouragement to teachers of Greek. [16]

The issue is not whether Boethius was capable of learning Greek at home in Rome or how many Greek tutors may have been available to him, but rather that the climate of education in late fifth-century Rome was not at all conducive to such study. But if we may believe contemporary evidence, such as a letter of Ennodius, Bishop of Ticenum and Boethius's slightly older contemporary, which praises Boethius for his accomplishment "when he was but a schoolboy" of reading the outstanding works of both Greek and Latin authors, [17] it would seem that the young ward of Symmachus succeeded remarkably. Still, while Ennodius's words speak to the abilities of the young Boethius, they also say something about the quality of education in Rome at the time in that Boethius's accomplishments were not only remarkable but quite exceptional. For a Roman youth to achieve such competence in Greek and Hellenic culture, it seems likely that he would have had to go beyond the schools of Rome and study abroad.

Because Boethius was the ward of Symmachus, the probability of his studying in a Greek-speaking center of culture was especially high. Not only was Symmachus himself a philologist, historian, and philosopher well versed in Hellenic culture, but he and his family maintained contacts with the Eastern Empire. Perhaps more so than anyone else in Rome at the time, Sym-

machus was responsible for encouraging Hellenic culture, and
Boethius's own training may reflect his guardian's zeal and sense
of purpose. [18]

An old view, recently revived, is that Boethius as a boy studied
in Athens. Although the famous School of Athens had declined
with the death of the Neoplatonist Proclus in 485, it was not
dormant; and, moreover, Athens itself continued to enjoy a reputation as the traditional center of classical culture in general and
of philosophical studies in particular. [19] Unfortunately, the *De
disciplina scholarium,* which reports that Boethius "got strength"
at Athens when he was eighteen years of age, has been proved
spurious; and a letter of Theodoric, stating that Boethius, "in
spite of the distance, entered into the schools of Athens," where
he penetrated so deeply the doctrine to be found there that he
made it the possession of the Romans, is too ambiguous to be
conclusive. [20] That is, Theodoric may have meant that Boethius,
even though studying at home in Rome, had through his dili-
gence accomplished as much as he would have had he entered
the Athenian schools. The most that can be said in support of
Boethius's studying in Athens is, first, that it would have been
wholly in accord with Symmachus's interests and, second, that
in his later writings Boethius cites several Neoplatonic philosophers—notably Plotinus, Porphyry, Iamblichus, and Proclus—
whose ideas were particularly available at Athens in the late fifth
century.

Regardless of whether Boethius studied in Athens, it is also
possible, perhaps even probable, that he studied in Alexandria,
which after 485 replaced Athens as the center of Hellenistic
studies. As Pierre Courcelle has made clear, Boethius is heavily
indebted to the teachings of the master of this school, Ammonius
Hermiae; and his writings are very much in accord with those
of Ammonius's disciples, men who were Boethius's immediate
contemporaries. [21] Moreover, recently discovered evidence indicating that someone named Boethius was Prefect of Alexandria
from 475 to 477 makes the connection between Boethius and
Alexandria all the more possible. But if this prefect were Boethius's father or some other close relative who brought back to

Rome manuscripts containing the writings of Ammonius and his disciples, Boethius could have learned about Alexandrian Neoplatonism without going to North Africa. [22]

According to the synthesis of possibilities offered by C. J. de Vogel, Boethius might very well have spent a few years in Alexandria, probably from age eighteen to age twenty or so, perhaps after studying as a boy, say from ages eight to eighteen, in Athens. [23] Though pure speculation, this chronology at least accounts for Boethius's familiarity with the thought and writings of both Athenian and Alexandrian Neoplatonists.

A Program of Education

Regardless of how Boethius acquired his learning, he was being celebrated for it by the time he was in his early twenties. Although no record exists of Theodoric's first meeting with Boethius, or of the chain of events that led to his taking the young man into his employment, Boethius was apparently in the king's service soon after the turn of the sixth century. It is not unlikely that the young nobleman's accomplishments in Greek language, thought, and culture came to Theodoric's attention when the king made his only visit to Rome. This was in the year 500, and in the course of the six months of his residence in the city he might naturally have met the ward of the important Senator Symmachus, regardless of any special talents possessed by the youth.

That Theodoric may have immediately given the young Boethius an important position should not be surprising in the light of what we know of his other appointments. The young Cassiodorus, for instance, who was already in Rome working as a civil servant, came to Theodoric's attention when, sometime after 503, he delivered an oration in praise of the king. Largely because of this eulogy, so it would seem, Cassiodorus was elevated to the office of Quaestor, an important position amounting to Cabinet rank. As Quaestor, Cassiodorus had to clothe in fitting language everything receiving Theodoric's signature. This correspondence, which he wrote in the king's name and collected later in his life, not only offers a major record of the reigns of Theodoric and the later Gothic kings, but also provides a unique source of details about Boethius.

In one of these letters, probably an early one, circa 504, Theodoric asks Boethius to select a harper for his brother-in-law, Clovis, King of the Franks, who, apparently attracted by the fame of Theodoric's court banquets, had requested one for his court. Theodoric says via Cassiodorus that he can comply best with this request if Boethius, who is accomplished in music, would take it on himself to choose a skilled man.[24] Although this request might seem to have little to do with the knowledge of Hellenic culture, it should not be regarded as either strange or trivial. From the beginning Theodoric seems to have prized Boethius for his culture in general and for his skill in the arts and sciences of the day in particular. Not only was culture revealed in good taste and in the ability to discern, but for both Goth and Roman the proper end of theoretical learning was its practical application. For Theodoric the harper sent to the Franks would be a means of establishing further the cultural superiority of his court. As he says at the conclusion of the letter, Boethius should be sure to find someone who would be able "to charm the beastlike hearts of the Barbarians." In fulfilling his request, he adds, Boethius will also render himself famous.

A comparable practical application of learning may be found in another letter of Theodoric to Boethius, where the king cites the complaint of his Horse and Foot Guards that the coins being paid to them were not of proper weight.[25] It is not Boethius's expertise as a scholar that is being addressed here but rather his apparent ability in knowing how to handle a problem of weights and measures. Regardless of what Boethius himself valued in his learning, it would appear that for Theodoric learning was less its own reward than a practical tool.

It is this pragmatic attitude that underlies another letter to Boethius in which Theodoric writes about a request of the King of the Burgundians for two clocks, one a water clock and the other some kind of intricate sundial. Complicated as this request seems, and though it necessitates more than a theoretical understanding of physics and mechanics, there is no question in the

king's mind about Boethius's ability to effect the construction
of these clocks. In fact, Theodoric's main concern seems to be
to impress the Burgundians with the culture at his court. As he
writes, stating how politic it would be to fulfill their request,
"It will be a great gain to us that the Burgundians should daily
look upon something sent by us which will appear to them little
short of miraculous." As the next letter in Cassiodorus's collection
makes clear, the gift was apparently sent.[26] It would seem that
the young master of Hellenic culture was indeed able to carry
out the king's wishes in such matters.

When asking Boethius to construct these clocks, Theodoric
praises the young Roman's erudition in general. The passage,
already cited for what it says about Boethius and the schools of
Athens, is a famous one that deserves to be quoted in its entirety:

In your translations Pythagoras the musician, Ptolemy the astronomer,
are read by the Italians; Nicomachus the arithmetician, Euclid the
geometer, are heard by the Ausonians; Plato the theologian and Aristotle
the logician dispute in the Roman tongue; and you have given back
Archimedes the mechanician in Latin to the Sicilians. And whatever
disciplines or arts the eloquence of the Greeks has taught through
various men, Rome has received on your authority alone in the speech
of the fatherland. You have rendered these clear with such luminous
words and marked with such propriety of expression that one who had
learned them both might have preferred your work.[27]

Even allowing for hyperbole, for the various rhetorical formulas
designed to flatter Boethius and make him willing to take on
this task, and for the florid excesses that are not infrequent in
Cassiodorus's style, Theodoric's praise may be based on actual
accomplishments of the young Roman—beyond those of selecting
a harper and checking the weight of coins. In fact, the various
translations attributed to him here would seem to bear out Boethius's plans as he set them forth in a letter to Symmachus that
functions as a preface to the *De institutione arithmetica* [Principles
of Arithmetic], dated circa 503, which Boethius terms his first
work. Addressing Symmachus, Boethius states that he undertook
this writing at his request so as to make Latin readers acquainted
with the riches of Greek culture.[28]

What Boethius may be referring to here is Symmachus's long-range plan to bring Greek learning to Rome. We know of such an educational program through the dedicatory letter to Symmachus that Priscian, a Latin grammarian of Constantinople, wrote to accompany three treatises apparently commissioned by the Roman nobleman. As Priscian suggests, these treatises—on the Greek source of Latin numerical signs, on the Greek basis of Latin meter, and on Greek rhetoric—may have been designed to aid in a revival of culture in Rome.[29] Though written fifteen to twenty years after Boethius's letter accompanying his *Arithmetic,* Priscian's words may allude to the same educational program of Symmachus suggested by Boethius, and both writers may have participated in the same great plan.

Although we do not know when Symmachus began his program, we might wonder about its relationship to both Boethius's work and his education. On the one hand, Symmachus may have developed his ambitious plan after he saw what his ward was capable of accomplishing; on the other hand, Symmachus may have designed the full, and apparently unusual, education Boethius received—perhaps in Athens and/or Alexandria—as a means of preparing him to carry out this program. In any case, as Boethius makes clear in the preface to his *Arithmetic,* his plans had their impetus in Symmachus's concern with reviving classical culture by making Greek learning available to the Romans.

In this work Boethius also states his plans to treat not only arithmetic but also those other subjects—music, geometry, and astronomy—that lead to the study of philosophy. Between this statement of his intent (ca. 503) and Theodoric's praise of his accomplishment in the letter asking for his help with the clocks (ca. 507), it would seem that the young man had already gone a long way in carrying out his plans.[30] Unfortunately, we do not know precisely which works of Boethius Theodoric had in mind. Although the reference to his translation of "Nicomachus the arithmetician" is clearly to the work prefaced by Boethius's letter to Symmachus, and although extant fragments of Boethius's work on geometry bear out the king's reference to his translation of "Euclid the geometer," it is not clear that the treatise on music by Boethius which has come down to us is the translation of "Pythagoras the musician" cited by the king, although Boethius's expertise in music was the cause of his being asked to select the harper for Clovis's court.

Still, rather than think that Theodoric—or Cassiodorus, for that matter—was really concerned with stating the precise source of each of Boethius's renditions from the Greek, we should view the letter as a commendation to Boethius for his works on various subjects, in which its author uses the rhetorical device of linking each subject to a traditional authority. Regardless of Boethius's actual sources for his work on music, Pythagoras may be seen as a traditional authority, just as Ptolemy is for astronomy, Euclid for geometry, and Archimedes for mechanics. Rather than provide a bibliography of Boethius's works, Theodoric's letter may serve at most as a general indication that Boethius had already written treatises on the four subjects which represented for him steps to the study of philosophy. Moreover, the king's allusions to "Plato the theologian and Aristotle the logician" may suggest that Boethius had actually gone beyond these preliminary subjects to philosophy itself.

More important than providing a chronology of Boethius's accomplishments, Theodoric's praise suggests that Boethius's plan—and perhaps his involvement in Symmachus's program—of making Greek learning available to the Latin-speaking people of Italy was not at all a private endeavor. It was apparently known to the king and supported by him. While Theodoric's views of education may seem to be as inconclusive as his own educational attainments, we may say with confidence that he wished not only to impress his Germanic neighbors with the culture in his realm but to have the admiration of the East; and, for Theodoric, Hellenic culture was a necessary means of rivaling the Eastern Emperor. Although Cassiodorus's words suggesting Theodoric's desire to appear as a philosopher-king must make the Goth seem foolish, his concern with Hellenic culture was more than superficial, and, notwithstanding his official attitude toward Roman schools, he seems to have made sure that his daughter Amalasuntha, who succeeded him on the throne, knew both Latin and

Greek.[31] While the motives of Theodoric and Symmachus for bringing Greek culture to Italy may have been quite different, the two men seem to have been in agreement about the need for acquiring it.

The Liberal Arts

The course of studies advocated by Boethius at the beginning of his *Principles of Arithmetic* is hardly original with him or with Symmachus. It is by and large an application of the study of the Liberal Arts, which can be traced back to the educational programs of the fourth-century-B.C. Greek philosophers Isocrates and Plato. The notion of the Liberal Arts was an attempt to organize the sum total of knowledge so that it could be transmitted and applied effectively. From the beginning it seems to have been a "philosophers' curriculum," but in Roman times this *encyclios paideia* ("encyclopedic learning") was regarded, theoretically at least, as the necessary preparation for all forms of higher culture.[32] Although the actual number of the Liberal Arts varied in the different schemes—Varro, for instance, writing in the first century B.C., listed nine—it was St. Augustine, writing at the end of the fourth century of seven arts—grammar, logic, rhetoric, geometry, arithmetic, astronomy, and music—who was responsible for establishing this number as the norm. And after Martianus Capella followed Augustine's division in his influential allegorical encyclopedia *De nuptiis Philologiae et Mercurii* [The Marriage of Philology and Mercury] at the beginning of the fifth century, the number was permanently fixed at seven.[33]

In time it became customary to distinguish the first three of these subjects—all of which dealt with language—from the latter four—which treated mathematics. But the term customarily used to describe these latter four subjects, the *quadrivium,* apparently originates with Boethius's discussion at the beginning of his *Principles of Arithmetic* of the four disciplines that prepare one for the study of philosophy. These subjects, which cover the study of nature, represent for him "the quadruple way" to wisdom. Because they involve the acquisition of particular knowledge, they are, in Boethius's view, preparatory both to the study of theoretical philosophy and to the study of language—mainly logic, but also grammar and rhetoric—which teaches methods of expounding what is known.[34]

While Boethius may have intended to compile a complete course of study of the seven Liberal Arts, with renditions in Latin of the most important Greek authorities on these subjects, he was equally concerned with establishing a proper order of study. And his statement at the beginning of the *Arithmetic,* offering what amounts to an outline of "the fourfold way" and its purposes, presents what he views as the necessary sequence of its disciplines. As he says, "arithmetic is the first of the four disciplines comprising mathematics"; as the study of number, or magnitude, per se, it is basic to the other numerical studies, which are to be studied in the following order: music, the study of the relationships between numbers, or magnitudes; geometry, the science of quantity at rest, or immovable magnitude; and astronomy, the science of quantity in motion, or movable magnitude. Each of these four numerical subjects represents a necessary and distinct step along the path to wisdom, each depending on that which precedes it and each leading to that which follows it.[35]

It should be emphasized that the *quadrivium,* necessary as it is, does not represent for Boethius a discipline to be studied for its own sake. The mathematical subjects comprising it are justified insofar as they prepare one to understand philosophy, which is for him, as for Plato, the subject of pure form, and which he defines in the *Arithmetic* as "the love of wisdom." As he writes, "whoever rejects these subjects, that is, these paths to wisdom, I cannot rightly call a philosopher."[36] Regardless of Theodoric's concern with the practical application of study—its usefulness in enabling one to construct clocks, determine weights of coins, and even to select a harper—for Boethius, the *quadrivium* if effective would actually deliver the mind from the uncertainties of the sensory world to the certainty of intelligence and prepare it for abstract reasoning. What has come down to us of Boethius's work on the *quadrivium* gives us a fairly clear idea of his procedure and, moreover, enables us to understand how he uses his Greek authorities.

The Arithmetical Basis

The *Principles of Arithmetic,* as Boethius himself acknowledges, is based on the *Introduction to Arithmetic* of Nicomachus of Gerasa, who flourished at the beginning of the second century A.D. Nicomachus's work was not an original mathematical treatise but rather, as its title indicates, an introduction to the subject. It should in fact be regarded as a textbook or manual, offering a concise description and a systematic exposition of the elements of arithmetic. As such it makes use of a theory of numbers that goes back through Aristotle and Plato to the earliest discoveries of Pythagoras and his school in the sixth century B.C. As a Neopythagorean, Nicomachus was very much interested in the philosophical and mystical theory of number; and it is not coincidental that his work should have interested Neoplatonic thinkers, who were likewise attracted to numerology: Apuleius (second century) translated it into Latin; Iamblichus (fourth century) wrote a commentary on it; and Boethius's contemporary John Philoponus wrote glosses on it that are extant.[37]

For the ancient Romans, who were interested mainly in the practical applications of mathematics and not, like the Greeks, in mathematical theory, geometry—because of its importance to surveying—had been the primary science, with arithmetic but an ancillary one useful merely as a tool for computation. Roman interest in Nicomachus's *Introduction* was so great, however, that this work soon became a standard manual in Roman schools and preempted the position long held by Euclid's *Elements of Mathematics,* the basic work for the study of geometry. Moreover, arithmetic came to replace geometry as the basis of mathematics. This shift may be due in large measure to the increasing interest in the Latin West in Pythagorean number symbolism, manifested in the inherent relationship between Neopythagoreanism and late Roman Neoplatonism, and to the interest of Christian thinkers—including St. Augustine—in the symbolic sense of numbers as well as in the practical application of arithmetic to compute the movable feasts of the Church, such as Easter. Still, it was the particular accomplishment of Nicomachus in his *Introduction* that was the efficient cause of the new interest in arithmetic.[38]

The version of Nicomachus's work made by Boethius amounted to a free translation of it. As Boethius writes at the outset, his purpose was to translate, to paraphrase, to abridge, and in general to clarify the Greek treatise for his Latin audience.[39] Although he has been criticized for ignoring some of the fine points of Nicomachus's treatise and for displaying "too little originality, independence and progressiveness, and too much prolixity," he may have been purposely trying to simplify his source.[40] Boethius more often expands than condenses the Greek, but these additions by and large spell out what has already been stated or provide further numerical examples and charts. While Boethius's "exhaustive explanation" alters the succinctness of Nicomachus, his method demonstrates not a lack of understanding on his part but a desire to make this textbook on arithmetic available to an audience which lacked a knowledge not only of Greek but of the basic science of numbers.

Regardless of whether or not Boethius intended his work to rival the earlier—now lost—Latin version of Apuleius,[41] it seems clear that his translation was designed for an audience quite different from that addressed by the eminent Neoplatonist a few decades after Nicomachus's original. In his attempt to bring classical learning to his Roman audience, Boethius was preparing them to think and reason clearly, and he was hardly concerned about being original or profound. At the same time, Boethius's version does not seem to have replaced Apuleius's translation immediately. That Apuleius's rendition was still extant in the sixth century may be attested by Cassiodorus in Book 2 of his *Institutes*, the program of secular studies he established late in his life. In his chapter on arithmetic—which is, as it was for Boethius, at the head of his treatment of the mathematical sciences—Cassiodorus notes that the first scholar to provide a Latin translation of Nicomachus's "diligent explanation of this science" was Apuleius, and the second was Boethius.[42] Since Cassiodorus's procedure in the *Institutes* is to cite Latin translations that his readers might use, it is likely that Apuleius's version was still available. If so, it may be significant that Cassiodorus himself chose to base most of his chapter on arithmetic on Boethius's rendition, perhaps indicating further that Boethius's procedure of simplification and clarification was precisely what the Latin speakers of Italy needed.

It was, moreover, by and large through Boethius's version of Nicomachus that the Latin Middle Ages received its understanding of numbers. In fact, the *Principles of Arithmetic* remained an authoritative textbook for more than a thousand years. Whatever else Boethius's claim to fame may be, it is necessarily as an arithmetician. Not only do medieval allegories depict him as an authority, but a sculpture of the Liberal Arts on Chartres Cathedral seems to portray him as the representative of arithmetic.[43]

Numerical Proportion and Harmony

The second discipline in Boethius's program of study, music, is fully treated in his *De institutione musica* [Principles of Music]. As with his treatment of arithmetic, Boethius is interested in the subject at hand less as a discipline to be investigated for its own sake than as a way of preparing the mind for the study of philosophy. Because, on the surface at least, this work seems to be an amalgamation of several Greek and Latin works on the subject of music, it is not as easy to describe as the *Principles of Arithmetic.* Still, inasmuch as it regards music as mainly an expression of numerical proportion, the work may be understood as being wholly within Platonic and Pythagorean tradition. Regardless of the various authorities cited, the first three—if not the first four—books comprising the *Music* are closely connected in their mathematical theory and may well represent a complete unit with a single source. This source is most likely Nicomachus of Gerasa, who seems to have been the only pertinent author to have been a Pythagorean and to have had access to the different authorities cited by Boethius. Not only does Boethius again use his *Introduction to Arithmetic,* he may be following a compilation of Nicomachus's works that included this *Introduction* along with an *Enchiridion* [Manual] *of Music*—a short, rather superficial summary of the science of music—and an *Introduction to Music*—a longer, more general treatise on the subject, available now in only a few brief fragments.[44]

Along with using Nicomachus, Boethius in the fifth and last book of his treatise translates and paraphrases the first book of the *Manual of Harmonics* of Ptolemy (second century A.D.). But while this work is compatible with Pythagorean tradition, it does not offer a natural conclusion to the first four books. Moreover, Boethius's rendition of this first book of the *Harmonics* is incomplete, although the fact that he includes headings for several of Ptolemy's final chapters would seem to indicate that he intended to finish it. Still, even a completed Book 1 of the *Harmonics* would not offer a logical conclusion to the *Principles of Music.* Perhaps Boethius had intended to translate all three books of Ptolemy's work, and, indeed, had he done so, he would have gone beyond the harmony of sonorous music to the harmony of human beings and the universe, which, although touched on by Boethius with a promise of further treatment, is never referred to again.[45]

Although we shall probably never know why Boethius did not finish translating Ptolemy, it is not likely that he lost interest in the mathematical disciplines as he himself moved to the philosophy of Plato and Aristotle. If Boethius's work was indeed part of a program—perhaps one inaugurated by Symmachus and supported by Theodoric—the educational level of Boethius is incidental. And if Boethius was indeed working on the various disciplines of the *quadrivium* in the order given in his letter to Symmachus—arithmetic, music, geometry, and astronomy—he must have done more after his treatise on music since his work on geometry and astronomy is well attested. Perhaps, given the complexity of the *Principles of Music,* Boethius was unable to unify his sources in a way totally satisfactory to him; and the unfinished state of the work may indicate that he intended to return to it to put everything together more effectively. Still, we should appreciate what Boethius attempted and indeed what he accomplished in this work. Moreover, had he completed it, perhaps adding the two additional books of Ptolemy's *Harmonics,* he would have produced the most comprehensive musical work of classical antiquity.[46]

As to Boethius's method of rendering his sources, we may say—especially on the basis of Book 5, which may be easily compared to Ptolemy's treatise—that he generally paraphrases. Sometimes he condenses or amplifies greatly, but when basic premises are involved and when technical matters are being discussed, he tends to offer literal translation. In other words, his method in the *Principles of Music* would seem to be essentially that of the *Principles of Arithmetic*. Indeed, given the common source represented by Nicomachus's *Introduction to Arithmetic*, Boethius's *Music* may not only have been composed soon after the *Arithmetic* but may also represent a direct continuation of the earlier work, with differences in style and vocabulary in the two works largely due to differences in subject matter.[47]

The fact that this work on music is no more an original treatise than that on arithmetic should not cause us to conclude that Boethius is, even at this point in his literary career, essentially a compiler, limited to paraphrasing authorities and linking them together but unable to provide a synthesis of his own.[48] We must remember that Boethius's point is less to write his own contribution to the science or theory of music than to make traditional Pythagorean views of the subject meaningful to his uninformed Latin audience. Like the *Principles of Arithmetic*, the *Principles of Music* was meant to be a textbook, not a scholarly monograph. To say that because Boethius compiled a textbook he was unable at the time to produce an original work on the subject is not to give him his *donné*. We should also realize that differences between Boethius's words and those of his sources represent most likely not errors of translation on his part but conscious alterations; for along with offering traditional Greek musical authorities to his Latin audience, Boethius wishes to show the proper role of music in the *quadrivium*. When his authorities are not in accord with his own Pythagorean position, he evaluates and criticizes them and even alters their words.[49]

In particular Boethius wishes to take the student of music— that is, one who has already mastered his *Principles of Arithmetic*— to an understanding of numerical proportion and harmony. As he states in his *Arithmetic* and as he reaffirms in his *Music*, proportion, not sound, is the basis of music. Although one may discern musical proportions through sonorous music, recognizing tones and harmonics is but the first step to understanding the numerical proportions that are the source of all music. Boethius insists that his reader go beyond sonorous, or instrumental, music (*musica instrumentis constituta*) to the music of man himself (*musica humana*), the harmony of proportion in human beings, and even further to the music of the universe (*musica mundana*), where one may comprehend pure proportion or the idea of harmony itself.

Whereas instrumental music is audible, the other two kinds of music are inaudible, representing the harmony that is the basis of sonorous music. The music of the universe, the highest kind of music, may be discerned in the relationships that hold together the elements, that cause the variation of the seasons, and that determine the movements of the stars. This music is the principle of creation and the source of all other music. Human music, the human expression of natural harmony, is in effect man's participation in the music of the universe and a duplication in the microcosm of what exists in the macrocosm. Though the instrumental music produced by man is an external music, it has extraordinary power over man's physical and mental condition and causes responses in man's soul. While lascivious men naturally delight in lascivious melodies and martial men in martial melodies, the behavior of these men can be altered by the music they hear. Since this music has the power to change the vicious into the virtuous, it is an especially powerful force. As a moral force, capable of healing illnesses of both the body and the soul, instrumental music imitates the harmony that governs the universe.[50]

While this threefold division of the kinds of music is hardly original with Boethius—it is implicit in Platonic and Pythagorean thought—it is clearly expressed in Latin for the first time here. For Boethius this division represents a real hierarchy, as may be seen in his discussion of the true *musicus* ("musician"), who, through his reason, not his senses, knows the proportions of music. One is not a *musicus* through being involved in the playing of music. Performers, in fact, are mere manual workers, even slaves, governed by their tasks of performance and by the instruments they play; and composers—including poets—are little better since they are impelled to music not by reason or philosophy but by a certain natural instinct or inspiration. The *musicus,* on the other hand, is he who studies music as a rational science, not he who is involved in the laborious skill of manufacturing it. The *musicus,* wholly concerned with reason, is able to know and judge modes and rhythms, varieties and combinations of melodies, and the achievements of composers. For Boethius, the true "musician" is thus what we might term a critic or musicologist.[51]

Music, like the other disciplines in Boethius's *quadrivium,* must be understood as basically protreptic, or exhortatory. Instead of being simply an introduction to the subject of music, focusing on such matters as its invention, divisions, and uses, the *Principles of Music* uses the subject as a means of expressing numerical proportion. It is Boethius's exhortation to his reader to contemplate and judge the harmonious relationships of quantity, to go beyond tangible expressions of proportion—as may be discerned in sonorous music—to the essence of harmony. Mathematics for Boethius functions first and foremost to set the mind free from matter, and while arithmetic introduces the student to the numerical expression of quantity, music takes the enlightened mind a step further toward reasoning about the pure and incorporeal essences of philosophy.[52]

Boethius's procedure is wholly Platonic in its desire to go beyond the senses to reason and to arrive at an essence. For Boethius as for Plato music is a tool of philosophy, not as for Aristotle a part of philosophy. Had Boethius approached music as an Aristotelian, he would doubtless have proceeded inductively, speculating on practical problems such as performance, analysis, or composition. Instead, he proceeds deductively, using mathematical laws of related numbers to deduce and judge harmony. Rather than conclude from this that at the time of his *Music* Boethius had not as yet confronted Aristotle, we should recognize that the exigencies of his *quadrivium,* where all the subjects are designed to take the student to philosophy, make his procedure necessarily Platonic. To look in the *Principles of*

Music for an account of the actual musical practices of the early sixth century, or to criticize Boethius for neglecting the practical aspects of music and for treating it in "an excessively theoretical way as a sub-division of mathematics" is to fail to understand the purpose of the work.[53] It is also to fail to appreciate Boethius's accomplishment in rendering the ancient authorities into Latin.

The *Principles of Music* shows that Boethius had a thorough knowledge of Greek musical theory, but he should hardly be thought of as "a mere translating machine." While he limited himself to transmitting in Latin a few particular texts by Nicomachus and Ptolemy, he, at the same time, added and deleted material and qualified and corrected his sources according to his own understanding and his Platonic purpose.[54] It is difficult to take seriously the suggestion that Boethius himself was not responsible for synthesizing the Greek material, that he actually copied another Latin writer—probably Albinus, whom he twice cites—who brought together all of this material shortly before Boethius, and that he himself wrote only the introduction.[55]

At the same time, it is not clear what to make of the fact that Cassiodorus, in the chapter on music in his *Institutes,* after listing Greek and Latin authorities, cites as first among Latin writers "Albinus, a man of distinction," whose "compendious work" on music Cassiodorus says he read in Rome. The chapter does not mention Boethius at all, though the title *vir magnificus* ("man of distinction"), applied here to Albinus, is otherwise used by Cassiodorus to refer only to Boethius.[56] Perhaps Cassiodorus is alluding to a treatise by Albinus—a minor, even an obscure, writer whose treatise on music is now lost—and to another by Boethius, the "man of distinction." Or, on the other hand, perhaps Cassiodorus means to cite an authoritative work that appeared in the Latin of Albinus and also in that of the "man of distinction," Boethius. In any case, the notion that Boethius merely copied a work by another Latin writer is not at all in accord with what we know about his practice elsewhere. It is "somewhat improbable," to say the least, that Boethius would have written a treatise on music that had exactly the same contents as that of a recent Latin predecessor. Moreover, Boethius's sources were Greek, not

Latin, and if satisfactory Latin texts of these already existed, neither Boethius nor Symmachus would have been likely to include them in a program making Greek sources available to the Latin world.[57]

The Latin writer on music who best provides a perspective for understanding Boethius's accomplishment is St. Augustine, whose *De musica* dates from the late fourth century. Both writers, insofar as they are Neoplatonists and Neopythagoreans, explore the mathematical character of music and advocate what may be termed the music of judgment. Aware of the moral function of music, both denounce the illusions of sensory response and the dangers of the music that appeals to the senses. But while meeting as theoreticians on the terrain of musical aesthetics, Augustine and Boethius are far apart in their technical concerns. On the basis of what Augustine actually wrote—his work is even less complete than Boethius's treatise—he would seem to be mainly concerned with rhythm, while Boethius, neglecting this element, offers a thorough examination of musical consonances and scales. Although we do not know how the completed works might have compared, as they stand, they give little indication that Boethius knew the musical work of his great predecessor. Both works were in fact standard reading for the Middle Ages, but Boethius's work remained, even for the practitioner of music, the most authoritative work on musical theory for almost a thousand years. It was so standard an authority that at the end of the fourteenth century Geoffrey Chaucer could use it for comic purposes by having the fox in his *Nun's Priest's Tale* cite Boethius as the yardstick for measuring the musical abilities of the cock.[58]

Continuing the *Quadrivium*

The only other portion of Boethius's *quadrivium* extant are fragments of what may be his *De institutione geometrica* [Principles of Geometry], apparently a redoing of the *Elements* of Euclid (third century B.C.). This work is attested not only by Theodoric's reference to Boethius's translation of "Euclid the geometer" but also by Cassiodorus's chapter on geometry in the *Institutes*. Boethius—again called the *vir magnificus*—is the only Latin translator of Euclid to be cited here, and Cassiodorus adds that if Boethius's volume is read carefully, the subject of geometry "will be distinctly and clearly understood." Even more significantly, Cassiodorus's organization of Euclid's fifteen books into four parts, an organization that becomes the standard way of approaching the study of geometry, stems from Boethius's version.[59]

Unfortunately, neither the translation of "Ptolemy the astronomer" nor that of "Archimedes the mechanician" alluded to in Theodoric's praise of Boethius's accomplishments now exists. Still, there is strong evidence that the *Astronomy*, perhaps called *De astrologia*, a rendition of some version of Ptolemy's *Almagest*—if not of the original, perhaps of a shorter manual by Ptolemy or of a handbook in the Ptolemaic tradition—existed not only at the time of Cassiodorus, whose chapter on astronomy in the *Institutes* may contain excerpts from it, but also in the tenth century.[60] The evidence for the existence of a *Mechanics,* based on works of Archimedes (third century B.C.), is less certain; and after all, the subject of mechanics was not a part of Boethius's *quadrivium.* Still, someone able to construct an hydraulic water clock and an elaborate sundial might well know the basic writings on both astronomy and mechanics, and recent authorities consider it "probable" that Boethius did indeed paraphrase some work of Archimedes.[61]

Models of Synthesis

Cassiodorus's *Institutes,* an outline of learning that serves as an introduction to the study of the Liberal Arts, not only shows something of how Boethius's translations and paraphrases were viewed by a contemporary, but it also illustrates what an encyclopedic synthesis of the arts was like after Boethius. But along with recognizing the immediate influence of Boethius's scientific program, we might also examine some of the syntheses of learning that existed before him. Although he knew educational programs from as early as Plato's *Republic,* we must limit our brief inquiry to those that may have been actual models for him.

The corpus of writings of Nicomachus of Gerasa may seem to be such a model. Not only did Boethius use his work in his

Arithmetic and *Music,* but it has recently been suggested that Nicomachus may have played a dominant role in Boethius's *Geometry* and *Astronomy* as well.[62] Whether or not this influence is real, we should note that Boethius chose to go beyond Nicomachus and use other Greek sources in compiling the works in his *quadrivium,* and, even more important, that because Nicomachus was not concerned with translation, his work and that of Boethius were of necessity significantly different. More immediate models for Boethius's educational program would come from the world of Latin letters.

Two likely candidates for models are Martianus Capella and St. Augustine, both flourishing in the early fifth century and both the authors of works well known by Boethius. But Martianus's account of the Liberal Arts, incorporated in his allegorical poem *De nuptiis Philologiae et Mercurii,* is limited and elementary, offering little more than is found in a manual like that by Cassiodorus. Moreover, since Boethius's level of competence was "distinctly higher" than that of Martianus, there is little prospect of finding definite traces of Martianus's influence on Boethius's program.[63] Augustine, on the other hand, along with setting up educational programs in several works, notably his *De ordine* and *De doctrina Christiana,* began an actual project of compiling individual manuals on the Liberal Arts. As Augustine explains in his *Retractions,* he desired to attain to spiritual truths through secular knowledge, and while awaiting baptism at his retreat outside Milan, he occupied himself with this project. What he actually completed was a treatise on grammar and six books of his work on music. Unfortunately, he explains, his notes on the other five arts were lost.[64]

What is most important about this project of Augustine is not the individual works he wrote but the point he makes clear— that secular knowledge is an essential part of Christian studies. It is this principle, as stated in the *De doctrina Christiana,* that justifies Cassiodorus's procedure in his *Institutes,* where Book 1, on sacred learning, is followed by a book on secular knowledge. And it may also be this principle that inspired the young Boethius. Regardless of what Greek Neoplatonic syntheses of knowledge Boethius may have known, the famous synthesis attempted by Augustine may have provided a justification as well as a procedure for his work.

We know that Boethius was a practical administrator, capable of handling all sorts of daily difficulties during the reign of Theodoric. Constructing clocks, ascertaining weights, and selecting harpers most likely represent only three of many tasks given to him and successfully accomplished by him. But regardless of his practical abilities and regardless of how Theodoric valued his work, we should see in Boethius one who understood the proper nature of "arithmetic by which earth and the heavens are ruled" and who in his *quadrivium* set forth for the Latin world a program of studies that would enable the work of the greatest minds of the past to be continued.[65]

Chapter Two

The Explorer of Language

The Porphyrian Introduction

What most likely follows Boethius's work on the *quadrivium* as the next step in his program of studies leading to philosophy is a series of works based on Aristotle's logic. Although Boethius wrote that he was determined to translate and comment on all the works of Aristotle that came into his hands and that he wished to show the fundamental philosophical agreement between Plato and Aristotle, the only Aristotle he seems to have translated are treatises comprising the *Organon,* a collection put together by Aristotle's pupils after his death in 322 B.C.[1] While the term *logic* apparently did not acquire its current sense until used in the second century A.D. by Alexander of Aphrodisias, the scope of the study called logic was determined by the contents of this *Organon,* the first systematic examination of the formal structure of reasoning. Although the works comprising it—the *Categories, On Interpretation,* the *Prior* and *Posterior Analytics,* the *Topics,* and its appendix, *On Sophistical Refutations*—were written by Aristotle at different dates and without being part of a single plan, they came to form an ordered whole; and Boethius's intention seems to have been to proceed through them in what was probably in his time the traditional order.[2]

Although Boethius's plans are audacious, they are not unique to him. Before him, others, notably the third-century Greek philosopher Porphyry, had been concerned with harmonizing Plato and Aristotle; and Boethius's mid-fourth-century Latin predecessor Marius Victorinus seems to have anticipated his plan of translating and commenting on the *Organon.*[3] Moreover, Porphyry wrote an introduction, or *Isagoge,* that, though intended to introduce the first of Aristotle's collected works, the *Categories,* became the standard introduction to the entire *Organon* and was translated into Latin by Victorinus. While Boethius knew the prefatory nature of the *Isagoge,* he purposely began his study of Aristotle's logic with it, using Victorinus's translation as the basis of his commentary. As Nicomachus seems to have been most responsible for Boethius's entry into the mathematical works of the *quadrivium,* so Porphyry and Victorinus—who was himself guided by Porphyry—provided Boethius with his entry into the logical works of the *Organon.*

Boethius's initial commentary on the *Isagoge* is interesting for several reasons including the fact that it represents Boethius's first attempt at creating a fictional framework for his thought. Although Porphyry at the outset of his work addresses one Chrysaorius, who had asked him for help in understanding Aristotle's *Categories,* the account that follows is in the form of straightforward exposition without any further mention of Chrysaorius. Victorinus echoes this form in his rendition even though he more freely adapts than translates, and even though he changes Greek names to Latin ones, including replacing the name of Chrysaorius with that of Menantius. Boethius, however, extends the fiction, and in his commentary establishes a fictional dialogue between himself and a friend called Fabius. This dialogue is in the literary mode of the Socratic and Ciceronian dialogue, though if Boethius had a particular model in mind, it may well have been not one of Plato's or Cicero's works but rather Porphyry's commentary on Aristotle's *Categories,* the *Exposition through Question and Answer,* which is likewise in the form of a dialogue.

Boethius's extension of the fictional dialogue is surely original with him. He shows Fabius and himself meeting one winter night in the mountains of Aurelia outside Rome, and there, while the wind blows violently, they begin to discuss the usefulness of commentaries in which learned men interpret and clarify difficult matters. The friends focus in particular on Marius Victorinus, described as "quite the most learned orator of his time," and his translation of the *Isagoge,* which Fabius asks Boethius to explain to him. As E. K. Rand describes this opening, "Never had a dialogue been given such a setting; it suggests that the passion of these friends for the eternal verities was such that they forgot that it was night and winter." Indeed, Boethius seems to have chosen as his setting the wilderness on a cold, stormy night precisely because of its inappropriateness as a context for a placid discourse on the mind. Instead of explaining this setting, or relating it to Boethius's life—as Luca Obertello does by saying that Boethius's family probably had a villa off the Aurelian road and that the dialogue occurred before he got married—we should realize that the setting is a purposeful fiction designed to contrast the physical with the intellectual.[4]

The parallel between Porphyry's explanation of Aristotle to Chrysaorius and Boethius's explanation of Porphyry to Fabius would also seem to be intentional. What follows, however, is more than an explication of Porphyry; it is also a criticism of Victorinus. After reproducing much of Victorinus's text in his explication—so much in fact that even though the translation itself is now lost, it can be reconstructed on the basis of Boethius's quotations and allusions—Boethius criticizes him for modifying Porphyry's definitions and classifications, for being imprecise and obscure, and for lacking understanding of the Greek original.[5] Although scholars have thought that during the course of working with Victorinus's translation, Boethius increasingly realized its inadequacies, we should also recognize the possibility that the fictional setting of his *Dialogue* may in part have been designed to establish Victorinus as a target for this criticism. If, moreover, as Pierre Hadot has suggested, Victorinus had actually tried to pass himself off as author of the *Isagoge*, presenting it as in effect *his* introduction to Aristotle—which may explain his substitution of names—Boethius may well have intended to correct this impression. At the beginning where Fabius asks specifically to know what the learned Victorinus wrote on "the *Isagoge* of Porphyry, that is, on the introduction to the *Categories* of Aristotle which he is said to have translated," we may see that Boethius's point is to do more than explain the *Isagoge* itself.[6] The initial focus on Victorinus and praise of him may represent an ironic way of proceeding. The young Boethius, while purporting to pay respect to this venerable translator—who was so much in regard during his own lifetime that his statue was erected in a Roman forum—may set the stage so that his readers can see for themselves the inadequacy of Victorinus's approach in general and of his translation in particular.

A major problem with Victorinus's work is his inadequate understanding of the function of philosophy. As Boethius defines philosophy early in his *Dialogue,* it is the science which, proceeding from the wisdom of God and leading back to Him, illuminates and purifies the mind with the light of truth. As in the *Arithmetic,* Boethius calls philosophy the love of wisdom, but here he emphasizes that the proper pursuit of it is not a concern with "particular arts or other skills" but with "the enduring intelligence which alone is the primeval principle of things." For Victorinus, however, philosophy was "a certain kind of discourse," one included in the standard fifteen rhetorical figures. And on the basis of this presupposition he seems to have translated not only the *Isagoge* but other treatises in the *Organon.* Given the definition of philosophy that Boethius offers near the beginning of his commentary, there can be little doubt that he intended for his *Dialogue* to undercut Victorinus's treatment of the subject and to highlight the defects of his grammatical-rhetorical stance.[7]

It is not at all surprising that after this work Boethius went on to write his own translation of the *Isagoge* as well as a second commentary. What is surprising is that the first commentary is extant, for if Boethius had indeed been so unhappy with what he could do using Victorinus's translation, he might well have wished to leave the *Dialogue* unfinished or at least to suppress it. But not only does this work still exist, it is extant in a great number of manuscripts, some of which include the *Dialogue* along with Boethius's second commentary.[8] The explanation would seem to be that in using his initial explication of Porphyry to disassociate himself from Victorinus—who is not even mentioned in the second commentary—Boethius provides a basis for his own work of translation. In looking at this initial commentary, with its citations of Victorinus's translation, and then at Boethius's own translation and second commentary, his audience could see for themselves how original and how useful Boethius's work really is.

At the same time, for all of Boethius's desire to detach his work from that of Victorinus, some of his basic distinctions use the terminology of his predecessor. For instance, after making the traditional division of *philosophia* into theoretical and practical, Boethius discusses the object of *theoretica* as knowledge of three kinds of beings, which he calls *intellectibilia, intelligibilia,* and *naturalia*. As Boethius explains, the intellectibles refer to immutable or pure forms (which are the proper subject of theology) that exist outside matter; the intelligibles comprise all created spiritual beings, including human souls which, though originally intellectibles, have become imprisoned in matter; and the natures, or natural beings, are those beings whose forms are inseparable from matter and which cannot exist except as corporeal entities. Because these distinctions are in neither the *Isagoge* nor Victorinus's translation—insofar as the reconstructions reveal—they have been thought to be original with Boethius. But not only do the concepts have their roots deep in Neoplatonic thought, the terms themselves would seem to have been coined by Victorinus in his theological treatises. Boethius's major contribution here is to remove much of the obscurity found in Victorinus.[9]

In the two books that comprise the *Dialogue* Boethius by and large offers a literal comment on the various sections of the *Isagoge*, responding to the questions of Fabius—who from time to time reads a brief part of Victorinus's translation—and explaining Porphyry's notion of the five predicables, or ways of designating what can be attributed to any subject. These—genus, species, difference, property, and accident—are borrowed by Porphyry from terms found in Aristotle's *Topics* and used by him to explain Aristotle's *Categories*. Subsequent commentators, however, including Boethius, found it necessary in turn to explain these terms.[10]

The explanation of these predicables concerns Boethius even more in his second commentary on the *Isagoge*—which may be called the *Commentarius* to distinguish it from the *Dialogue*—but now he is able to use his own translation. In this second commentary he does away with all sense of a fictional framework and with all pretense of dialogue, and instead gives his attention exclusively to the continuous exposition of Porphyry's ideas. As he explains at the beginning, when one is seeking understanding, he should be concerned not with "the wit and charm of splendid oration" but with "the expression of unadulterated truth."[11] While this statement suggests the inadequacy of Victorinus, whose translation of Porphyry, though deficient in philosophy, was rich in rhetoric, it may also apply to Boethius's own *Dialogue,* which he has now gone beyond. But while recognizing that Boethius chose to reject the dialogue format, we should not necessarily conclude that he found it an inadequate way of treating serious philosophical matters, since after all he was familiar with the dialogues of Plato, Cicero, and even Porphyry. Rather, Boethius may have felt that a method of continuous exposition— which he perhaps learned from the commentary on the *Isagoge* made by the Alexandrian Neoplatonist Ammonius Hermiae[12]— was most appropriate for approaching logic since this was Aristotle's own method as well as that of Porphyry after the opening of the *Isagoge.*

Spelling out his new method of translation, Boethius writes, "I am afraid I have fallen victim in my translation to the fault of the faithful interpreter, in that I have rendered every word, expressed or implied, with a word." This statement represents in effect a continuation of Boethius's correction of Victorinus, who was in the habit of not only using a great variety of Latin words to render a single Greek term, but of failing to make clear the real significance of the original term. While Boethius's first commentary, the *Dialogue,* demonstrated the need to consider the *Isagoge* on other than traditional grammatical-rhetorical grounds, Boethius's second commentary shows how it really works as philosophy.[13]

But notwithstanding his claim of being "the faithful interpreter" of Porphyry, Boethius proceeds in his translation by paraphrasing, amplifying, summarizing, and simplifying as he wishes. To make certain that his reader can follow him without great effort, he frequently alters the arrangement of details and repeats himself, either to clarify Porphyry's arguments or to shore them up when he thinks that they are too brief. While Boethius's verbosity and relentless spelling out of points cause the tight logic and fine precision of Porphyry's arguments to disappear, and while Boethius's proud statement that he used a word for every word expressed *or implied* in his original may be taken to show what is wrong with his work and why it has been judged inferior to its original, we should realize that Boethius is concerned not with matters of style but, as he states, with "unadulterated truth"; to get at this, he does not feel that he can leave anything in Porphyry's thought uncertain or even implicit.[14] In Boethius's view his method here represents a principle of translation that he would like to see established, as his statement of procedure at the beginning of the *Commentarius* suggests: "I would think I had been successful if books of philosophy could be composed in Latin by painstaking and complete translation, until nothing more were missing from the Greek." While reaffirming his view in the letter to Symmachus at the beginning of the *Arithmetic* about making Greek learning available to Romans, this statement insists further that Latin translations be accurate and complete.[15]

   Although it is not our intention to discuss the philosophical issues brought out in Boethius's commentaries, we can hardly avoid one of these, for Boethius's words on the nature of general ideas, or universals, may well be the most far-reaching contribution made in all of his logical works. At the beginning of the *Isagoge,* Porphyry announces his intention to put aside the investigation of "certain profound questions" concerning genera and species: first, whether these exist in themselves or are simply conceptions of the mind; second, supposing they exist, whether they are corporeal or incorporeal; and, third, supposing they are incorporeal, whether they exist apart from sensible objects or only as united with them. Instead of taking up these matters, says Porphyry, he will make clear how the ancient philosophers dealt with genus, species, and the other predicables. The "profound questions" avoided by Porphyry amount to choosing between the views of reality associated with Aristotle on the one hand and

Plato on the other. But rather than follow Porphyry's discretion in avoiding problems of advanced metaphysics at the outset of a treatise designed for beginners, Boethius in both of his commentaries chose to comment on the "profound questions"; and in doing so, he triggered a controversy that marked Western philosophical thought for most of the next thousand years.

Part of the difficulty is that Boethius would seem to offer two opposed views. In the *Dialogue* he makes the point that "it is impossible to doubt that genera and species really exist," apparently acknowledging the two as separate. In the *Commentarius*, however, Boethius says that although genera and species "exist in connection with sensible things, we know them separate from bodies," suggesting that even though genera and species do not exist separately, we may think of them as such.[16] Whereas Boethius's first position is in accord with the views of Plato, his second, as Boethius acknowledges, is borrowed from Alexander of Aphrodisias, a second-century interpreter of Aristotle. But this second position should not be regarded as Boethius's own view, for as he says in the *Commentarius* he is following Aristotle and not offering his own opinion:

Plato thinks that genera, species and other universals are not only known separately from bodies, but also that they exist and subsist outside them; while Aristotle thinks that incorporeals and universals are really objects of knowledge, but that they exist only in sensible things. I had no intention of deciding which of these opinions is true, for that rests with a higher philosophy. I clung to Aristotle's opinion, therefore, not because I favored it particularly but because this book happened to be written in view of the *Categories,* whose author is Aristotle.[17]

Even though Boethius seems to have proceeded most commendably by deferring to Aristotle, whose positions he is after all concerned with explaining, his fairness—which has been criticized as fence-sitting—led to the issue's being raised over and over throughout the Middle Ages; and most of these discussions began with a reference to Boethius and his translation of Porphyry's questions. In choosing to comment on Porphyry's "profound questions," Boethius stimulated great interest in the signification of terms and in the problems of meaning; and regardless of his intention, the interest and subsequent discussion went beyond his answers.[18]

Aside from the matter of universals, the beginning of Boethius's *Commentarius*—indeed most of Book 1—is dominated by his consideration of the nature of logic, an issue merely touched on in the *Dialogue*. Boethius is specifically concerned with whether logic should be viewed as a part of philosophy—as it was for the Stoics—or as its instrument—as it was for the Aristotelians. After offering arguments for both positions, Boethius states that surely nothing prevents logic from serving at the same time as both part and instrument. In that it is the art of distinguishing what is true from what is false or merely probable, logic has its own object and is therefore a part of philosophy. At the same time, since logic is useful to all the other parts of philosophy, it may be viewed as their instrument. As such, he says, it is like the hand and the eye, which, while being parts of the body, are also aids to it: "So too the logical discipline is a part of philosophy, since philosophy alone is the mistress of it, but is an instrument too because by it the sought-for truth of philosophy is investigated." This solution—which he may have taken from Ammonius's commentary, where credit for the synthesis is given to Plato—may be seen justifying Boethius's including the study of logic as preparation for the study of philosophy, and his working in particular on Aristotle's *Organon,* a term meaning "instrument of science."[19]

Both of Boethius's commentaries on the *Isagoge* indicate that he meant this work to be part of a larger endeavor. At the conclusion of the *Dialogue,* Fabius says now that Porphyry has been explained to him, he hopes Boethius will sometime teach him the logic of Aristotle. And Boethius answers that he will happily do so, but since it is dawn and—as Petronius says—"the sun is smiling on the rooftops," they should postpone their discussion until a later time.[20] Since Boethius established his commentary in the framework of a fiction, however, and since the *Isagoge* itself leads to Aristotle's *Categories,* this ending may not offer any hard evidence of Boethius's purpose. Its point may rather be the symbolic one of indicating that with wisdom has come a return of light, calm, and indeed civilization.

The beginning of the *Commentarius,* where Boethius reaffirms his wish that all the learning in Greek be translated into Latin, may offer better evidence that Boethius did indeed view his exposition of the *Isagoge* as part of a larger plan. But whether Boethius began his work on Porphyry with an eye to translating and commenting on Aristotle or whether he came to such an intention after writing on the *Isagoge* we can never know. On the one hand, since Boethius was clearly influenced by Porphyry's writings, it might be argued that he began the *Isagoge* because of interest in Porphyry, not in Aristotle. But, on the other hand, since Boethius's program of education seems to have involved moving from the sciences of the *quadrivium* to the study of language, which teaches how to expound knowledge, the *Organon* was the obvious body of material for such a study. Moreover, because Boethius's *Dialogue* was influenced by Porphyry's dialogue-commentary on Aristotle's *Categories,* the *Exposition through Question and Answer,* it seems likely that Boethius's study of Porphyry was integrally linked to his study of Aristotle. And, significantly, Porphyry's Neoplatonic stance would seem to be Boethius's own position in relation to the Aristotelian material.

Understanding the *Organon*

While we may tend to agree with R. W. Southern that the logical works of Boethius are "immensely difficult to understand and repellent to read," we must keep in mind that for Boethius logic was an instrument that could bring order to a chaotic world and that his program necessitated moving through the *Organon* until the student was sufficiently prepared to take the next step toward philosophy.[21] Thus Boethius moves from the *Isagoge* to the work it properly introduces, Aristotle's *Categories,* again both translating and commenting. As the *Isagoge* was concerned with classifying the objects that are external to the mind, so the *Categories* intends to classify all the remarks that can be made about any object whatsoever. The notion of categories, and the ten categories themselves, can be understood by noting everything that may be said about a pen. The pen itself is a substance; it is long and thin (quantity); it is black (quality); it belongs to me (relation); it rests on its point (position), on a piece of paper (place), at noon (time); it is filled with ink (state); it makes a blue mark (action); and it is being held by my hand (affection). Such classification, enabling one to understand what can be signified by simple signs, represents the proper starting point for the study of logic; and inasmuch as treating of signs necessitates treating of the things they signify, these categories are the proper starting point for all philosophy.[22]

In his work of both translation and commentary Boethius employs the method of continual exposition, which, perhaps as adopted from Ammonius Hermiae, he had used in his second commentary on the *Isagoge*. Whereas it might seem natural for Boethius to use this method again, in this particular instance it is surprising since Porphyry's commentary on the *Categories*, the *Exposition through Question and Answer*—to which Boethius was so indebted that he sometimes followed it point for point—is in dialogue form. By choosing to employ continuous exposition, Boethius would seem to be reaffirming his principle of avoiding rhetoric and of faithfully rendering his original. And though he again adds details and alters constructions for the sake of clarity, his translation admirably reflects Aristotle's original.

It may be more accurate to speak of Boethius's *translations* of the *Categories* since Lorenzo Minio-Paluello—who spent decades identifying and isolating all of Boethius's translations and commentaries from the hundreds of medieval manuscripts offering Latin versions of Aristotle—believed that he wrote at least two translations: first, a preliminary one, extant in complete form in two manuscripts; and second, a revised version, available only as fragments imbedded in manuscripts of Boethius's commentary.[23] In any case, none of these gives any indication of a Latin authority for Boethius's renditions. Since earlier Latin translations of the *Categories*—by Varro (first century B.C.) and, perhaps, by Victorinus—are now lost, the only Latin versions of the work extant before Boethius's are two condensed paraphrases—one falsely attributed to Augustine and the other included in Martianus Capella's *De nuptiis Philologiae et Mercurii*—neither of which can meaningfully be compared with Boethius's version.[24] While not the first Latin translator of the *Categories,* Boethius seems to have been concerned—as he was in the *Isagoge*—with making the treatise meaningful in a way it had not been before him, that is, as a work of philosophy.

Boethius's concern for his reader extends to his commentary on the *Categories* where he seems to have used Porphyry's *Exposition* as a primary source mainly because, as he states, it, more than any other available Greek commentary, "is easier for beginners to comprehend."[25] But important as it is, and while it may be the source of Boethius's citations of earlier commentators, the *Exposition* cannot be the source for such later authorities Boethius alludes to as Iamblichus, who was a pupil of Porphyry, or for Ammonius Hermiae, whose influence may pervade the work. Although Pierre Courcelle maintains that Ammonius is Boethius's primary source here, James Shiel theorizes that the actual influence is marginalia, representing teachings of the School of Athens, which Boethius found in a copy of the *Organon.* As an alternative to these views, C. J. de Vogel has suggested that Boethius knew Ammonius but took "a rather independent attitude towards him," just as he did with such other Greek sources as Porphyry, Nicomachus, and Ptolemy. She feels that although the commentary on the *Categories* contains "quite a good part of Porphyry's work," it is mixed up with other later sources, and these are more from the school of Athens than that of Alexandria.[26]

As if the current confusion about Boethius's sources were not enough, Minio-Paluello has also suggested that Boethius actually wrote two commentaries on the *Categories*—again perhaps following the lead of Porphyry, who seems to have written not only the extant *Exposition* but a longer work now lost. The argument for the existence of a second commentary by Boethius—likewise lost—is based in part on the fact that early in the commentary which has come down to us he states his intention to write another exposition addressed to those who are advanced students *(doctiores).*[27] This suggestion may be strengthened by the fact that

Boethius actually wrote two commentaries on the *Isagoge* and two also on the next work in the *Organon*, the treatise *On Interpretation*.

The possibility of two commentaries on the *Categories*—and indeed a fragment of a second one may have been uncovered[28]— has led scholars to wonder whether Boethius may not have arrived, at some point at least, at a plan to translate the *Organon* into Latin—with perhaps two redactions of translations—and to write two different kinds of commentaries—one essentially simple, designed for beginners; the other more complex, for advanced students—as part of his educational program. Rather than reduce Aristotle to the level of his Latin audience, Boethius might have tried to raise his audience to the level of his material, first by offering them a basic introduction and then by providing a more sophisticated and probing analysis.[29]

If Boethius actually had such a plan, it is unlikely that his second commentary on the *Isagoge*, the result of his unhappiness with Victorinus's translation, was part of it; and since in the prolegomena to the *Categories*—which he wrote after finishing the commentary itself—Boethius does not speak of any second commentary, the idea to write two commentaries may not have occurred to him for some time.[30] It may well have been his plan when he wrote his two commentaries on the treatise *On Interpretation*, for not only does he here oppose the beginner *(simplex intellectus)* and the more advanced reader *(altius acumen)*, he even refers in his first commentary to his second one. At the same time, because *On Interpretation* is so difficult—Cassiodorus quotes the famous statement that when he was in the process of writing it, Aristotle "dipped his pen in his mind"; and Boethius himself acknowledges its complexity—what Boethius does with it may well represent a special case.[31]

In this treatise—called by Aristotle *Peri Hermeneias*, meaning "On Exposition," but known since the Renaissance by its Latin name, *De Interpretatione*—Aristotle's main purpose is to discuss the notion of statement, or proposition, and to determine what pairs of statements are opposed and in what ways. Moving from the classification of objects that exist outside the mind, as seen in the *Isagoge*, and from the classification of the remarks that can be made about any object, as found in the *Categories,* Boethius in his translation of *On Interpretation*—which also apparently exists in at least two redactions—follows Aristotle's concern with the classification of the various statements that can be made on any subject.[32]

The basic difference between Boethius's two commentaries may be understood by noting their lengths in the standard Meiser edition. Whereas the translation itself occupies twenty-five pages, and the first commentary, in two books, almost two hundred pages, the second commentary, in six books, comprises five hundred pages. Beyond the fact that it is two and a half times longer than the first commentary, the second is more elevated in tone and would seem to be designed, as Boethius said at the beginning of his first commentary, for a learned audience, one already expert in philosophical matters and capable of being raised to an even higher level of understanding.

But the principle governing Boethius's plan—that whereas the first commentary will represent a relatively simple kind of interpretation, the second will be far more analytical and critical—is not entirely successful. The second commentary does not always succeed in attaining the high level he promised, and, notwithstanding its sophisticated tone and great length, it frequently does not represent an enrichment of the original Aristotelian text. For instance, Book 2 of this larger commentary—presenting affirmative and negative propositions, the relationship between universal and particular propositions, and the rules of opposites and contraries—does little more than present Aristotle's text, although in many more words than were used by Aristotle. Similarly, the last three books of this commentary (Books 4–6)—treating indefinite propositions, the ordering and inversion of terms in propositions, and contradictory and antithetical terms—do not add meaningfully to Aristotle's discussion. In fact, the criticism made earlier about Boethius's presentation of Porphyry's text in his second commentary on the *Isagoge*—that his efforts do not really help the original but instead cause its tight logic and fine precision to disappear—may justly be made here. Boethius's second commentary on the treatise *On Interpretation* rarely surpasses the level of simple interpretation found in his much shorter first commentary, and Boethius himself seems to have been aware that his wordiness may not be justified, for several times he speaks apologetically about his prolixity and about the inordinate length of his discussion.[33]

Elsewhere in this second commentary, Boethius occasionally does enrich his original. In Book 1, on the signs of interpretive language—that is, on the elements of discourse, such as nouns and verbs—the discussion moves beyond Aristotle's position as Boethius notes that these elements, while being signifiers, express at the same time the reality being signified. In other matters Boethius moves outside *On Interpretation*. In Book 3, for instance, the discussion of propositions and syllogisms—hypothetical (or conditional) and, mainly, categorical (or necessary)—he goes beyond what is found in this treatise of Aristotle and uses material that would seem to come from the *Prior Analytics,* the next treatise in the *Organon*.

In making a synthesis of points found in these two works of Aristotle Boethius may have been following a tradition seen in a work attributed to, if not by, Apuleius (second century). Although this treatise—called *De syllogismis categoricis* and representing either the earliest Latin translation known of *On Interpretation* or a translation of another Greek work focusing on propositions and syllogisms—is quite different from Boethius's work, a comparison of it and Book 3 of Boethius's second commentary suggests that both authors employed a scheme which may be based on a synthesis of points found in Aristotle's *On Interpretation* and *Prior Analytics*. Because such a scheme may also be found in Martianus Capella's *De nuptiis* and perhaps in the now-lost translation that Marius Victorinus seems to have made of *On Interpretation,* it may have represented by Boethius's time a standard way of discussing propositions and syllogisms.[34]

For other particulars in his commentaries, Boethius would again seem to be relying on Porphyry—whose commentary on the treatise *On Interpretation* is now lost—and also on later Greek thought of both the School of Athens and that of Alexandria.[35] Although in his second commentary Boethius refers to two Latin commentators—Praetextatus, who, he notes, plagiarized the work of the Greek Themistius (fourth century), and Albinus, whose work, he says, he was unable to find—his point in alluding to these virtually unidentifiable figures is not to suggest any affinities but to emphasize that he is again doing something in his work on Aristotle never before done in the Latin world.[36] As with the *Categories*, the previous Latin translators and commentators offer no direct influence on Boethius; and the most that can be said about relationships is that the work of Apuleius and Martianus Capella may indicate a tradition of synthesizing in which Boethius participated.

The consideration of terms in the *Categories* and of propositions in *On Interpretation* may be seen to be leading to the treatment of inference in the remaining works of the *Organon*. The *Prior Analytics* treats syllogisms in general; the *Posterior Analytics* concerns scientific (or apodictic) syllogisms; the *Topics*, dialectical syllogisms; and the *Sophistical Refutations*, false (or sophistical) syllogisms. Although Boethius seems to have translated almost all of these treatises, the manuscripts of his renditions of these later works of the *Organon* offer few pure texts. Rather, Boethius's work is most often mixed with other later Latin versions, and only recently has an attempt been made to ascertain and publish Boethius's actual translations.[37]

For the *Prior Analytics*, two redactions of a translation by Boethius may exist.[38] Whereas no commentary as such is extant, numerous references attest to such a commentary. And, interestingly, a preparatory collection of scholia has been found—corresponding to passages in extant Greek commentaries by Alexander of Aphrodisias, Ammonius Hermiae, and John Philoponus—that would seem to be by Boethius and that may represent the first stage of a commentary. At the same time, the very fact that this preparatory scholia has been handed down through the centuries suggests that Boethius never actually completed this commentary.[39]

Statements by Boethius referring to his translations and commentaries are most trustworthy when they are in accord with other evidence, since they may represent his intentions as easily as his accomplishments. Although Boethius refers to a translation of the *Posterior Analytics,* the next treatise in the *Organon,* and though Minio-Paluello thinks that he indeed wrote one, if not two, none has yet been found.[40] Similarly, there is no indication of a commentary on this work by Boethius, though in this instance Boethius's other works offer no references to any. Since Boethius seems not to have completed his commentary on the *Prior Analytics,* it is unlikely that he began another on this next work.[41]

Boethius's translation of Aristotle's *Topics*—attested to both in other works by him and in Cassiodorus's *Institutes*—may exist in two versions, a complete one of eight books and a fragment, offering part of Book 4, imbedded in another logical work of Boethius, the *De divisione.* As for a commentary on this work of Aristotle, notwithstanding three citations in Boethius's writings to such a work, no trace of this commentary exists today.[42]

For the last work in the *Organon,* the *Sophistical Refutations*—which represents an appendix of sorts to the *Topics*—Boethius's other writings offer no references at all, although a twelfth-century manuscript refers explicitly to a version by Boethius. The Latin manuscripts of this work of Aristotle are so impure, showing a mixture of different translations, that it has been difficult to determine Boethius's actual text—although recently an edition of this translation has been published in the *Aristotles Latinus.* As for a commentary on the *Sophistical Refutations,* no reference exists, either by Boethius or by anyone else, to such a work; and it is generally agreed that—as seems to have been the case with the *Posterior Analytics* and the *Topics*—Boethius never wrote a commentary on it.[43]

Beyond Aristotle and Logic

Along with translating and commenting on the *Organon,* Boethius also wrote several treatises that obviously stem from his study of Aristotle's logic, notably two works on categorical syllogisms, one on hypothetical syllogisms, one on division, and two on topics. The two treatises on categorical syllogisms—*De syllogismis categoricis* and *Introductio ad syllogismos categoricos*—are concerned with the theory of logical propositions and with those propositions and syllogisms based on premises that are necessarily true or factual. Inasmuch as these works seem to be continuing points already touched on by Boethius in his commentaries on the treatise *On Interpretation,* it has been suggested that one or both of these represent the synopsis of his discussion which, at the beginning of Book 4 of his second commentary on this work of Aristotle, Boethius indicated he intended to write—"bringing together what has been presented diffusely and expanding what has been offered too briefly." At the same time, Boethius may have intended his work on categorical syllogisms to serve as an introduction to his translation of the *Prior Analytics* since in combining points found in both this treatise and *On Interpretation,* these treatises may be considered as—if not actually designed to be—a bridge between these two works of the *Organon.*[44]

Boethius's two treatises have presented a problem for scholars in that while seeming to do much the same thing, they are also quite different. Whereas they agree even to the point of containing identical passages, *De syllogismis categoricis* employs a "definitely older terminology" than the *Introductio,* one that may be related to the rhetoric found in the work of Marius Victorinus. Also the *Introductio,* comprising one book, duplicates the first of the two books making up the *De syllogismis categoricis,* except that it is twice its length.[45] The relationship between these two works may be understood as that between Boethius's two commentaries on the treatise *On Interpretation,* where the second, so much longer than the first, analyzes in much greater detail. But at the same time, the *Introductio* may well represent a later revision of the first book of *De syllogismis categoricis,* and the finished revised work would probably have included a second book representing an expansion of material found in Book 2 of this earlier work. If either of these treatises is the synopsis of *On Interpretation* spoken of by Boethius, it would have to be *De syllogismis categoricis,* or at least its first book. If this is the case, the second book of the treatise may represent a similar résumé of material which would have been included in Boethius's commentary on the *Prior Analytics.*[46]

The titles given to these two treatises, coming from late manuscripts, are misleading. *De syllogismis categoricis* should most
properly be called an *Introductio,* and indeed in this work Boethius
refers to it as such seven times. What we know as the *Introductio,*
on the other hand—actually the longer, more detailed work—
might well be viewed as an *Institutio,* as Boethius terms it, perhaps
even as *De institutione categorica,* paralleling Boethius's earlier titles
for his work on arithmetic and music.[47]

Necessarily joined to these two treatises is Boethius's work on
hypothetical syllogisms, *De syllogismis hypotheticis,* in which he
begins by distinguishing between categorical (or necessary) and
hypothetical (or conditional) syllogisms, which stem from premises that, though commonly accepted as true, lack absolute and
necessary certainty. Although Boethius's discussion uses Aristotelian principles and methods as well as points touched on in the
Prior Analytics, it is quite different from Aristotle's analysis, which
is mainly concerned with categorical syllogisms. In fact, in an
epistolary preface Boethius stresses the uniqueness of his work
on hypothetical syllogisms, "about which Aristotle wrote nothing." Whereas two of Aristotle's disciples, Theophrastus and
Eudemus, did write on this subject, Boethius does not find their
work especially useful. Thus, as he says, he will explain what he
has found "discussed summarily and confusedly by the Greeks
and not at all by Latin writers." And his method is to offer
detailed analyses to illustrate one particular aspect of the problem,
one method that is objectively valid, or one traditional explanation of the argument.[48]

Notwithstanding Boethius's statement to the contrary, Latin
precedents for his work do exist. In particular, Cicero (first century B.C.) included a section on this kind of propositional logic
in his *Topica;* and Marius Victorinus wrote a treatise called *De
syllogismis hypotheticis* which, though now lost, is cited by Cassiodorus and may be the source of Martianus Capella's discussion
in his *De nuptiis.* Since these earlier Latin works include several
kinds of syllogisms not found in Boethius's treatise, however, it
is unlikely that either of them provided him with a model.
Boethius's source is most likely a Greek commentary on the *Prior*

Analytics, though the extant work of Alexander of Aphrodisias, Ammonius Hermiae, and John Philoponus differ significantly from Boethius's treatise. What seems most clear is that Boethius is reflecting a kind of syncretism of positions advanced by Aristotelians, Stoics, and Neoplatonists; and probably the leading candidate as his source is again Porphyry—though he does not seem to have written a work specifically on the subject of hypothetical syllogisms.[49]

It is noteworthy that the *De syllogismis hypotheticis* begins with a letter addressed to an unnamed friend who, having already acquired a comprehensive knowledge of categorical syllogisms, has inquired about hypothetical syllogisms. Although Symmachus has been suggested as the person being addressed here, this identification does not seem likely, for not only do the several expressions of mutual friendship suggest a younger contemporary of Boethius, but the deference toward his guardian and father-in-law expressed in other addresses to Symmachus—such as that at the beginning of the *Arithmetic*—is lacking here.[50] Regardless of any particular identification, however, this unnamed friend should also be seen as following in the steps of Fabius, who in Boethius's *Dialogue* on the *Isagoge* asks for particular instruction. But whereas the request at the end of that work was to move to an explication of Aristotle, here it is to move beyond Aristotle to a subject that is largely outside his authority. Whether or not Boethius intended any parallel, it is interesting that years after writing the *Dialogue*—during which time he translated and commented on Aristotle's logic, using the method of continual exposition—Boethius, when he is for the first time purportedly moving beyond Aristotle, may again be using a fictional device, that is, a device offering a framework for the discussion at hand.

Like his work on categorical and hypothetical syllogisms, Boethius's treatise *De divisione*—on division, or what may be understood as the breaking down of a whole into its essential parts—seems to be an outgrowth of his work on Aristotle's *On Interpretation* and *Prior Analytics*. But not only is Aristotle's discussion of division quite brief, it is designed to show that division is only a weak or inadequate syllogism and to deny its demonstrative capability. Similarly, when Aristotle uses division in his *Topics* and *Sophistical Refutations,* it is only as an instrument of dialectic, capable of proving arguments but not of producing knowledge.[51]

Inasmuch as it goes beyond Aristotle to discuss a matter he did not consider sufficiently, the *De divisione* resembles the *De syllogismis hypotheticis.* Also like this work, the *De divisione* seems to represent a synthesis of Aristotelian, Stoic, and Neoplatonic views. It is probably based on Porphyry's commentary on Plato's *Sophist,* though here Plato considers division as simply a method allowing one to construct proper definitions. Boethius in fact cites this work by Porphyry at the beginning of his treatise where he states that his purpose is to make available to the Romans material for clarifying the division of the whole into its parts. He is especially concerned with the division of genera into species and with the concomitant distinction between essential and accidental forms that is the basis of such division.[52]

Boethius's work on topics would also seem to have grown out of his work on the *Organon,* but instead of being in the form of an actual commentary on Aristotle—notwithstanding Boethius's references to such a work—it takes instead the shape of a commentary on Cicero's *Topica (In topica Ciceronis)* and an original treatise called *De topicis differentiis.* Aristotle's *Topics,* concerned with finding arguments that can be used by either side in a disputation, is wholly taken up with dialectic and not with demonstration. Though in his *Rhetoric* Aristotle is interested in topics as an aid to memory and as a tool of rhetoric, in his *Topics* he uses this subject as a basic principle capable of supporting a variety of arguments and a strategy of argumentation. But his main concern is with citing the topics themselves—he cites hundreds—and not with analyzing the theory behind them.[53]

Although Cicero's *Topica* has been taken as an explication of Aristotle's work, it is, in being concerned only with the method of finding arguments and not at all with the arguments themselves, actually quite different. Not only is Cicero, even more so than Aristotle, uninterested in the theoretical foundation of topics, for him dialectical disputation is incidental. His concern is with the art of discourse *(ars disserendi),* and he takes up topics as elements in this art, particularly useful for making speeches and for arguing cases of law.[54]

We may well wonder why Boethius should have chosen to write a commentary on the *Topica* of Cicero. Although the ascription to Cicero of a rendering of Aristotle's *Topics* extends to the sixth century—Cassiodorus cites Cicero as the author of such a translation—Boethius, who had translated Aristotle, certainly knew that Cicero's treatise had little to do with that in the *Organon*.[55] But regardless of whether or not Boethius thought Cicero's work to be a translation, it is unlikely, given his aversion to using previous Latin work and his desire to replace earlier Latin translations and commentaries with his own work, that he would have written a commentary on Cicero's rather slight work. The issue is not resolved by suggesting that Boethius wrote his commentary on the *Topica* as a way of rendering homage to the greatest representative of Roman philosophical and rhetorical culture, for this commentary is more than a mere tribute. Not only long, it is noticeably careful, clear, and precise. Moreover, because Boethius begins his work by acknowledging favorably the now-lost commentary on the *Topica* by Marius Victorinus, it would seem that, whether or not he wished to rival Victorinus, Boethius intended to place his work wholly within the context of the Latin grammatical-rhetorical tradition that he had scorned in his early work on the *Isagoge,* when he sought to detach his writings from those of Victorinus. And finally it seems clear that Boethius wished to use the occasion of commenting on Cicero as an opportunity to write a sizable treatise on a subject pertinent to both logic and rhetoric.[56]

Unfortunately, Boethius's treatise is incomplete; the intended seven books of commentary break off at the beginning of Book 6. As Cicero's work begins with an epistolary address to a friend, Trebatius, who had asked for an explanation of the topics, so Boethius's commentary begins with a preface in which Boethius says that he is writing this work for his friend Patricius who has asked him about topics. He then proceeds in Book 1 to analyze Cicero's definition of topics—"the discipline for finding arguments"—and classifies these topics according to whether they are

part of the *ars rhetorica* or *logica*. Book 2 treats of the origins of
arguments that are topics and classifies these according to whether
they are intrinsic—and pertinent to logic—or extrinsic—and
pertinent to rhetoric. Book 3 clarifies, with various examples,
the concept of definition, noting its two forms, *divisio* and *partitio;*
Books 4 and 5 further discuss intrinsic topics and the various
elements comprising the *ars topica;* and Book 6, after summarizing
the matter of intrinsic topics, is on the verge of discussing extrinsic topics when it breaks off.

Lengthy as this commentary is, it is still elementary when
compared with Boethius's other treatise on the subject of topics,
De topicis differentiis—probably best translated as *On Differences
in Topics* or *On Different Topics*—in which he intends to show that
all the systems of topics known to him may be reduced to the
same basic set of distinctions, or, as he terms them, *differentiae.*
Although at the outset of this work Boethius cites Aristotle's
Topics, "which we translated into Latin," and Cicero's *Topica,*
"for which we with a great deal of effort produced a clear and
complete commentary," *De topicis differentiis* is quite different
from both of these works.[57]

Whereas Aristotle focuses on oral disputation, Boethius con-
centrates on the arguments themselves, divorced from both disputation and its participants. And, unlike Aristotle, Boethius
recognizes two different kinds of topics: maxims, which are self-
evident propositions, and *differentiae,* mechanisms for grouping
principles, which are for him the real instruments for finding
arguments. Moreover, for all his analysis of Cicero, not only in
his commentary on the *Topica* but also in his discussion in Book
3 here, Boethius goes far beyond him. Although he is able to use
what Cicero offers in his lists of topics and in his examples
showing how these topics may be used in argumentation and
jurisprudence, his discussion and point are far different from
Cicero's. In fact, Boethius's method for discovering arguments
is unlike the extant work of any of his predecessors, including
Aristotle and Cicero and such Greek intermediaries as Alexander
of Aphrodisias (second century) and Themistius (fourth century).[58]

After a general introduction in which he defines his terms (Book 1), Boethius proceeds to an analysis of division and of the twenty-eight *differentiae,* as found in the writings of Themistius (Book 2). In Book 3, he discusses Cicero's *Topica,* with which he compares and reconciles Themistius's work; and in Book 4, after moving to rhetorical topics, which he compares with logical ones, he concludes with a theoretical discussion of the nature of rhetoric, which he claims is original. As Eleonore Stump writes, the more one studies this analysis of rhetoric the more one is inclined to believe him; and, moreover, the coherent and elegant system for finding arguments represented by *De topicis differentiis* is unequaled in any of the material that has come down to us from antiquity.[59]

A question little considered by scholars is why Boethius, who was so concerned with translating and commenting on Aristotle's *Organon,* should also have written several original treatises, that is, work not precisely commentaries. This question may be related to that already touched on—why Boethius commented on Cicero. Boethius's other non-Aristotelian works on language—his translation and commentaries on Porphyry's *Isagoge*—are easily explained as his entry to Aristotle; but after he is involved with Aristotle, it seems unlikely that he should have taken time to write on Cicero or even to make further analyses of points already brought out in his work on Aristotle.

The lack of extant commentaries by Boethius on Aristotle's works after his *On Interpretation* may indicate that Boethius decided not to comment further on the *Organon* but, instead, to write a series of treatises on points he felt needed clarification or additional emphasis. Possibly Boethius may have determined after his two commentaries on Aristotle's *On Interpretation* that he could not effectively convey more of Aristotle to his Latin audience. Or possibly Boethius may have decided that what he had offered on the *Isagoge,* the *Categories,* and the treatise *On Interpretation* was indeed sufficient for his program of demonstrating how logic could be employed as an instrument of philosophy. His commentary on Aristotle's *On Interpretation* had in fact touched on the discussion of syllogisms found in the *Prior Analytics,* and the

Posterior Analytics, with its emphasis on scientific reasoning, may have struck him as not only exceedingly difficult but irrelevant to his plan. Boethius may have felt that it was time to get on with matters other than logic.

If, for whatever reason, Boethius indeed decided to stop working on Aristotle, his original treatises might then represent surrogates for actual commentaries. The translations he made of the remainder of the *Organon*—with the apparent exception of the *Posterior Analytics*—would then function as authoritative statements; and Boethius's original treatises would offer, through synopses and syntheses on the one hand and additional analysis on the other, what amount to his commentaries, but now on principles, not on works. His two treatises on categorical syllogisms clearly isolate and syncretize points found in both Aristotle's *On Interpretation* and *Prior Analytics;* his *De syllogismis hypotheticis* represents, according to Boethius, an inquiry into a matter on which Aristotle wrote nothing; his *De divisione* is designed to correct Aristotle's view of the value of division; and his works on topics move beyond Aristotle's concern with dialectic to rhetoric. Also all of these original treatises reveal a pattern in that Boethius moves from the study of proposition to that of syllogism, both categorical and hypothetical; to division, the principle of breaking down syllogisms; and finally to topics, which represent the *differentiae* produced by division.

For all of his expertise in logic, Boethius was not primarily a logician. The fact that he began his study of language with logic does not necessarily mean that he had no use for grammar and rhetoric. Rather, he may have been simply trying to show how logic—which had for centuries in the Latin world been immersed in grammar and rhetoric—could be useful as an instrument of philosophy. Although Boethius did not get to grammar, he was clearly moving to rhetoric; and it is hardly accidental that his *De topicis differentiis* concludes with an analysis of topics as they could be used in rhetoric, as well as with an innovative reconciliation of logic and rhetoric. Although rhetoric here is subordinated to logic, it too functions as a useful tool for the study of philosophy.

Moreover, in commenting on a treatise by Cicero, Boethius in fact focused on the prince of rhetoricians, whose work represented for the Latin world both the standard view on rhetoric and the epitome of classical rhetorical theory. Although the *Topica* is a lesser work, it may represent a link to Cicero's major rhetorical works; and, indeed, the discussion of rhetoric in Book 4 of *De topicis differentiis* would seem to include what amounts to a commentary on Cicero's *De inventione*. Also, in being ostensibly linked to Aristotle, and in viewing dialectic as a part of the *ars disserendi,* the *Topica* provides for Boethius a transition from logic to rhetoric.

At the same time, because of Cicero's affinities with Plato—he is, as E. K. Rand writes, "in the best sense of the term, the first of the Neoplatonists"—he offered Boethius a means of moving from Aristotle to Plato. And, indeed, from the beginning of Boethius's first commentary on the *Isagoge*—where philosophy is defined as "the science which proceeds from the wisdom of God and which leads back to Him"—Plato has been an essential part of his work.[60] As Etienne Gilson perceives, "the logic of Boethius is a commentary on Aristotle's in which the desire to interpret it according to Plato's philosophy frequently shows through." And with Cicero, as with Boethius, it is Aristotle who is harmonized with Plato and not vice versa.[61]

Boethius's plan to move from Aristotle to Plato may be suggested in his statement of purpose at the beginning of Book 2 of his second commentary on Aristotle's *On Interpretation*. His "fixed intention," he writes, is "to translate into Latin every work of Aristotle that comes to my hand and furnish it with a Latin commentary." He goes on as follows:

Thus I may present, well ordered and illustrated with the light of comment, whatever subtlety of logic's art, whatever weight of moral experience, and whatever insight into natural truth, may be gathered from Aristotle. And I mean to translate all the dialogues of Plato, or reduce them in my commentary to a Latin form. Having accomplished this, I shall not have despised the opinions of Aristotle and Plato if I evoke a certain concord between them and show in how many things of importance for philosophy they agree.[62]

If Boethius had indeed finished with the instrument provided by "Aristotle the logician," he may have been moving toward "Plato the theologian"—to use the terms in Theodoric's letter praising his work. [63] As Boethius had begun his study of logic by focusing on the work of the Neoplatonist Porphyry, so he concludes it by examining in detail the work of another follower of Plato, Cicero. The study of philosophy toward which Boethius's educational program aimed was clearly the study of wisdom as understood by Plato, and Cicero would seem to have represented for him a further step toward this end.

Chapter Three

The Concerned Christian

The Philosopher as Public Administrator

The preceding discussion of Boethius's works may have inadvertently led to an unwarranted conclusion—that after fulfilling the task he set for himself of writing on the subjects of the *quadrivium,* Boethius then began his logical work, on which he labored systematically and solely for a period of more or less twenty years. The matter is far more complex than this, and the chronology of Boethius's work, determined largely on the basis of internal evidence such as peculiarities of vocabulary, similarities of style, and references to particular writings, is necessarily controversial. Scholars are still not in agreement on the question of whether Boethius's first work was his *Dialogue* on the *Isagoge* or his *Principles of Arithmetic,* or on the issue of the relationship between his logical and his scientific writings. On the one hand, Boethius may have been writing his scientific treatises while he was commenting on Porphyry; on the other hand, he may have turned to his *Principles of Music* and his version of Euclid's *Geometry* after writing most of his work on Aristotle. And although Boethius's original treatises on logic seem especially meaningful when viewed—as they were in the preceding chapter—as synopses and expansions of points that concerned Boethius after he wrote his commentaries on Aristotle's *On Interpretation,* some scholars have regarded these treatises as in effect sprinkled through the corpus of Boethius's writings. The *De syllogismis categoricis* has even been placed—perhaps along with the *De divisione*—at the beginning of Boethius's literary efforts, soon after his first commentary on the *Isagoge.* [1]

To be sure, few scholars would wish to suggest that Boethius wore blinders as he worked, that he looked only straight ahead as he plodded relentlessly through his self-appointed task of translating, collating, and commenting, working up to the point where he, like the students who would be following his educational program, could arrive at philosophy and, no longer constricted by preliminary matters, range freely. The picture of Boethius sitting at his desk for two decades with Aristotle's logic propped before him is not a pleasant one; nor fortunately—regardless of the actual chronology of his scientific and logical writings—is it an accurate one.

We know that Boethius continued in the service of Theodoric and Rome. One of the few certain dates in Boethius's life is 510, when records indicate that he was named Consul of Rome for the year. A passage at the beginning of Book 2 of Boethius's commentary on the *Categories*, referring to the cares of his consular office, not only serves to date his work on the *Categories*, but also makes clear that Boethius's work on Aristotle coexisted with his public service:

Although the cares of my consular office prevent me from devoting my entire attention to these studies, yet it seems to me a sort of public service to instruct my fellow-citizens in the products of reasoned investigation. Nor shall I deserve ill of my country in this attempt. In far-distant ages, other cities transferred to our state alone the lordship and sovereignty of the world; I am glad to assume the remaining task of educating our present society in the spirit of Greek philosophy. Wherefore this is verily a part of my consular duty, since it has always been a Roman habit to take whatever was beautiful or praiseworthy throughout the world and to add to its lustre by imitation. So then, to my task.[2]

Not only does this passage offer an explicit statement of Boethius's point in translating and writing on Aristotle—"the products of reasoned investigation"—as well as a reaffirmation of the educational program he had laid out in his letter to Symmachus at the beginning of his *Arithmetic*, it also reveals his insistence on a synthesis of thought and action. Without altering his intention to educate the Latin world in what he terms "the spirit of Greek philosophy," he cheerfully takes on himself the busy schedule of the Consul, a venerable office which, though without the power it enjoyed during the Roman republic, was still highly prestigious.

As E. K. Rand writes, alluding to classical and Christian predecessors of Boethius, philosophy was for Boethius, as it was for Lucretius, Cicero, and Lactantius before him, "a patriotic act." And indeed Boethius may not only have had in mind a passage at the beginning of the *Tusculan Disputations*, where Cicero declares his own program, he may also have intended to carry out Cicero's plan. It seems clear that for Boethius, Plato's words in the *Republic* were not merely theoretical, and he may even have felt himself bound to give practical illustration to Plato's theory that the happiest states are those governed by philosophers.[3]

Although in one sense Boethius's words in his commentary on the *Categories* may appear arrogant—as Rome rules the world, so he will instruct the world—in another sense his attitude is humble—as Rome has profited from taking and imitating whatever was good, so Boethius as Consul has the duty of continuing this act by finishing his task of teaching the spirit of Greek philosophy. Boethius's emphasis is on his work's being not an act of self-aggrandizement but "a sort of public service," a "task" which he gladly accepts. The implication is that the same could be said about the office of Consul: it is a "duty," and though its "cares" prevent him from devoting his entire attention to Aristotle, he gladly accepts it. The impulse toward synthesis that marks Boethius's gathering together of Greek thought obviously extends to his own life: as he amalgamates the wisdom of the past, he employs it in both his writings and his acts of public service.

Besides being elected sole Consul in 510—ordinarily two consuls were elected each year—Boethius was also introduced into the senate with the title of Patrician, an honor not ordinarily given to someone thirty or so years of age but usually reserved for faithful statesmen on their retirement from public life.[4] Extraordinary as they were, these honors were but precursors to still greater ones. As Boethius continued working for Theodoric and for Rome, the king rewarded him increasingly. In 522, his two young sons, named Symmachus and Boethius, were elected joint Consuls for the year. For this election to have been effected, the Emperor of the East—at this time Justin—must have waived his own right of nomination; and his doing so may be interpreted as indicating his good will toward both Boethius and Theodoric. At the same time, since Theodoric obviously supported this un-usual election, his action suggests his own desire to honor Boe-thius and his family in an exceptional way. Also, Boethius himself was apparently chosen to deliver the customary panegyric to Theo-doric, who then showed his further appreciation of Boethius by appointing him, apparently in 523, to the illustrious office of *Magister Officiorum* ("Master of the Offices"), a demanding posi-tion, combining the duties of a modern Secretary of State, several Cabinet offices concerning domestic affairs, Postmaster General, as well as Chief of the entire Civil Service, and Head of all the palace officials, including the guards.[5]

The evidence suggests that at least from 510 to 523, and most likely from 500, or whenever Boethius entered into the service of Theodoric, his time was increasingly taken up with matters of public administration. Moreover, his later administrative po-sitions were obviously quite different from his earlier tasks of selecting a harper, checking the weight of coins, and constructing clocks. The fact that even with his full-time work for Rome and the king he could continue to read Nicomachus, Porphyry, Ar-istotle, Cicero, and various other Neoplatonic philosophers, as well as translate and write commentaries on their works, and compose treatises on various points he wished to bring out more clearly or fully is, to say the least, incredible. But at the same time that we may marvel at Boethius's industry, as well as his obvious success, we should recognize that he was involved in still other study and writing—on matters of Christian theology.

On Christian Doctrine

Although the Middle Ages and Renaissance knew that Boethius was the author of several theological tractates, in the eighteenth century it became increasingly fashionable to doubt both his authorship of these *opuscula sacra* and his Christianity. As is now clear, however, Boethius, like his father-in-law, Symmachus, was not only a devout Christian, he was also very much concerned with Church policy and theological questions. Paganism had died in Rome in the fourth century, and in fact, the laws of the Theodosian Code against paganism were confirmed by Theodoric, who, although an Arian, was, it should be stressed, a Christian. In Boethius's lifetime it would have been virtually impossible for a non-Christian to have held public office. Moreover, Boethius's family, the Anicii, had been among the earliest of the great Roman families to be converted to Christianity, and were even singled out by St. Jerome at the end of the fourth century for their piety. While Symmachus's great-grandfather Quintus Aurelius Symmachus had been one of the last champions of paganism, the great-grandson was praised for being as much a champion of Christianity as his forebear had been its opponent.

The issue of Boethius's Christianity in general and his authorship of several *opuscula sacra* in particular was finally settled in the late nineteenth century when a fragment of a hitherto-lost work by Cassiodorus, recording the literary achievements of his family and kinsmen, among them Symmachus and Boethius, was published. This work, known as the *Anecdoton Holderi,* or more accurately the *Ordo generis Cassiodorum,* states explicitly in a paragraph detailing Boethius's public offices and honors that along with his "work on the art of logic, that is, dialectic, and the mathematical sciences"—in which "he either equalled or surpassed the ancient authors"—he also wrote "a book concerning the Holy Trinity, certain dogmatic chapters, and a book against Nestorius." Here, along with referring to Boethius's works on logic and the sciences of the *quadrivium,* Cassiodorus seems to be citing his theological tractates. The five that have come down to us include a work on the Trinity, two shorter essays on doctrinal questions, an affirmation of the orthodox Catholic faith, and a defense of orthodoxy against the Eutychian and Nestorian heresies. Of the five tractates extant, two—the work on the Trinity and the book against Nestorius—are most likely alluded to by Cassiodorus; and the two other short works by Boethius on doctrinal matters may well be what are described in the *Anecdoton* as "dogmatic chapters."[6]

While we may marvel that Boethius had the time to write these theological tractates, we should not be surprised that he turned his hand to theology. Although the writings that have come down to us from the fifth and sixth centuries include some historical works and collections of letters, the bulk of the prose literature of the time can be broadly classified under four headings: exegetical and hermeneutical writings, concerned with interpreting Scripture; homilies and pastoral dissertations, designed for moral instruction; *apologiae,* or affirmations of the faith; and dogmatic treatises, on matters of theological controversy.[7] Since the writings of Christians during Boethius's lifetime were almost entirely at the service of their religion, what is surprising about Boethius's literary output is that so many of his works are on non-Christian matters.

While noting how remarkable it is that the corpus of Boethius's writings should include so many treatises on scientific and logical matters, we should not, however, view these works as evidence indicating that Boethius was essentially not religious or that he was so taken up with classical philosophy that he had little time for Christianity. Rather, his educational program, like that of St. Augustine, began with secular studies, but incorporated these into a larger corpus that included religious writings. Although we might wish to make a separation between sacred and profane writings, it would seem, for Symmachus and Boethius at least, that such a division would have been no more meaningful than that between the activities of the private citizen and those of the public citizen. Their plan to bring about an ideal civilization meant both laboring with one's whole being and incorporating the learning of the classical world into a framework that was wholly Christian. In a sense, Boethius was able to proceed with his science and logic precisely because no conflict existed in his mind between the teaching of pagan Greeks and the faith of his religion. The sciences of the Greeks offered a way to philosophy, and their logic provided an instrument at the service of truth.

In like manner, for Boethius, the thought of such pagans as Plato, Aristotle, Cicero, Nicomachus, and Porphyry was to be brought to the service of Christianity.

The Logic of Theology

What one cannot help noticing in Boethius's theological tractates is that most of them seem to be extensions or applications of the concern with clear thinking that marked his logical work. And, in fact, they may properly be seen representing his application of the instrument of logic to the body of truth represented by Christianity. As E. K. Rand points out, Boethius's logical and theological writings "seem altogether of a piece. It is the same mind here as there, only exercising itself in a different field." The result is "a new method in theology, the application of Aristotelian logic to Christian problems."[8] As Boethius asserts at the end of his treatise on the Trinity, he has intended to furnish "some support in argument to an article which stands by itself on the firm foundation of Faith." And again, at the end of one of his short pieces on doctrinal matters, when he states what he has done, he asks the reader to "examine carefully what I have said, and if possible, reconcile faith and reason."[9]

At the same time, it would be a mistake to think that these treatises represented learned exercises, perhaps imposed by Symmachus on the young Boethius as part of his education.[10] Boethius's point in applying Aristotelian methods to Christian doctrine was not to practice his logic but, by using the precision of thought logic offered, to make certain theological points clear in a way they had not been before. In this sense, the *opuscula sacra* represent a fulfillment of Boethius's study of Aristotle. As has been seen, Boethius was concerned in his commentaries on the *Isagoge* with what could be said about objects existing outside the mind; in his work on the *Categories* with the remarks that could be made about any object whatsoever; and in his commentaries on the treatise *On Interpretation* with the statements that could be made on any subject. His theological tractates may be seen to represent a continuation of the process suggested here, for in these he goes beyond objects and words to pure form, or divinity, and to what can be said about this.

It should be understood that for Boethius theology represented not a marginal activity but the highest form of philosophy. As has been seen, in his *Dialogue* on the *Isagoge,* when speaking of theoretical, or speculative, philosophy—which is higher than practical philosophy—he divides it into three areas of study: the study of *naturalia* is physics; that of *intelligibilia,* the science dealing with souls, is psychology; and that of *intellectibilia,* concerned with the highest beings, is theology. He repeats this division in his treatise on the Trinity, where, though the science concerned with bodies apart from matter is termed mathematics, that dealing with forms which cannot be separated from their bodies is again called physics; and that concerned with the apprehension of pure form is again termed theology.[11] When in his various *opuscula sacra* Boethius applies the instrument of logic to matters of theology, he is both using logic in accord with its function as an instrument of philosophy and going beyond it to express his concern with the highest form of philosophy.

Something of Boethius's approach may be understood by glancing at the first three tractates—the order is traditional, not chronological. In Tractate 1, on the Trinity, Boethius uses the predicables of difference, number, and species, which he found in the *Isagoge,* to make meaningful the unity of the Trinity. Elsewhere in this work he applies the Aristotelian categories to God to make clear His nature: he distinguishes between categories of accident and those of substance—only the latter can be used in reference to God; and he employs categories of substance and relation to define and differentiate Unity and Trinity—"the category of substance preserves the Unity, that of relation brings about the Trinity."[12] Similarly, in the second tractate, where the argument is "whether Father, Son, and Holy Spirit may be predicated of the Divinity substantially or otherwise," the distinction is again one of the categories of substance and relation. And in the third tractate, on the question of "the manner in which substances can be good in virtue of existence without being absolute goods," he follows explicitly "the example of the mathe-

matical and cognate sciences" as he develops nine axioms to show
the difference between the good that is a substance and the good
that comes about through existence. [13]

In one sense, Boethius's procedure is not new at all. In the
second and third centuries such writers as Clement of Alexandria,
among the Greeks, and Minucius Felix, among the Romans, had
related Greek philosophy to Christian thought; and before them,
perhaps earliest of all, the author of the prologue to the Gospel
according to St. John had effected this synthesis. [14] Moreover, St.
Augustine had employed Plato and Aristotle as frequently as
Boethius had; and, indeed, in his treatise on the Trinity, Boethius
acknowledges his debt to Augustine, whose great work *De Trinitate* is the theological basis for Boethius's tractate. What is new
in Boethius's work, however, is the systematic application of the
terms and methods of philosophy, as seen in the logic of Aristotle,
to problems of theology. Although, for Boethius, using Aristotle's ten categories to view the Trinity may not have been extraordinary, for Augustine, who had attempted to apply Aristotle's
methods to God, the harmonizing of the two was impossible. As
Augustine reports in his *Confessions,* at about the age of twenty
he found that he was able to read and understand the *Categories*
without any assistance, even though others found the work quite
difficult. But, says Augustine, Aristotle's treatise is clearly an
example of false teaching since it misled him into supposing that
everything that exists, including God, could be placed into the
ten categories. Boethius, however, notwithstanding Augustine's
objections, had no trouble applying the categories both to God
and to the Trinity. [15]

By virtue of his applying to Christian doctrine a new method
of analysis and a foreign vocabulary, Boethius at the same time
brought into logical consideration a body of revealed truth that
was recognized as existing in its own right. While Christian
doctrine does not need the support that logic brings, logic may
still serve to corroborate its teachings. Although faith, which for
Christians was the ultimate truth, does not require the support
of rational thought, the principles of reason may still function
to confirm the doctrines of faith. And in early sixth-century Italy

matters of orthodox faith could use all the help they could get, not against paganism, but rather against the more dangerous enemy, heresy.

Theological Controversies

The theological controversies in Rome during Boethius's lifetime were of two sorts: Trinitarian and Christological. Although the Arian heresy—which involved a gradation of attributes of the members of the Trinity, with the Son inferior to the Father, and the Holy Spirit inferior to both—had been formally settled as early as 325, when the Council of Nicea offered the orthodox definition of the three persons of the Trinity, the heresy continued to be important in the West largely because of the Goths' conversion from heathendom to Arian Christianity. But by the sixth century, although the Goths were still Arians, the heresy itself had been superseded as the liveliest and most challenging of the theological controversies. Although the Arian Vandals in Africa and Visigoths in Spain persecuted orthodox Catholics, Theodoric's tolerance—which solved the problem of how an Arian king could govern a Roman people that were largely Catholic—certainly made the issue less pressing to the faithful in Italy, as did such gestures by the king as his worshipping in St. Peter's Cathedral on his visit to Rome in 500. Not only did all of the Catholics who chose to serve Theodoric know of his Arianism, the king also knew of their Catholicism. He certainly knew of Boethius's religious convictions before heaping honors on him. The point is that in early sixth-century Italy, there existed a mutual truce between Arians and Catholics; and consequently, the issue of Arianism was not a major one for doctrinal tractates. [16]

Although other heresies—Donatism, Manichaeism, and Pelagianism, all of which had occasioned famous tractates by Augustine—also continued into the sixth century, far more significant in Boethius's time were the Christological disputes prompted by the Nestorian and Monophysite heresies. The orthodox Christian position was that Christ contained two natures, divine and human, in one person. But according to Nestorius, Patriarch of Constantinople in the early fifth century, Christ contained two natures and possessed two persons. And opposed to this, according to Monophysitism, introduced in Constantinople by Eutyches in the mid-fifth century, Christ contained one nature and also possessed one person. Throughout Boethius's lifetime the controversies raged between heretic and orthodox as well as between the heresiarchs themselves. Although the Council of Chalcedon in 451 had defined the orthodox position, the decisions of the council were far from bringing a harmonious settlement of the issue. In 482, the Emperor Zeno, along with Acacius, Patriarch of Constantinople, had tried to reach a compromise through the *Henoticon* or Edict of Union. But instead of bringing the controversy to an end, it, by advocating tolerance of a form of Monophysitism, actually created a break between Constantinople and Rome, which could not accept its position. The situation within the Church was so grave that a rupture known as the Acacian Schism was precipitated in 484, with the bishops of Rome and Constantinople mutually excommunicating each other.[17]

In 512, the controversy resulted in a letter that certain Eastern bishops sent to the Pope in Rome, in which, while declaring their confusion, they proposed a new Christological formula— that the Incarnation of Christ is both from and in two natures *(et ex et in duabus naturis)*—which they hoped would heal the rupture between Constantinople and Rome. Instead of pronouncing on the theology of this solution, the Pope invited the bishops to come to Rome to present their views; and apparently their letter was read aloud to an assembly that seems to have included both Symmachus and Boethius. Although the assembly, including Boethius, was favorable to the formula, Boethius felt that most of those present did not really understand the issue. The result of his further musings on the subject of the natures and person of Christ was his *Contra Eutychen et Nestorium* [Against Eutyches and Nestorius], which is generally known as the Fifth Tractate, though chronologically it is most likely the earliest of the five.[18]

Unfortunately, the Schism between East and West remained, and, in 519, a group of Scythian monks came to Rome with another formula they hoped might resolve the controversy. This formula—that one of the Trinity suffered in the flesh (*unus ex Trinitate passus est carne*)—protected Christ's divinity while at the same time allowing for His suffering as a human being. Not only did this formula effectively end the Acacian Schism, but it seems to have been the occasion for Boethius's so-called First and Second Tractates, on the Trinity, written in the early 520s.[19]

The Question of Audience

Boethius's role in these theological disputes has engendered controversy in its own right. He has been described as an inactive disputant who wrote only for his own satisfaction, and his theological work has been evaluated as seeming "much more like a task conscientiously undertaken and efficiently carried through, than a labour of love." In opposition to such views, we may affirm that Boethius, an enthusiastic advocate of orthodoxy, was very much, though unofficially, involved in these theological controversies. Even though most of his theological tractates may represent pieces written because of particular occasions—as opposed to his scientific and logical writings, which were most likely part of an overall plan—they represent real concerns of Boethius. That he wanted them to be meaningful and effective may be seen in his Third Tractate, when he acknowledges that he is once again taking up a question he had already discussed because the method he had used was "not clear to all."[20]

The fact that he addresses three of his five theological tractates to contemporaries whose expertise he valued—Symmachus, his mentor, and John the Deacon, who may very well be the man who in 523 became Pope John I—may suggest further how important these treatises were to him. It may also indicate Boethius's hesitation at venturing into an area where, not being a cleric, he would necessarily be an amateur among professionals. As he writes at the beginning of his *Contra Eutychen,* he refrained from speaking at the assembly of clergy gathered to listen to the new Christological formula offered by the Eastern bishops: "I held my peace, fearing lest I should be rightly set down as insane." Although at the time of the assembly he had some thoughts and objections, he had no real contribution to make. But as he continued to ponder the issue at hand, he finally arrived at an understanding, which here, in the form of a "little essay," he submits to John the Deacon for his "judgment and consideration." If John feels that anything should be struck out, added, or altered in any way, Boethius will happily make the revisions and then "send the work on to be judged by the man to whom I always submit everything," that is, Symmachus.[21]

It would seem that John had, in fact, previously criticized Boethius's writings, for as Boethius says in the letter to him at the beginning of the Third Tractate, he has written this essay because John asked him "to state and explain somewhat more clearly" a question he had already dealt with. His concern with John's response would seem to be genuine. Similarly, in his letter to Symmachus at the beginning of the *De Trinitate,* Boethius writes that after long pondering the problem "with such mind as I have and all the light that God has lent me," he submits his essay to the judgment of Symmachus. Although the matter of the Trinity is difficult, Boethius says he has discussed it "only with the few," in fact with no one but Symmachus, and now he asks for Symmachus's assessment of his thinking.[22] Such hesitancy does not exist in Boethius's scientific and logical writings, and even the letter to Symmachus at the beginning of the *Principles of Arithmetic* is more full of self confidence than of humility. While, on the one hand, Boethius's humility may be the result of his awareness of venturing into an area outside his real expertise, on the other hand, this humility may be an expression of the *sermo humilis,* the lowly or humble style associated early with Scripture and with Christian writings in general. Whatever the reason for or point of this humility, we should realize that the *opuscula sacra* reveal profound thought and that, besides being a philosopher, scientist, and statesman, Boethius was "an accomplished theologian."[23]

At the same time, it should be emphasized that Boethius was purposely writing for a limited audience, and that he was being intentionally concise and complex. The obscurity and difficulty of his style in most of his theological tractates, far from being the result of immaturity or inexperience, are the deliberate intention of Boethius. He purposely uses scientific and philosophic methods and terms to make his thought impenetrable to those outside the faith. Only those who are properly equipped, that is, those who are both Christians and philosophers, will recognize the clarity of his thought. As Boethius writes in his letter to Symmachus at the beginning of his treatise on the Trinity, "I purposely use brevity and wrap up the ideas I draw from the deep questionings of philosophy in new and unaccustomed words," which are designed to be meaningful only to those whom, like Symmachus, Boethius respects. Likewise, in the Third Tractate, in his epistolary preface to John the Deacon, he acknowledges once again "the obscurity that waits on brevity," and justifies following "the example of the mathematical and cognate sciences." For him, "obscurity is the sure treasure-house of secret doctrine and has the further advantage that it speaks a language understood only by those who deserve to understand."[24]

In employing such language, Boethius's theological tractates are within a religious tradition which insists on the esoteric expression of doctrine so that only those who have been initiated into the faith are able to comprehend what is being said. The Christian basis for this practice may be seen in Matthew, where, answering the disciples' questions about why He speaks in parables, Jesus says that those who have been chosen to know the secrets of heaven will understand, but others hearing his words will not comprehend them. The authority for this attitude may be found in various Old Testament passages that criticize man for his inability to know truth, such as that reflected in Matthew: "This people's heart has grown dull, and their ears are heavy of hearing, and their eyes have closed."[25] This criticism would seem to be echoed in Boethius's sentiments about ordinary men, as in his letter to Symmachus at the beginning of his *De Trinitate,* where he appears to scorn "the common herd":

. . . apart from yourself, wherever I turn my eyes, they fall on either the apathy of the dullard or the jealousy of the shrewd, and a man who casts his thoughts before the common herd—I will not say to consider but to trample under foot, would seem to bring discredit on the study of divinity. So I purposely use brevity and wrap up the ideas I draw from the deep questionings of philosophy in new and unaccustomed words which speak only to you and to myself, that is, if you deign to look at them. The rest of the world I simply disregard: they cannot understand, and therefore do not deserve to read.

Similarly, in the letter to John the Deacon at the beginning of the Third Tractate, in reference to a work which he calls the *Hebdomads,* Boethius registers his scorn of the "pert and frivolous": "I confess I like to expound my *Hebdomads* to myself, and would rather bury my speculations in my own memory than share them with any of those pert and frivolous persons who will not tolerate an argument unless it is made amusing."[26]

From such criticism scholars have conjectured, first, that Boethius came to scorn his fellow Romans and, second, that all of his work interested no one but a few intimate friends.[27] But this language may very well have been more conventional than personal, more a way of introducing esoteric writing than of criticizing the age. Indeed, Boethius's attitude toward what he terms the "amusing" argument may be in accord with his decision in the second commentary on the *Isagoge* to do away with "wit and charm" of oration. There and here the "unadulterated truth" may not be for all. Moreover, Boethius's criticism of his contemporaries would seem to be a standard feature of the epistolary prefaces of his *opuscula sacra.* In his letter, again to John the Deacon, at the beginning of the *Contra Eutychen,* Boethius even criticizes the assembly responding to the letter from the Eastern bishops as a "mob of ignorant speakers" who, in their assumption of knowledge, "idly and carelessly slurred over" matters of gravity. But for all his "wonder" at "the vast temerity of unlearned men who use the cloak of impudent presumption to cover up the vice of ignorance," Boethius seems to respect those interested in matters of intellect.[28] Since in 512, the likely date of the *Contra Eutychen,* Boethius was also translating and commenting on Aristotle—most probably writing his first commentary on the treatise *On Interpretation,* in which he is particularly concerned with educating those who are beginners in the study of philosophy—it seems unlikely that he would have continued what amounted to his life's work of educating the Roman public if he actually scorned them.

The most important reason for Boethius's emphasizing that in his *opuscula sacra* he is writing for the few who are actually capable of dealing with theological disputation is that the Trinitarian and Christological subjects at hand are precisely the stuff of which heresy is made. Just as simple piety is not enough if one is to participate in theological controversy, neither is great intelligence. One must have both piety and knowledge, and be able to assess clearly the proper relationship between faith and reason.

In several of his works—certainly his two commentaries on Aristotle's *On Interpretation* and probably his two treatises on categorical syllogisms, as well as his double redactions of translations—Boethius reveals, first, a keen sense of his different audiences and, second, an ability to fit the work to the audience. His concern in his logical works with making the same material meaningful to both the advanced philosopher and the novice extends to his *opuscula sacra*, where, along with complex rational discourse, he offers a simple statement of faith, as may be seen in his so-called Fourth Tractate, *De fide Catholica* [On the Catholic Faith].

The Five Tractates

The *De fide* is notably different in its approach, style, and subject matter from the four other treatises that comprise Boethius's *opuscula sacra*. Instead of being obviously theological, it is religious, offering not a complex application of Aristotelian logic to Christian dogma but rather a succinct and simple statement of the principles of the Christian faith and of the history of salvation. Because, unlike the other theological tractates, it does not apply the principles of reason to confirm the truth of faith; and because in manuscript the work lacks title and statement of authorship, it has frequently been thought to be spurious. Since, however, it is included in two recensions of Boethius's theological works, and since, unlike the other tractates, it does not address anyone and therefore does not require a superscription, it should probably be accepted as authentic. Although E. K.

Rand had written a dissertation showing that the *De fide* was not by Boethius, he later changed his mind and was influential in shifting opinion about the question of authorship. While some recent scholars have wondered anew about the work's authenticity, we may agree with William Bark, who concludes in a detailed study of the piece that "the reasons for rejecting Boethius's authorship are flimsy; the reasons for accepting it are substantial."[29]

The work's superficial difference from the other *opuscula sacra* is not sufficient reason for doubting its place in the canon of Boethius's writings. Not only does Boethius demonstrate an exceptional versatility in passing from one kind of writing to another, but he seems to have cultivated, like Aristotle and Jerome before him, "an *esoteric* or technical style, intended for the inner circle of specialists, and an *exoteric* or popular style, intended for the general public."[30] The *De fide,* as an affirmation of faith, has no need for esoteric language. In moving from the creation of the world to the founding of Christianity to the Second Coming of Christ at the end of time, it stresses the bond between the Old and New Testaments in general and between the story of salvation before and after Christ in particular. And, in focusing on such basic tenets of Christian doctrine as the Unity and Trinity of God, the Incarnation of Christ, the union in Christ of human and divine natures, Christ's Resurrection and Ascension into heaven, the Virginity of Mary, and the manifestation of the Church on earth, the *De fide* resembles an expanded paraphrase of the Athanasian Creed.

Still, while it treats the fundamentals of Christianity, and while its style seems more liturgical than metaphysical, the *De fide* should not be thought to lack theological depth. Because its statements of dogma are laid down in conjunction with corresponding heresies—Arian, Sabellian, Manichaean, Pelagian, Nestorian, and Monophysite—Boethius may have intended this work to represent a compendium of Christian doctrine for the use of the orthodox Christians of his time, who may have had trouble distinguishing in doctrinal matters between the orthodox and the heretical. And perhaps, as Bark suggests, Boethius may have been employing his understanding of the issues, as well as his ability to simplify, to edify the Roman public and make them sympathetic to particular orthodox positions.[31]

It is also possible that Boethius intended the synthesis represented by the *De fide* to be a mere outline of points to be taken up and developed more fully, a preliminary classification of doctrinal points, not designed for publication, that would provide a basis for his further theological work. Still, in offering a "clear and admirably ordered account, not without touches of poetic intensity," the *De fide* may properly be considered as "a little masterpiece."[32] While its so-called "mystic manner" has been taken to suggest affinities with treatises by some of Boethius's Eastern contemporaries, the work is very much within the Augustinian tradition. As it stands, it resembles Augustine's *De catechizandi rudibus* [On Catechizing the Unlearned], a treatise offering basic religious instruction; though if the *De fide* were meant to be expanded, it might well have resembled Augustine's *City of God,* with its full picture of Christianity in relation to human civilization.[33]

The *De fide* demonstrates that the range of Boethius's Christianity extends beyond the application of Aristotelian methodology to vexing theological questions, and indeed the affirmation of faith found in this work may be understood as that which allows the philosophy-theology to come about, and that which is at the end of all the theological speculation.

Although the chronology of the *opuscula sacra* is moot, the *Contra Eutychen et Nestorium*—Tractate 5, written circa 512—is now generally agreed to be the earliest of the five tractates. In a sense—regardless of actual chronology—the *Contra Eutychen* is an appropriate successor to the *De fide,* for it takes up in detail the last two of the several heresies cited in this more general work. And here, in the course of clearing away the Nestorian and Monophysite heresies—showing that the one exalted the humanity of Christ at the expense of His divinity, and that the other emphasized the divine to the loss of the human—Boethius reasserts orthodox Catholic doctrine as he demonstrates that in Christ the human and divine natures were united in one person.[34]

Not only is the *Contra Eutychen* the longest of all Boethius's theological tractates—it is almost twice the length of the next longest, the *De Trinitate*—the work is, according to some scholars, "by far the most important and interesting of all." But regardless of whether we wish to praise it because Boethius seems "more at home in his subject, more master of his material" than in the other tractates, we should realize that Boethius's brilliant defense of the position of the Eastern bishops was actually one of the first notable contributions to scholastic studies. Besides refuting both the Nestorian and Monophysite positions, Boethius presents in a particularly effective way the notions of nature and person, and offers an especially memorable definition of person as "the individual substance of a rational nature." As adopted by St. Thomas Aquinas in the thirteenth century, this definition became the standard statement on the subject.[35]

Following the *Contra Eutychen,* though perhaps a decade later, were what are known as Tractates 1 and 2, the *De Trinitate* and the *Utrum Pater.* Although both of these works clearly go back for their understanding of Trinitarian matters to Augustine, whom Boethius even cites when at the beginning of the *De Trinitate* he says that Symmachus must examine "whether the seeds sown in my mind by St. Augustine's writings have borne fruit," it would seem that Augustine is less obviously present than Aristotle. Some scholars have even gone so far as to suggest that Boethius's tractates are in a sense opposed to Augustine's because all the elements which concur to give the wonderful balance between reason and faith in Augustine are omitted or turned around in Boethius. His procedure is more in accord with the intellectual principle, "I know so that I may believe," than with the fideistic principle, "I believe so that I may know."[36] But this critical judgment is based on the premise that Boethius intended to proceed as Augustine had, that he wished, in particular, to include the profound sense of the mystery of the Trinity earlier expressed by Augustine. Rather than blame Boethius for not doing what he never intended to do, we should recognize that he is concerned by and large with offering a metaphysical analysis of the terms of Trinitarian dogma. And although he employs arguments for the comprehension of revealed truth, Boethius does not presume to attempt to resolve rationally the mystery of the Unity and Trinity of Divinity, which is, as he says, a suprarational reality transcending human reality, that is, a "supersubstantial quality."[37]

Notwithstanding the traditional numbering of the First and Second Tractates, it has been suggested that Tractate 1, the *De Trinitate*, was most likely written after Tractate 2, the *Utrum Pater*, a work of but a few pages and the shortest by far of the five theological tractates. As Viktor Schurr argues, the *De Trinitate* extends the single argument presented in the *Utrum Pater*, which, as its full title indicates, concerns "Whether Father, Son, and Holy Spirit May Be Substantially Predicated of the Divinity." In one chapter of the *De Trinitate* (ch.5), on the categories of substance and relation, Boethius takes up this argument in detail and incorporates it into a larger analysis. Schurr thus concludes that the *De Trinitate* must have followed the *Utrum Pater*, for otherwise Boethius would have been returning to an argument he had already considered with particular care and thoroughness. Moreover, says Schurr, the *Utrum Pater* is clearer, simpler, and more direct than the complex *De Trinitate*, and although the contents of both go back to Augustine's work on the Trinity, the influence of Augustine is more apparent in the *Utrum Pater*.[38] Also, whereas Tractate 2 is addressed to John the Deacon and Tractate 1 to Symmachus, it might be argued, applying as Boethius's standard practice what he acknowledges in the *Contra Eutychen*—that after getting initial advice from John, he will send his work to Symmachus, "the man to whom I always submit everything"—that the *De Trinitate*, directed to Symmachus, therefore represents the more mature work.

While such a sequence is certainly possible, and while the *Utrum Pater* may represent a first stage of what later became the *De Trinitate*, it seems as likely that the *Utrum Pater* represents a clearer analysis of a point that had been made earlier in the *De Trinitate*, where Boethius had affirmed, on the one hand, that some qualities, notably goodness and justice, can be predicated from divine substance, and, on the other hand, that the relationship between Father, Son, and Holy Spirit does not refer to their substance. As Boethius acknowledged in his letter to John the Deacon at the beginning of Tractate 3, *Quomodo substantiae,* John had asked him "to state and explain somewhat more clearly that obscure question in my *Hebdomads* concerning the manner in which substances can be good in virtue of existence without being absolute goods"; and the Third Tractate represents just this clarification. Although the *Utrum Pater* begins with no epistolary prologue, it is addressed, like *Quomodo substantiae,* to John the Deacon, and may represent a comparable clarification of a point brought out in an earlier work, in this case, doubtless the *De Trinitate.*[39]

Moreover, as Boethius writes at the beginning of his Third Tractate, he can attest to the eagerness with which John has "already attacked the subject." What "the subject" refers to is not clear, though it would seem to be something found in the *Hebdomads;* but what this refers to is likewise not clear. In signifying literally a group of seven, *Hebdomads* may refer to seven works or to a work in seven parts, in this sense being comparable to the *Enneads,* or groups of nine, in which the different parts of Plotinus's work are arranged, and to the decads in which the historian Livy organized his material.[40] Although "the subject" that John has attacked eagerly may be the "obscure question" reflected in the full title of Tractate 3—"How Substances Can Be Good in Virtue of Their Existence without Being Absolute Goods"—it may also refer to a larger subject which has already concerned John. Indeed, the main theme of *Quomodo substantiae,* that in God qualities are substances whereas in man and other creatures they are merely accidents, would likewise seem to go back to the Trinitarian tractates. Not only were substances important in the *De Trinitate,* they were the entire subject of the *Utrum Pater,* where Boethius's concern was with distinguishing substantial predicates from relative ones. And, likewise, though the Third Tractate is taken up with the question of essential goodness, it is with the goodness of substances.[41]

Without intending to suggest that Tractate 3 continues the point of Tractate 2—although, as Luca Obertello among others points out, *Quomodo substantiae* was "certainly written in conjunction with the other two"—we may still recognize the possibility that this Third Tractate, like the *Utrum Pater,* refers to the issue of substance brought up in the *De Trinitate.* If this is so, we may consider the brief *Utrum Pater* as in effect an appendix to the *De Trinitate.* To the six chapters of this First Tractate would be added what amounts to a seventh chapter; and the composite work may represent what Boethius terms his *Hebdomads,* that is, his seven chapters dealing with substantial categories and their application to the Trinity.[42]

Joining East and West

Boethius's involvement in theological matters was not limited to his writing on Christian doctrine; it extended to his personal activity as well. Just as philosophy was something he not only read and wrote about but actually put into practice, so his religion was more than a matter of acknowledging the basic tenets of Christianity or of discussing such abstruse matters as the Unity of the Trinity and the Hypostatic Union of divine and human natures in one person in Christ. Moreover, as his educational program involved actual learning, so his theological concerns were both theoretical and pragmatic.

Although it has been suggested that for all his indebtedness to Augustine—who is the only Christian writer cited in all of his writings—Boethius, along with Symmachus and the other Romans who had succeeded in combining a genuine Christian faith with a devotion to the pagan heritage of Rome, would never have accepted Augustine's indictment of Rome in his *City of God,* it seems more likely that the point of Augustine's work, the need for man to become a citizen of the City of God instead of the city of man, would have seemed especially timely to Boethius.[43] Whereas the efficient cause of Augustine's treatise was the destruction of Rome by Alaric and the Goths in 410, the application of Augustine's views to the situation in early sixth-century Italy was easy to make. Augustine himself had insisted on the need for Rome to pay heed to its afflictions; as he says, addressing the Romans, "you have missed the profit of your calamity; you have

been made most wretched, and have remained most profligate."[44]
And in Boethius's lifetime Rome was still suffering from the
affliction of Gothic oppression. As long as the schism between
Rome and Constantinople lasted, it seems that the Romans accepted their domination by the Arian Goths. But in 519, with
the return of Constantinople to orthodoxy, some Romans apparently saw the possibility of bringing about a new and unified
world of orthodox Christianity, a City of God, as it were, where
Pope and Emperor, as well as Rome and New Rome—as Constantinople was called—would be joined together in harmony.

For men like Boethius and Symmachus, the East represented
more than the fount of ancient science and philosophy, and the
homeland of the Greek language. It also was the contemporary
center of culture and the seat of the Emperor. When in 519 the
relationship between East and West changed and the orthodox
emperor Justin submitted himself to the authority of the Pope,
the opportunity was at hand for Rome to regain its lost power
and glory and for a unified empire to be established, where the
combination of Pope and Emperor would insure the joining of
Faith and Reason and result in, as Boethius phrased it in his *De
fide Catholica,* the knitting together of a people who fill the broad
earth, governed by heavenly instruction through the Church, and
comprising one body whose head is Christ.[45] Such a cosmopolitan
City of God, far from threatening Boethius's classical interests,
would have represented for him, with its manifestation of truth
and goodness, the fulfillment of his educational and philosophical
plans, and the proper extension of his harmonizing of Aristotle
and Plato.

In the sixth century, when matters of religion were inseparably
bound up with political affairs, the doctrinal disputes in which
Boethius took an active interest were of the greatest political
importance. Regardless of how effective Boethius may have been
as transmitter of ancient learning or as clarifier of Christian doctrine, it was as Theodoric's Master of the Offices, where he could
actively work to effect a meaningful unification of East and West,
that he was best able to restore the prestige of Rome and achieve
harmony within the Church. Although Boethius's role in bring-

ing about unification is not at all clear, we should realize that anything he did to link Rome to the Empire would necessarily have been construed as being against the interests of the Goths in general and of Theodoric in particular. Justly or unjustly, not long after becoming Master of the Offices, Boethius was accused of being involved in a plot to bring Italy under the sway of the Emperor. He was deposed from office, imprisoned, brought to trial; and finally both he and Symmachus were executed as traitors.[46]

Incredible as this ending to Boethius's life might seem, it represents in one sense an obvious outcome of his political and theological activity, and even his great interest in Greek culture. And in the context provided by his apparent failure to make philosophers out of his fellow Romans and to restore Greek culture to the West, the fact that his efforts to create a unified empire were abortive is not surprising. As Boethius may have been too optimistic a judge of the abilities and interests of the Romans for whom he wrote his scientific and philosophical treatises, so he may have misjudged both the passivity and weakness of the Romans themselves and the strength of Gothic nationalism in Italy. As Pierre Riché suggests, the rupture between the Latin and Greek worlds may actually have been too complete to be healed. At the same time, it may be argued that had Theodoric followed the example of Clovis, King of the Franks, and converted the Ostrogoths from Arianism to Catholicism, not only would Italy probably have been spared the forthcoming horrors of war with the Empire and subsequent conquest by the Lombards, but Boethius's program of restoring classical culture may well have been successful, and, moreover, Boethius himself may have lived to extend his work.[47]

It is hardly sufficient to say that Boethius would have been better off had he remained in his library translating and commenting on Aristotle instead of working as an official in Theodoric's government, for as a public figure Boethius was only endeavoring to bring to fruition the cultivation he was involved with as a private citizen. All of his work, from his translations to his philosophical and theological speculations to his administration of the realm may be properly viewed as having the same end; and though Boethius finally failed in his plan, he cannot be accused of inadequate efforts. His words at the end of his *De Trinitate* may be aptly applied to his life's work in general and to his involvement in the attempt to join East and West in particular: "if human nature has failed to reach beyond its limits, whatever is lost through my infirmity must be made good by my intention."[48]

Chapter Four

The Martyr and the
Consolation of Philosophy

The Historical Record

Although it is something of an exaggeration to claim that the fall of Boethius has been "almost as much discussed as the fall of Adam," without a doubt, his downfall and subsequent death at a time when he was enjoying his greatest fame and power have fascinated the Western world. Notwithstanding all of Boethius's intellectual and literary accomplishments, he has in fact been most widely known and celebrated throughout the ages as a martyr. Although today scholars have by and large abandoned the old tradition that Boethius died a Catholic martyr at the hands of a persecuting Arian king, there seems to be little doubt that Theodoric was responsible for the downfall and death of both Boethius and Symmachus, most likely because he suspected that these important Romans were involved in a conspiracy against Gothic rule of Italy.[1]

Theodoric in 523 was seventy years old and clearly under great public and private strain. He had no son to succeed him, and his daughter's husband, who would have been the natural protector of his young grandson, had recently died. Another grandson had been murdered by his father, the King of the Burgundians, and Theodoric's sister, who was Queen of the Vandals, had been imprisoned by her husband's successor to the throne. Although the sixth century had begun auspiciously for Theodoric, who had already made his own peace with the Emperor in Constantinople; and although in 519, with harmony once again existing between Pope and Emperor, it seemed likely that his wish to renew the ancient glory of Rome under his leadership would be realized, by 522, the king was seeing the distinct possibility of the imminent destruction of everything for which he had hoped and worked. And, to be sure, Theodoric's anxiety was well founded, for within thirty years of his death in 526, the Ostrogoths were annihilated and Italy was made part of the Empire.[2]

Although through hindsight we might maintain that all of Theodoric's problems would have been avoided had he converted the Ostrogoths to Catholicism, the reality would seem to be that with the new harmony between Rome and Constantinople after 519, Roman hopes of a unification of East and West into one Empire and one orthodox Church increased dramatically, and Theodoric felt on the defensive in his relationship both with the Emperor and with his Roman Catholic subjects at home. But what actually occurred during the last two years of Theodoric's life, and what actually happened to Boethius, are not at all clear.

When in the first book of his *Consolation of Philosophy* Boethius the narrator tells Lady Philosophy of his fall, he notes in particular the accusation of treason: "you remember how at Verona a charge of treason was made against Albinus and how in his eagerness to see the total destruction of the Senate the king tried to extend the charge to them all in spite of their universal innocence; and you remember how I defended them with complete indifference to any danger, and you know that I am telling the truth."[3] Citing forged letters and perjured testimony used against him, Boethius says that if he could have replied to these charges, he would have said what Canius did when the Emperor Caligula accused him of being involved in a conspiracy: "If I had known of it, you would not." The precise charges are not clear, but along with being accused of practicing magic and seeking the assistance of evil spirits—charges apparently the product of ignorance about the study of philosophy—Boethius is supposed to have "desired the Senate's safety," to have prevented an informer from revealing papers which would show the Senate to be "guilty of treason," and to have "hoped for Roman liberty."[4]

Rather than be guilty of any crime, Boethius asserts that he took public office so as to put into practice his philosophical principles. He worked for what was right, and even when it meant opposing those who wielded greater power than he did, he protected the poor and helpless from the oppressions of the mighty. In particular, he says, he saved ex-Consul Paulinus from "the very mouth of the gaping courtiers, who like ravenous curs had already . . . devoured his riches." And in order to save ex-Consul Albinus from being punished wholly on the basis of presumed guilt, he risked incurring the enmity of Cyprian, Albinus's accuser. Such actions as these, which, insists Boethius, were based wholly on his love of justice, provoked resentment and opposition against him and led finally to his being struck down by false informers:

Yet who were the informers who struck me down? One was Basilius. He had previously been dismissed from the royal service and was forced into impeaching me by his debts. Two others were Opilio and Gaudentius. A royal decree had sentenced them to banishment because of their countless frauds, and to avoid complying they had protected themselves by seeking sanctuary. When the news reached the king he made a proclamation that unless they had left the city of Ravenna by the appointed day they would be driven out with their foreheads branded. There could scarcely be greater severity than that. Yet the very same day they laid information against me and the denunciation was accepted. Surely my actions didn't deserve that? And surely the fact that my conviction was prejudged didn't make just men of my accusers? Fortune should have blushed at the sight of innocence accused, or at least at the depravity of my accusers.[5]

Boethius's overt concern in this impassioned defense is less with clarifying the charges against him or with recording the events leading to these charges than with protesting his innocence and with lamenting the injustice done to him. What he offers is obviously neither an impartial nor a complete account of what actually happened. This he says he has offered elsewhere: "That posterity may not be ignorant of the course and truth of the matter I have put it down in writing." But since no such account has come down to us, we can only wonder how much of what Boethius includes of his fall in the *Consolation* can be taken at face value.

While the actual chain of events leading to the fall and death
of Boethius will probably never be known, it may be something
like the following: Sometime after the East returned to orthodoxy,
the Emperor Justin began to persecute Arians in the East, taking
their churches and forcing them to convert to Catholicism. In
response to these actions, Theodoric, probably alarmed at the
possibility of repercussions in Italy, initiated measures against
the Roman Catholics and sent Pope John I to Constantinople to
persuade the Emperor to modify his decrees against the Arians.
During the Pope's absence, letters from Roman senators to the
Emperor came to light. These indicated the existence of a conspiracy in Rome against Theodoric and implicated Albinus in
particular. But when Boethius rose to Albinus's defense, he too
was accused of treason. Whether Boethius was immediately imprisoned and soon executed is not clear. He may have been
stripped of his offices and property, and exiled, and then after
a while put to death. Because Boethius enjoyed the good favor
of the Emperor—who must have been partially responsible for
Boethius's two sons being named Consuls in 522—Theodoric
may have delayed executing Boethius to avoid jeopardizing the
Pope's negotiations with the Emperor. But when Pope John returned only partially successful, Theodoric not only imprisoned
the Pope—who died in prison—he also executed his former
Master of Offices. At this time the king probably arrested and
then executed Symmachus also, whom he may have recognized
as likewise involved in the conspiracy, or, because of his likely
desire to avenge the death of his son-in-law, as a danger to the
realm. Theodoric, moreover, planned to seize several Roman
Catholic churches; but before he could carry out this plan, he
himself died in 526.[6]

While recognizing that Boethius's fall was due to political, not
religious, causes, most recent scholars tend to take at face value
the impassioned words in the *Consolation* where Boethius, insisting on his innocence, says that he became involved in the matter
only because he genuinely felt that Albinus was falsely accused
and that the incriminating letters were forgeries designed to
implicate the Senate. A minority view, but one that deserves to

be noted, is William Bark's that Boethius not only was far from being a martyr to his faith but, along with Symmachus, was actually guilty of treasonable activities.[7] A union of Rome with the Empire would have represented the culmination of their desire to bring Greek thought and culture to Rome, and would have meant ridding Rome of Arian heresy and Gothic dominance. In working for these great ends, Boethius and Symmachus may not have intended either to be pawns of the Emperor or to work to depose Theodoric, but their interests were clearly not on behalf of the King of the Ostrogoths. While from their point of view they may have been working only for the good of Rome and of Christianity, from Theodoric's point of view they were guilty of conspiring against his control of Italy. The protestations of innocence in the *Consolation* may indicate only that Boethius fully believed he was working for "the common good."

The few extant historical sources do not offer much help for our understanding of these matters. The official letters written by Cassiodorus when he was Theodoric's Quaestor and collected by him in his *Variae,* though otherwise providing valuable details about Theodoric's reign, say nothing about the fall of Boethius. The *History of the Gothic Wars,* written later in the century by Procopius of Caesarea, says only that when "men of worthless character" laid false information against Boethius and Symmachus, the king believed they were guilty and after confiscating their property had them put to death on the charge of treason. Procopius is more concerned with the subsequent marvels that supposedly showed Theodoric his error than with the facts of Boethius's fall:

Symmachus and Boethius his son-in-law, both of noble and ancient lineage, were leading men of the Roman Senate and had been Consuls. Their practice of philosophy, their unsurpassed devotion to justice, their use of their wealth to relieve the distress of many strangers as well as citizens, and the great fame they thus attained caused men of worthless character to envy them. And when these laid false information against them to Theodoric, he believed them and put Symmachus and Boethius to death on the charge of plotting a revolution, and confiscated their property. And when Theodoric was dining a few days afterwards

his servants placed before him the head of a large fish. This seemed to
Theodoric to be the head of Symmachus newly slain. Indeed with its
teeth set in its lower lip, and its eyes looking at him in a dreadful
frenzied stare, it had a most threatening appearance. Greatly alarmed
at this extraordinary portent and shivering with cold, Theodoric has-
tened to his bed, and bidding his servants pile clothes upon him he
rested a while. But later he revealed all that had happened to his
physician Elpidius and wept for his sin against Symmachus and Boethius. Then having lamented and felt great sorrow for the calamity,
he died not long afterwards—this being the first and last act of injustice
he had committed against his subjects—and the reason of it was that
he had not, in the case of these two men, made the thorough examination he was accustomed to make before passing judgment.[8]

The marvelous also permeates the fragmentary chronicle known
as the *Anonymous Valesii,* which, because the pertinent section
about Boethius was apparently written within ten years of his
death, might otherwise seem to be of inestimable value. The
work reports that when the devil found a way to subvert Theodoric, who had hitherto governed well, he became alienated from
the Romans and even forbade them to bear weapons. The account
goes on to emphasize the supernatural as it notes that a woman
gave birth to four dragons, a comet fell for two weeks, and
earthquakes were commonplace. Such is the setting for Boethius's
fall:

The King began to show anger against the Romans wherever there
was opportunity. Cyprian, who was then Referendarius and afterwards
Count of the Sacred Largesses and Master of Offices, driven by greed,
laid an information against Albinus the Patrician that he had sent letters
to the Emperor Justin hostile to Theodoric's rule. Upon being summoned before the Court, Albinus denied the accusation and then Boethius the Patrician, who was Master of Offices, said in the King's
presence: "False is the information of Cyprian, but if Albinus did it,
both I and the whole Senate did it with one accord. It is false, my
lord, Oh King." Then Cyprian with hesitation brought forward false
witnesses not only against Albinus but also against his defender Boethius. But the King was laying a trap for the Romans and seeking how
he might kill them; he put more confidence in the false witnesses than

in the Senators. Then Albinus and Boethius were taken into custody to the baptistry of the Church.

But the King summoned Eusebius, Prefect of the city of Ticenum, and, without giving Boethius a hearing, passed sentence upon him. The King soon afterwards caused him to be killed on the Calventian territory where he was held in custody. He was tortured for a very long time by a cord that was twisted round his forehead so that his eyes started from his head. Then at last amidst his torments he was killed with a club.[9]

In both Procopius's *History* and the *Anonymous Valesii,* because of the mixture of history and legend, it is difficult to ascertain what is valid.[10] Even if we assume to be factual only those details that are in accord with the account of Boethius's fall included in the *Consolation,* we are faced with a further problem, for we do not know that the accounts in these chronicles are independent of that in the *Consolation.*

Even the scant evidence we have is not without ambiguity. Notwithstanding his identification in the *Anonymous Valesii,* it is not clear that at the time of Albinus's accusation Cyprian would have been Referendarius, the official who made an impartial statement of law cases that came before the King's Court. Furthermore, the historicity of the main actors in the drama of Boethius's fall is not at all certain. Cassiodorus's collection contains letters to a Cyprian, written on the occasion of his being appointed Count of the Sacred Largesses, or finance minister, and again when he is named Patrician, and to an Opilio, brother to this Cyprian, when he succeeds him as finance minister. Also, one of the letters praising this Opilio cites the noble family of Basilius, with whom Opilio has allied himself in marriage.[11] The striking differences between these figures celebrated by Cassiodorus and those reviled by Boethius have been explained by saying, on the one hand, that Cassiodorus, who was serving as Theodoric's mouthpiece, was not offering his private opinion, and, on the other hand, that Boethius's assessment was hardly impartial. As John Moorhead has argued, Boethius's opinions of the Romans who served the Goths clearly differed from the opinions they held of themselves.[12]

A further possibility, which should at least be considered, is that the eminent citizens of Cassiodorus's letters and the false accusers of Boethius's *Consolation* only coincidentally have the same names. Not uncommon at the time, these names may not refer to the same people at all. This is what is customarily said about the name Basilius, which in Cassiodorus is both that of a member of a noble family and that of a senator charged with practicing magical arts. Perhaps Cyprian, Opilio, and Basilius should be joined to Gaudentius, about whom, all scholars agree, nothing is known outside Boethius's account.[13]

While the identities of the rogues cited in the *Consolation* may be understandably unclear, we might expect more positive identification of the two noble ex-Consuls whom Boethius says he aided. Unfortunately, the situation is no better. Though an Albinus is addressed in several of Cassiodorus's letters, none of these records any accusation against him. In fact, aside from what is said of the accusation and arrest in the *Consolation* and the *Anonymous Valesii*—which may be based on the *Consolation*—no record exists of his fate. Paulinus, the other ex-Consul whom Boethius says he helped, may seem to be the Paulinus who, according to Cassiodorus, was Consul in 493 and later prosecuted by certain senators—perhaps explaining Boethius's reference to the "ravenous curs" who had already devoured Paulinus's wealth. But since Symmachus was one of the senators involved in prosecuting this Paulinus, it is hardly likely that Boethius would have celebrated him or criticized his father-in-law in this manner.[14]

Rather than take at face value Boethius's account of his fall, we should realize that it is part of the fictional account of a conversation between the victim Boethius and Lady Philosophy, who has come to console him and, indeed, to teach him a proper understanding of happiness. While several of the specific details of the *Consolation* may very well be factual, these are included mainly as part of the picture, created by the author at the beginning of his work, of man, here the narrator, grieving over undeserved misfortune. All of the details—whether or not they are historically accurate—seem to have been selected for their effectiveness in offering a meaningful account of one who has suffered unjustly. At the same time, we should recognize that in moving beyond the sorrowful and the emotional to the rational, the *Consolation* takes the narrator beyond the personal to an understanding of man's place in God's creation. It is hardly accidental that after the narrator finishes his long lament, Philosophy responds by saying unsympathetically that she had not realized how far he had been led astray by his grief (1:pr.5). Inasmuch as Boethius the philosopher proceeds by "ruthlessly exposing Boethius the natural man," the work should be understood less as a personal autobiography than as a manifestation of the didactic literature common in the sixth century. [15]

Symbolism and Tradition

Without going into the matter of genre or literary analogues at this time, we may still note that in its movement from the personal to the universal and from passion to reason, the *Consolation* may be seen in terms of a familiar pattern, found, for instance, in the well-known *Confessions* of Augustine, written at the turn of the fifth century. While the *Confessions* apparently details the story of Augustine's life before his conversion to Christianity, the author's point is actually to employ the personal to make meaningful the journey of the mind to God and, finally, to emphasize the hidden workings of the divine in human thought and effort. The last three books of the *Confessions*—books too frequently neglected by readers who turn to this work for personal details about the sinner-saint—are not at all about the man. Freed of the personal, Augustine is able to get to his main point; and the last three books move from the memory of the narrator and the present state of his soul to the ultimate meaning of human life in the divine plan of creation.

While Boethius's *Consolation* begins as though it too is a personal autobiography—particularly an account of the author's misfortunes—we soon realize that the autobiographical element is but the springboard for the work. Although, for the narrator, his undeserved misfortune is initially of paramount importance, as he begins to understand what Philosophy is saying, he moves beyond his concern with self. The personal element becomes decreasingly significant, and, in fact, in the last of the five books comprising the work, the concern is with issues that are not immediately pertinent to the character whose fall was the apparent subject of the first book. To say this is not to deny that the *Consolation* has as its starting point the situation of the fallen virtuous man, Boethius. Rather, it is to insist that the personal details should be taken less as historical facts than as details chosen by Boethius the author—not the character who changes in the course of the narrative—for their thematic significance. Their point is finally not to assert the innocence of Boethius but to justify the ways of God to man, to show that evil cannot happen to the good, and to affirm that everything occurring in God's creation is for the best.

Symbolic details are the norm in Book 1 of the *Consolation,* and the personal details about Boethius should be understood as having no more literal significance than those describing Lady Philosophy. Notwithstanding the abundance of specific details in her description, we have no doubt that those showing her to be both old and ageless, both of average height and higher than the very heavens, are to be taken metaphorically as revealing the nature, scope, and purpose of philosophy itself. Similarly metaphoric are the personal details found in the opening song, where the narrator—whose depiction may derive from that of the gray-haired narrator at the beginning of Martianus Capella's *De nuptiis Philologiae et Mercurii*—speaks of being old, with white hair and loose skin quaking on his bones. It is unlikely that Boethius, probably in his early forties at the time of writing, is giving a realistic picture of himself. As with the details in the description of Lady Philosophy, age is to be seen metaphorically as linked to sorrow: "Old Age, unlooked for, sped by evils, has come, and Grief has bidden her years lie on me."[16]

Comparable to the details associated with Lady Philosophy, which make philosophy itself meaningful, and those associated with the woebegone narrator, which suggest the plight of the fallen innocent, are the details of Boethius's fall, including references to figures who would seem to be historical personages. Whatever the historicity of the victimized ex-Consuls and the false accusers, Boethius may be using them symbolically. Names like Cyprian and Albinus may have been chosen more for their typicality and their symbolic potential than for their historical accuracy. Even if Albinus was indeed the actual name of the ex-Consul whom Boethius protected, it was especially appropriate in its connotations, seen in its Latin root, of whiteness and, by extension, of innocence.

Looking at the names of Boethius's false accusers in terms of their symbolic significations, we find that the Latin roots of the names Basilius, Opilio, and Gaudentius suggest respectively Power, Wealth, and Pleasure. The allegorical sense of the names Basilius and Gaudentius is especially apparent, for these names are synonymous with the Latin words for power and pleasure. But Opilio presents some difficulties. As a variant form of *ovilio* or *upilio,* both terms meaning "shepherd," the name Opilio would suggest the opposite of wealth. A name like Opulentius would have been much more suggestive of riches, but it would have functioned only to create an allegorical personification. Boethius seems to have been concerned with choosing for his accusers names that were actual Roman names, as Basilius and Gaudentius were. Opilio, containing the root *op-* and suggesting a reference to the Roman goddess Ops, associated with wealth and money, may have been selected as an actual Roman name that could function to suggest wealth.

Viewed symbolically instead of historically, Basilius, Opilio, and Gaudentius take on quite different significances. Basilius, who is described as having been dismissed from royal service, returns to accuse falsely; and Opilio and Gaudentius, having been banished because of "their countless frauds," return also to work against truth. It seems more than coincidental that Power, Wealth, and Pleasure, here figures of corruption and fraud, are precisely those false gifts of Fortune later singled out by Lady Philosophy in Books 2 and 3 of the *Consolation.* While appearing to give man happiness, they are actually deceptive, for they bring only misery.

In focusing here on Power, Wealth, and Pleasure—whereas later in the *Consolation* these false bringers of happiness are joined by High Office and Fame as well—Boethius would seem to be following a Hellenistic tradition of three false goods or false states of being, related perhaps to the commonly understood three parts of the soul. Included in this tradition are Aristotle's discussion in the *Nicomachean Ethics* of the three kinds of life—honor, money-making, and pleasure—which one could mistakenly think good; Plato's criticism in the *Republic* of the three concerns—with honors, wealth, and indulgence of appetite—that cause the decline of the State; and the Christian idea of the three temptations of man, as listed in 1 John—pride of life, lust of the eyes, and lust of the flesh—which were the subject of notable exegesis by the Church Fathers, including Augustine, not only in his Commentary on the Epistle of John but also in his *Confessions*. [17] Boethius's point in the *Consolation* is not necessarily to identify his three false accusers with any one set of these false concerns or temptations but, rather, to relate them to a familiar tradition that would have made clear the significance of their adversary relationship.

Precedent for Boethius's using details that though apparently autobiographical are actually symbolic may be found in both Neoplatonic and Christian tradition and in his own writings as early as his first commentary on Porphyry's *Isagoge,* where he establishes a fictional dialogue between himself and a friend who supposedly meet one wild winter night in the mountains outside Rome and discuss the usefulness of commentaries. And statements like Augustine's in the *Confessions* and *De doctrina Christiana* about the need to get beyond the name to the thing reflect a general awareness of the symbolic significance of names throughout the centuries immediately preceding Isidore of Seville's *Etymologiae.* Even names found in the New Testament were taken symbolically. Origen and Ambrose, for instance, in their commentaries on the Gospel according to Luke, matter of factly explain the significance of Luke's addressing his work to someone named Theophilus, a name meaning lover of God. As they make clear, this is what one must truly be if one is to understand Luke's message. Moreover, Boethius himself in his second commentary on Aristotle's *On Interpretation*—in what has been described as the first explicit recognition in Western writing that proper nouns express essences—speaks of fabricating names "so that the form of what is proposed would become clearer."[18]

To refer to Boethius's false accusers as symbols of Power, Wealth, and Pleasure is not to negate the reality of his fall, but rather to insist that, as Boethius presents his predicament, it is to be understood as more than something personal or individual. In the fiction that Boethius has created, his downfall functions as an object lesson of how a good man may be destroyed by relying on the impermanent and illusory goods of this world. Moreover, we should note the close similarity between the story of Boethius's fall and the account Plato gives in the *Republic* of the transition from timocracy—government based on love of honor—to oligarchy—government based on appetite. The timocratic man, in Plato's description, finds himself thrown down from power: "he may have held some high office or command and then have been brought to trial by informers and put to death or banished or outlawed with the loss of all his property."[19] We may well wonder whether Boethius consciously employed his own misfortune as an exemplum also making meaningful the degeneration of society or even whether the pattern described by Plato affected his presentation of his own predicament. In any case, we can hardly avoid feeling that in the *Consolation* Boethius uses his fall primarily for its instructive value.

As the story of the unhappy and unjust fate of Boethius may reflect a pattern for understanding the dissolution of society and its rulers, so it may be understood as offering an instance of the continual persecutions of philosophers, those who seek truth and justice. Lady Philosophy cites from early Greek times the poisoning of Socrates as well as the exile of Anaxagoras and the torture of Zeno, and she refers in more recent Roman times to the persecutions of the philosophers Canius, Seneca, and Soranus (1:pr.3). In insisting on man's recognizing the way of the world and, at the same time, his need to go beyond self-exoneration, the *Consolation* moves beyond the emotional to the rational and from personal experience to the truth revealed by it.

Far from being an autobiographical account of the persecutions of Boethius, the *Consolation* is more precisely a representative of the literary genre of *confessio* and should be linked to the various autobiographical confessions—of both sin and faith—that appeared in the fifth and sixth centuries, doubtless due to the influence of Augustine's own *Confessions*. Some, like the anonymous *confessio* attributed to Prosper of Aquitaine and the *Eucharisticos* [Thanksgiving] of Paulinus of Pella, both of the fifth century, show how the trouble brought about by the invading Goths led the authors to contemplation and to a recognition that their misfortunes had brought them to God. Others, like the *confessio* of Boethius's contemporary Ennodius of Ticenum, are more personal than public. This work was ostensibly the result of a serious illness which made Ennodius aware of death: praying for life, he vowed to repent and, moreover, to publish a literary statement of his repentance.[20] Whatever the personal or autobiographical elements may be in these writings, they function in all instances to show the need for proper understanding. The narrator, invariably a man who because of his own particular suffering has been unable to see clearly, in the course of the work demonstrates his new awareness.

While Boethius's *Consolation* is very much a *confessio,* it is explicitly—as its title indicates—a *consolatio;* and as such it reflects another established literary form, that had become by the time of Seneca's *Consolations* (first century A.D.) a kind of moral medication. Also, as used by early Christian writers, the *consolatio* pointed to trustworthy values beyond this world and stressed the workings of Providence in all of creation. For instance, in the fifth century, the important *De civitate Dei* [City of God] of Augustine offered a *consolatio* of sorts in its discussion of human suffering and its concern with the prosperity of the wicked; and the *De gubernatione Dei* [Governance of God] of Salvian was designed to reassure Christians who, faced with the defeats of the orthodox by invading Arians and pagans, wondered how God could permit the faithful to suffer, especially at the hands of unbelievers. Besides being comparable to these works, Boethius's *Consolation* may also, in its emphasis on the personal, be related to that form of the genre seen in Latin literature as early as Cicero's *Consolatio*, written after the death of his daughter, when he sought consolation in the study of philosophy.[21]

In the light of the way personal details are employed in the different works comprising the genres of *consolatio* and *confessio*, we should recognize that the *Consolation of Philosophy*, for all of its power and originality, is very much a traditional and conventional work of literature. And, in fact, literary—as well as philosophical—references fill the work. Although Lady Philosophy's first act when she appears before the disconsolate narrator is to drive the Muses of Poetry from his bedside, her speeches are full of poetry and song, as well as allusions to such Greek poets as Homer, Sophocles, Euripides, and Menander, and to such Latin writers as Catullus, Claudian, Juvenal, Lucan, Ovid, Seneca, Statius, and Virgil.[22]

Fact and Fiction

Far from being the spontaneous overflow of the powerful emotions of one who viewed himself as unfairly persecuted, the *Consolation* is a planned, contrived, and artful creation whose every detail of literary structure and philosophical content seems to have been carefully considered. Recognizing this, we should address two questions still bothering many readers of the work. First, if Boethius was actually in exile or prison—the narrator bitterly asks Philosophy if the place he is in looks like the library of his house in Rome (1:pr.4)—we are faced with the difficulty of explaining how he could have alluded to and quoted from so many works of literature and how he could have brought together such a wealth of material from Stoic, Aristotelian, and Neoplatonic sources. Furthermore, we might wonder how he had the leisure and peace of mind to create a prose style which is the nearest thing to the Ciceronian ideal that had been written in Latin for five hundred years, and how he could have penned thirty-nine poems that employ not only virtually every meter known in the sixth century but two or three apparently invented by Boethius himself.[23]

If we wish to avoid the problem, we may try to explain away the complexity of the work and say—as Hermann Usener did in the late nineteenth century—that the *Consolation* is merely a pastiche of some now-lost Greek works, put together either by Boethius or by an unknown Greek author whose synthesis Boethius then translated, prefacing to it a personal introduction and interspersing throughout the whole a number of poems.[24] If, however, we wish to claim that the *Consolation* is not a mere composite—"not a thing of shreds and patches, of clippings and pilferings, of translatings and extractings"—but a carefully designed piece of literature, we may try to get around the problem of the library by stating with E. K. Rand and others that Boethius must have possessed a power of memory far beyond that of most moderns. At the same time, given how syncretistic and structured the *Consolation* is, how "intensely artificial," as H. F. Stewart says, and smelling "of the lamp," memory alone is an unlikely answer to the question of how this work could have been written by someone with a limited number of books at hand.[25]

The problem is easily avoided if we view the *Consolation* as essentially a fiction, or, more accurately, if we recognize that the dramatic setting used by Boethius is essentially a literary device designed to provide a framework for the philosophy. Moreover, if we assess the thought of the *Consolation* not as the result of Boethius's fall but as the product of his life's work, the book does not seem at all surprising or strange. Nothing in it is antithetical to Boethius's thoughts elsewhere, and indeed its combination of Aristotelian and Neoplatonic elements is wholly in accord with the principle of harmonizing the two philosophies which he affirmed in his second commentary on the *On Interpretation* to be the ultimate aim of his writings.

Even though we may recognize this, we are faced with a second question: Why in his last work would Boethius, a practicing Christian, not have turned to the consolation offered by his religion? To rephrase this question, how could he, awaiting torture and death, have written a work that, while full of Aristotle and Plato, of elegant poetry and references to classical literature, never once mentions Christ and, for that matter, never presents teachings and conceptions that are unequivocally Christian?[26] Though an extensive collection of possible allusions in the *Consolation* to the Bible has been made, only one citation—and that to the Apocryphal *Wisdom of Solomon*—has been accepted as even likely.[27] Whereas certain elements, like the words on the power of prayer in 5:pr.3, may be understood as Christian in spirit; and whereas the powerful prayer to God in 3:m.9 may, for all its obvious Platonic features, have Judeo-Christian parallels in the Lord's Prayer and the liturgical *Gloria*, we are still faced with a paucity, if not a complete lack, of anything clearly Christian.[28]

To assert, as C. S. Lewis does, that Boethius was writing a consolation of philosophy, not one of religion, and that he purposely "wrote philosophically, not religiously," is unfortunately to beg the question, for it does not address the issue of why, on what has been taken to be the threshold of death, Boethius was concerned with matters of reason instead of faith, with thoughts of the providential order instead of the eschatological ultimates.[29] Similarly unhelpful for this question are views demonstrating that Boethius purposely blended philosophy, mainly Neoplatonism, with Christianity. No matter whether we agree with C. J. de Vogel that this blending amounted to an unconscious syncretism, or with Pierre Courcelle that it represented a purposeful adaptation of Christianity to philosophy, we are still faced with a work that is neither overtly nor, it would seem, essentially Christian.[30] When Augustine, for instance, blended Neoplatonic and Christian thought, his point was clearly to adapt the pagan philosophy to his Christian faith; and, indeed, this is what Boethius did in his *opuscula sacra*, when he used Aristotelian logic to affirm Christian dogma. But the *Consolation* would seem to be another matter.

The lack of Christian elements in the work is especially noticeable if we come to it from the *opuscula sacra*, where Boethius was very much concerned with Trinitarian and Christological matters, and where he offered—if Tractate 4 is indeed authentic—a full confession of faith. But readers throughout the Middle Ages and Renaissance were by and large not bothered by this lack. Although in the tenth century Bovo of Corvey felt that the

Consolation "did not at all deal with Christian doctrine" but rather with the opinions of philosophers, mainly Neoplatonists, the more representative analysis of the time was that of Remigius of Auxerre, who explained the work in terms of Christian doctrine and who greatly influenced subsequent interpretation.[31]

Those concerned with the lack of overt Christianity in the *Consolation* have offered over the centuries three basic explanations. The first, as stated in the twelfth century by Conrad of Hirsau, is that Boethius chose a purely rational form so that the *consolatio* he was offering could be understood not only by Christians but also by Jews, Muslims, and unbelievers. Although we might understandably be skeptical about such an explanation, this actually seems to have been the procedure of Minucius Felix when, in writing his dialogue *Octavius*—an apologia which has been termed the first monument of Christian Latin literature— he carefully excluded Biblical quotations and the very name of Christ. The second explanation, as suggested in the late Renaissance by Petrus Bertius, is that the *Consolation* as it stands is actually unfinished. According to this view, if Boethius had lived to complete the book, he not only would have returned to the plight of the narrator with which the work opened but certainly would have included Christian doctrine.[32] The third explanation for the lack of Christianity in the *Consolation* is that although Boethius was nominally a Christian, at the end of his life he found consolation not by turning to Christ but by continuing the intellectual activity that had been his main interest throughout his life. As he had written in the *De syllogismis hypotheticis,* he considered philosophy his "chief solace in life"; and this solace may have proved most effective when Boethius was most in need of it.[33]

The premises of all of these explanations—not only that the *Consolation* reflects Boethius's actual state of mind after his fall but that it was written while he was awaiting death—are suspect. Although death is mentioned in the poem that opens the work, it is there a desideratum: the unhappy narrator laments that "happy death" is deaf to his cries (1:m.1). And although the narrator says later in Book 1 that without a trial or conviction

he has been "condemned to death and proscription," the reference
is more likely to exile—a symbolic death—than to execution,
for, as he says in the same passage, he has been "conveyed five
hundred miles" from his home (1:pr.4). In like manner, the
narrator asks Philosophy why she has come down from heaven
to his "place of solitary banishment" (1:pr.3); and Philosophy
later remarks that "this very place, which thou callest banishment" is home to others (2:pr.4). Notwithstanding Philosophy's
sense that the narrator fears he will be killed (2:pr.5), the general
tone of the *Consolation* is, as Lewis notes, "not that of a prisoner
awaiting death but that of a noble and a statesman lamenting his
fall—exiled, financially damaged, parted from his beautiful library, stripped of his official dignities, his name scandalously
traduced." Not only is the language not that of "the condemned
cell," the consolation sought is apparently "not for death but for
ruin."[34]

The literature of imprisonment and banishment enjoyed in
Boethius's time a long tradition dating back to Plato's *Apology*
and *Crito,* dialogues whose setting was the prison where Socrates
awaited death, and in Roman times to, notably, Ovid's sorrowful
Tristia and *Dialogus ex Ponto,* written while he was in exile. In
Christian times this literature also took the form of theodicies,
or affirmations of divine justice, such as Dracontius's *De laudibus
Dei* [Praises of God], written at the end of the fifth century after
the author, who was imprisoned by the Vandals, was able to see
beyond his personal misfortune. At the same time, imprisonment
and exile were common metaphors in both Neoplatonic and early
Christian writings for the condition of man in this world, in that
the soul imprisoned in the body and man trapped in the world
of matter were both exiles from their proper spiritual homeland.[35]
Whatever the actual condition of Boethius after his fall from
power, we might wonder whether as author of the *Consolation* he
was not using the facts of his fall as a basis for developing the
metaphysical condition of imprisonment and exile.

In any case, there is absolutely no indication that Boethius
himself viewed the *Consolation* as his final piece of writing. Regardless of whether or not it is finished as it stands—and I will

argue that it is—Boethius may well have intended to write other works after it. The philosophical contents of the *Consolation* seem out of place only when readers insist that the work should represent a religious consolation. And the lack of overt Christian elements becomes significant only when readers insist on regarding the work as Boethius's farewell address to the world.

Moreover, the *Consolation* may represent the memorializing of work Boethius had been involved in for some time and may be considered an important part of his educational program in its investigation of such basic moral and metaphysical issues as the role of Fortune in the world, man's true and false happiness, evil, the relationship between Providence and Fate, and between God's foreknowledge and man's free will. If, as is likely, Boethius had already been thinking about these issues, his own personal fall from power, loss of wealth, and general unhappiness would have provided an apt context for making the issues particularly meaningful. Regardless of whether, by using the fiction of consoling the good man who had fallen, Boethius hoped to regain what he had lost, this fiction provided him with the opportunity to record his investigations of issues that were at the heart of philosophy and that he clearly felt must be considered by one seeking truth.

In his *Dialogue* on the *Isagoge,* Boethius had taken the role of teacher, instructing his friend Fabius about Porphyry's introduction to Aristotle's *Categories.* Although in his subsequent writings he rejected the dialogue format in favor of continuous discourse that would reveal "unadulterated truth," in the *Consolation* he not only creates another fictional dialogue but puts himself in it as the person requiring instruction from a teacher who is now Philosophy incarnate. While this role of pupil may be related to that assumed by Boethius in his letters at the beginning of several theological tractates, in the *Consolation* it is generalized and allegorized, perhaps because his concern here is with communicating to a wider audience than he wished to reach in most of the *opuscula sacra.* To say this is not to imply that Boethius is now addressing those whom he referred to at the beginning of the *De Trinitate* as "the common herd." As Hans von Campenhausen writes of the *Consolation,* "the refinement of its methods, its organization, its emphases, and its connections, the Greek quotations that are thrown in, and the countless reminiscences and echoes of older literature would even at the time be wholly clear only to the most learned reader."[36] The *Consolation* is anything but a naive piece of writing, though we may say that once again Boethius recognized the advantage of couching his truth in an attractive or compelling fiction. The fall of Boethius offered just such a fiction, as the fall of Socrates did for Plato's analysis of whether, even to preserve his life, the good man should return evil for evil, and as Augustine's early life did for his analysis in the *Confessions* of the journey of the mind to God. In all three instances the biographical or autobiographical elements function not as ends in themselves but as means of making clear the ideas of the philosopher.

That Boethius apparently died before writing anything more than the five books comprising the *Consolation* does not mean that he wrote the work in the shadow of execution. But we can hardly ignore the fact that the account of the execution—stemming from that in the *Anonymous Valesii*—has given the work a special poignancy and point. The last words of great men and martyrs are especially compelling, and the recognition that the *Consolation* contains the last words of Boethius in a sense assured the book's appeal to the Western world for more than a thousand years. Although we should not necessarily think that the autobiographical elements in the *Consolation* were what most interested Boethius, they clearly fascinated many readers, and in the Middle Ages led to the composition of several apocryphal lives *(vitae)*.

Although Cassiodorus says nothing about the death of Boethius, or his guilt or innocence, referring to him in his *Institutes* only as *vir magnificus;* and although Procopius, who thought Boethius innocent of the charges against him, says only that Theodoric confiscated his property and put him and Symmachus to death for crimes against the State, the legend of Boethius the Christian martyr, who endured a terrible torture at the hands of a barbaric Arian king, begins early. The details of the *Anonymous Valesii*—that Boethius was tortured by a cord twisted around his head so that his eyes popped out of their sockets, and then clubbed to death—may be related to the grim accounts in the medieval *vitae,* where Boethius is treated as a Christian martyr and saint. The detail of the clubbing is found in altered form in a tradition depicting Boethius as decapitated by a sword, carrying his severed head in his hands, even as he receives the Eucharist. Moreover, his bones are supposed to have been transported in the eighth century—along with those of St. Augustine—from Pavia, where he had been executed, to the Church of San Pietro in Cieldoro. His name is included as that of a saint in certain registers, including the official *Acta Sanctorum,* where he has the title of Saint Severinus and the feast day of 27 May; and in 1883, Pope Leo XIII sanctioned his being venerated in the diocese of Pavia and his being given the feast day of 27 October.[37]

The identification of Severinus Boethius as Saint Severinus doubtless reflects a traditional popular association and may explain much about the legends that came to be associated with Theodoric's deposed Master of Offices. Indeed, a famous Saint Severinus, who lived in Italy in the fifth century and died about 482, was the subject of a notable saint's life, written in 511 by Eugippius, a Roman contemporary of Boethius. In this work, in which Severinus is said to have forecast the reign of Odovacar and the number of years he would rule, even Theodoric figures, though briefly. Although we might be tempted to make a case for the influence of this particular saint's life on the legend of Boethius—and it has been suggested that Boethius was actually named after this saint—we should realize that before the seventeenth century there were upwards of a score of saints having the name Severinus. Still, it is likely, as E. M. Young among others has suggested, that Severinus Boethius became confused early in the popular mind with at least one Saint Severinus, and that the details of the philosopher's life became mixed up with details from the lives of saints and martyrs.[38]

Regardless of the various confusions that have existed, it seems clear that the story of Boethius's life and death developed in the popular mind and became, with little justification, the basis for interpreting Boethius's last work, the *Consolation.* But while we may legitimately lament that fascination with Boethius the martyr has prevented proper interpretation of his work, we must also recognize that the identification of Boethius as martyr surely attracted readers to the work. Without the legend, the *Consolation* would certainly not have fascinated men throughout the centuries as it did, and would not have exerted the influence it did on medieval and Renaissance thought, literature, and art. Admitting this, we should recognize that it is now time to study the *Consolation* apart from the fall of Boethius and see just how it merits its reputation as one of the greatest books ever written.

Chapter Five

The Argument of the *Consolation*

Notwithstanding the importance of Boethius's other writings, the *Consolation of Philosophy* so dwarfs them that it has come to represent its author to the world, much as the *Commedia* represents Dante, the *Faerie Queene* Spenser, and *Don Quixote* Cervantes. Not only the culmination of Boethius's literary activity, the *Consolation* is in its own right a great work of literature, fully the "golden volume," that Edward Gibbon termed it, "not unworthy of the leisure of Tully or Plato." Although in it Boethius works on many levels simultaneously, we should realize that as the *Consolation* is hardly the record of how its author recovered from being overwhelmed by grief and indignation, so its literary merit is not linked to this recovery. To say, as Helen Barrett does, that as Boethius regained his "mental poise and serenity," he increased "in power and independence of thought," is misleading at best.[1]

Before we can appreciate the complexity of Boethius's blend of drama and allegory, verse and prose, and philosophy and fiction, we must understand the *Consolation* as it functions to take the reader through five books and thirty-nine passages of alternating verse and prose to truth, specifically to an understanding of how to view the good and bad fortune of this world in the light of Providential order. The following summary-analysis is concerned with showing how the dialogue at hand is organized and with examining how the various sections of the work are constructed and interrelated.

Establishing the Problem

Book 1, the opening act in the "metaphysical drama" Boethius has created, presents a speculative problem which the following books are to solve.[2] Beginning with a depiction of the narrator as a man distraught by grief, the opening poem in elegiac couplets contrasts his present sorrow with past happiness.[3] The only constant in his life would seem to be the muses, who, the narrator says, inspired his present sad songs as they did the happy ones of his youth. These muses, however, although "partners of my weary way" (6), are to be understood not as steadfast friends but as reflections of the narrator's own passions, and the comfort they bring is false. Although the narrator asserts, "The art that was my young life's joy and glory / Becomes my solace now I'm old and sorry" (7–8), the sad songs his grief drives him to compose offer little solace. Providing the narrator with words to accompany his tears, the muses perpetuate his despair and bring him closer to death. Their "fruitless thorns of affections" kill "the fruitful crop of reason." Instead of "remedies," they offer only "poisons" in that they "accustom men's minds to sickness" (1:pr. 1). Philosophy's act of banishing these muses—within a long tradition extending back to Plato's *Republic,* though its immediate antecedent may be Augustine's *City of God*—is a basic step in the process of restoring the narrator's reason. Insofar as Philosophy reflects something within him, it is his latent reason—E. K. Rand calls her "naught but the idealization of his own intellect"— and, as she says, she comes to save the narrator precisely because he has previously been nourished by her.[4] But it is only in the third section of Book 1 that the narrator recognizes his physician as Philosophy, "in whose house I had remained from my youth."

Blindness, in fact, along with sorrow, dominates the first three poems of Book 1. In the initial poem the narrator's perception is so unclear and distorted that neither his analysis nor his evaluation of his problem can be trusted. Although he can report what Philosophy looks like (pr. 1), he is not able to use these details to identify her. In the second poem, Philosophy presents the narrator's condition by linking the contrast between past and present with the imagery of despair and blindness. The poem, in two parts, employs as a frame the present condition of the narrator's mind, within which it places a contrasting picture of the past. As the first lines make clear, his mind is sunk in despair and immersed in darkness (1–5); and as the concluding lines reaffirm, it is held down by heavy chains, prisoner of both night and earthy (24–27).[5] In contrast, the middle part of the poem shows the narrator's mind when it was turned to the heavens, contemplating the celestial bodies and the principle behind their movement and behind the change of the seasons in this world (6–23). The variety and brightness of creation here contrast with the "sullen earth" that is the object of the narrator's vision in the frame section, and the movement—of narrator, spheres, and seasons—is juxtaposed against the immobility that dominates in the frame. In particular, the eager searcher after wisdom of the central section of the poem is contrasted with the torpid, melancholy man of the frame, whose troubles blind him to anything other than his own condition.

After Philosophy, counseling remedies and not lamentation, wipes away the narrator's tears with a fold of her dress, he finally recognizes her (1:pr.2). Although the third poem, again put in the mouth of the narrator, would seem to be a continuation of his first poem, the two actually contrast. As the first two lines of m.3 make clear, darkness is replaced by light as the narrator's eyes recover their former strength. The remainder of this poem— the next eight lines in the form of an expanded simile—relate the new sight of the narrator to the coming of light to the world. The division between nature and man, highlighted in m.2 in terms of the difference between what is and what used to be, ceases, and in the last two lines the union of nature and man is suggested by the newly returned sun's dazzling with its rays the wondering eyes of man. The simile in fact continues into the third prose section as the narrator applies it to himself: "In like manner, the mists of sadness dissolved, I came to myself and recovered my judgment." He is now ready to listen to Philosophy's words, which resemble in pr.3 the kind of diatribe, or learned discussion, common in the writings of the Cynics and Stoics.[6]

Philosophy's next poem (m.4), celebrating the man who is unmoved by change in his earthly condition, insists on a distinction between change as a reflection of the mutability of this world and that which involves a movement of man to God and a metamorphosis of the self. As the first four lines state explicitly, the serene man is impervious to whatever happens to him, no matter whether good or bad. Again employing images linking the worlds of nature and man, Boethius makes clear that man should not be moved by either the storms and upheavals of nature or the rage of tyrants. The man who is master of himself cannot be ruled by "hope or terror" (13), passions which will only bind and enslave him. Whereas in m.2 the free man is he whose spirit ranges outside the body throughout the universe, here it is he who with firm spirit placidly withstands all that happens. The apparent paradox is purposeful, for in both poems the mind is the controller of man's condition. In depicting man as firm and serene—as in effect a manifestation of the Stoic ethical ideal—Boethius shows him as being able to encompass the world.

This fourth poem leads to pr.4 and Philosophy's direct question to the narrator: does he understand what she has said, or is his condition such that he is deaf as well, it would seem, as blind? What follows amounts to the first stage of healing in that the narrator's wound is being revealed. The language, which shows him defending himself, agrees with the principles of classical forensic discourse. According to the narrator, his loss of fortune has made it impossible for him to be in accord with nature. Though previously, with the aid of Philosophy, he could relate the manner of his life to "the pattern of the celestial order," now Philosophy has rewarded his endeavors with misfortune. The culmination of this section is a lengthy verse complaint in the form of a prayer which addresses the "creator of the starry heavens" (1:m.5) who, sitting on his everlasting throne, moves the heavens and orders the stars (1–13). God is depicted first as lord of the universe, then, inasmuch as he orders the seasons, as lord of nature (14–24); He rules everything except man, whose actions, says the narrator, are controlled instead by Fortune. The second part of the poem (25–41) focuses on the way of human society, where, as opposed to God's universe, the wicked rule and persecute the innocent. In the final lines the narrator prays that God will extend his rule from the stars and guide the earth as well (43–48).[7]

Although the prose section in which the narrator reveals the injustice done to him (1:pr.4) is three times longer than any other prose section in Book 1, and although the poem culminating this speech (m.5) is likewise the longest poem in Book 1 of the *Consolation,* we should not conclude that this length necessarily means that we are now seeing Boethius's point in this Book. Even though this speech is at the heart of Book 1, and even though it changes from the elegiac meter of the narrator's first two poems and approximates that of Philosophy's first two poems, we are still seeing the confusion of the narrator. For all his expressions of "continued grief," Philosophy remains, in accord with the ideal presented in m.4, placid "with an amiable countenance and nothing moved" (pr.5). Her response is to state that though she had known the narrator to be "in misery and banishment," until she heard these remarks, she had no idea how far astray he had gone, how much he had wandered of his own accord from his homeland.

Full of errors about human society and Providential order, the narrator's long speech serves in general to reveal the extent of his illness and in particular to provide a focal point for Philosophy's teachings.[8] His "sorrow raged against fortune," his complaints about not being rewarded, and his final "bitter verse," where he prays that "the earth might be governed by that peace which heaven enjoyeth," lead her to recognize that "the multitude of affections, grief and anger" afflicting him have made him unable to receive "more forcible remedies." Her subsequent poem (m.6), on the recognition of order in all of creation, offers three examples of the perversity of not being in accord with nature. As man would not think to sow wheat in the summer (1–6), search for violets in the winter (7–10), or look for grape clusters in the spring (11–15), so he should not think to upset God's established order: "He that with headlong path / This certain order leaves, / An hapless end receives" (20–22). This poem, with these concluding lines, offers both Philosophy's evaluation of the narrator's criticism of divine order and her prescription for curing the narrator.

What follows (pr.6), though the closest thing to a Socratic dialogue seen yet in the *Consolation*, is actually a catechism in which Philosophy, by questioning the narrator, further diagnoses his ailment. Along with exiling himself from his proper homeland, he has forgotten his true nature: "another, and that perhaps the greatest, cause of thy sickness: thou hast forgotten what thou art." Moreover, because he is ignorant of the purpose of things, he thinks that the wicked are powerful and happy, and that changes of fortune occur by accident. These errors—concerning the nature of man, of good and evil, and of universal order—are to be corrected in the instruction that follows. Proper understanding will not only restore the narrator's health, it will lead him back to his proper homeland.[9]

Book 1 of the *Consolation* ends with a poem by Philosophy (m.7) that, using the images which have dominated the book, restates its major theme—the need for man to avoid being dominated by passions—and also looks forward to the concerns of the next book. Again the structure is a three-part metaphoric statement—that stars hidden by clouds yield no light (1–4), that waters muddied by storms are no longer clear (5–13), and that streams flowing down mountains are apt to be blocked by rocks (14–19)—followed by an application to man. He would be able to see the clear light of truth and arrive at it if only he could rid himself of joy and fear, hope and sorrow: "The mind is clouded / And bound in chains / Where these hold sway" (29–31).[10]

The Goods of Fortune

At the beginning of Book 2, Philosophy diagnoses further "the causes and condition" of the narrator's "disease," which is the result of his having lost good fortune (pr.1); and the whole of this second book is "an exposition of the essentially fickle nature of Fortune, whose only law is that of constant mutability." In what may be viewed as an allegory of Fortune, Boethius connects three themes: the instability of human affairs, the ephemeral nature of worldly goods, and the vanity of earthly glory.[11] That change is the very nature of Fortune is clear with the first poem of Philosophy, where the dominant image is the Wheel of Fortune that the goddess constantly turns (m.1). The depiction of the tyrant ruler here provides an ironic echo and contrast with those images from Book 1, of God the unmoved mover and of man, who should be unmoved by whatever fortune is his.[12]

Although Philosophy is the dominant speaker throughout Book 2—all the poems are in her voice—Boethius gives a sense of variety by having her first speak as though she were Fortune, turning the narrator's accusations back on himself. Since "riches, honours, and the rest of this sort" are under the jurisdiction of Fortune, what right does man have to claim them (pr.2)? Should "the insatiable desire of men" tie Fortune to a constancy that is contrary to her very being? The poem Philosophy utters in Fortune's voice (m.2) is a further indictment of man for his essentially avaricious nature. Even if man should have as many gifts as there are grains of sand or stars that shine, he would still make his miserable complaints (1–8); even if God should answer his prayers with gold and honors, these would not suffice "since ravenous minds, devouring all, for more are ready still" (9–14). The rapacious greed of man is such that it can never be satisfied, and the conclusion of the poem is that the man who is not satisfied cannot be rich no matter how much he has: "He is not rich that fears and grieves, and counts himself but poor" (19–20). While shifting the responsibility of happiness away from Fortune to man himself, the poem also reaffirms Philosophy's teachings of the need for man to be free of such concerns.[13]

Invited to answer this indictment against mankind, the narrator can only reassert his misery (pr.3). But Philosophy berates him, pointing out the great amount of good fortune he has already enjoyed: a noble father-in-law, a chaste wife, and fine sons, along with honors—including having his sons made co-Consuls—rarely granted to men. Why, after such good fortune should he not expect to suffer a little trouble? Since at the end of his life man must necessarily leave all of his fortune, what does it matter if good fortune leaves him? As the next verse stresses, instability is the way of the world (m.3). Again the structure is a series of three illustrations from nature followed by an application to man. When the sun appears, the stars grow dim (1–4); when the cold blasts of wind come, the roses lose their buds (5–8); when the north wind blows across the deep, the waves are no longer calm (9–12). Since the world rarely stays the same for long, man should not trust things that are transitory (13–16). As the last lines state, "An everlasting law is made, / That all things born shall fade" (17–18).

These lessons of Philosophy lead to considerations of human happiness: "The nature of human felicity is doubtful and uncertain, and is neither ever wholly obtained, or never lasteth always" (pr.4). Moreover, human happiness is such that it does not last long with those who are contented, and it does not satisfy those who are discontented. Instead of seeking happiness in the world, man should look within himself; and m.4 is Philosophy's praise of the prudent man, who makes his home away from the threat of blasting winds and dangerous waves, as well as away from the extremes of mountain peaks and shifting sands (1–12). Choosing a place which is low and firm, he will live a serene life "scorning the air's distempered rage" (13–22). The poem would seem in its theme and imagery to be a purposeful echo of the last poem of Book 1, but there the point was that if man wished to see clearly, he should avoid being dominated by passions. Now the application is to man's happiness and to his relationship with Fortune. The similarity of passion and Fortune is not accidental; man must be immune to the dangerous attractions of both.

Noting that her soothing arguments have begun to be effective, Philosophy says that the time has come for arguments that are "somewhat more forcible" (pr.5). And so she begins to discuss particular gifts of Fortune and their inability to bring man happiness. Riches are essentially barren and troublesome; not only do men who "have much need much," but the quest for riches debases man. Again Philosophy insists that instead of searching outside himself for what is good, man should look within. When man knows himself, he surpasses the rest of creation; when, however, he forgets who he is, he is worse than the beasts.

Though, she says, the narrator fears now to be killed, he would not be afraid of anyone had he set out on the path of this life like a poor pilgrim. The fifth poem, continuing the point that man should prefer the simple life without wealth, gives a picture of the Golden Age—based on passages in Virgil's *Georgics,* Ovid's *Metamorphoses,* and Tibullus's elegies—when man was content with nature's ample bounty and not ruined by slothful luxury (1–3). Because man's desire for gold, burning like the fires of Mount Etna, has resulted in his plundering the world, he needs more than ever to return to the ancient ways and renounce his passion to possess gold and diamonds (23–26).

The sixth prose section turns from wealth to the dignities and power which man in his ignorance exalts to the heavens. But like all the other goods of Fortune, high office and power are not worth striving for. They are not intrinsically good, they are possessed by men who are not good, and they do not make good those who possess them: "neither can riches extinguish unsatiable avarice, nor power make him master of himself whom vicious lusts keep chained in strongest fetters." The sixth poem demonstrates the inadequacy of power in particular by detailing the vices and mad rage of the emperor Nero. It also serves to illustrate the degeneration that has come to the world since the Golden Age.

In pr.7 Philosophy shows the inadequacy of man's concern for earthly fame and glory, whose insignificance may be perceived when they are related to the infinite extent of eternity. Also when the mind "freed from earthly imprisonment" goes to heaven, it will disregard all earthly concerns, including fame. As m.7 makes clear, not only is fame trivial (1–6), it neither keeps man from death (12–14) nor offers him immortality. Notwithstanding man's hopes to live on by having his name remembered, the day will come when this too will be forgotten: "When length of time takes this away likewise,/A second death shall you surprise" (25–26).

In the eighth and last section of this book, Philosophy changes her argument and shows how man may properly use Fortune, specifically how, paradoxical as it may seem, bad fortune is more useful to man than good fortune, which is more apt to deceive him. The final point of pr.8, that through adverse fortune man may distinguish false friends from true ones, provides a link to m.8, which summarizes the several points of Book 2, and identifies the principle of harmony that binds everything together as love. The thirty lines of this poem may be meaningfully divided into two equal sections. In the first fifteen lines, a four-line statement showing that *concordia* is the principle making the changing world stable is followed by two four-line illustrations: Though day and night are apparently in opposition, one leads to the other (5–8); like land and sea each has its proper place in creation (9–12). The next three lines apply these illustrations to show that order is achieved through "love ruling heaven, and earth, and seas" (13–15). The second fifteen lines of this poem make clear the power of love. This section is subdivided into two six-line passages which show love first as a cosmic power controlling the reins of everything that moves in the universe (16–21), and second as a unifying principle in the world of men, expressed as alliances between peoples, union in marriage, and the bond of friendship (22–27). The concluding lines—"How happy mortals were, / If that pure love did guide their minds which heavenly spheres doth guide" (28–30)—extend the last lines of the first fifteen-line section, where love is identified as the controlling principle of the universe (13–15), and reaffirm the need for men to participate in cosmic harmony.[14]

Although we may marvel how Boethius has moved in Book 2 from Fortune to Love, his point is clearly that the gifts of Fortune—specifically wealth, power, and fame—are deceptive in that they cause strife, not harmony, and that the peace found in man during the Golden Age, along with the tranquillity found in the individual free of such concerns, are best understood as manifestations of love, the first principle of creation and order.

The Search for True Happiness

Refreshed by Philosophy's "weighty sentences and pleasing music," the narrator evaluates his condition and requests the sharp remedies for the assaults of fortune that she had referred to earlier. Though in Book 3 Philosophy examines the contrary of true happiness, her point is to show the narrator how to discern what is true. The principle of this procedure is spelled out in m.1, which offers a series of illustrations taken, as earlier, from nature and the cosmos. The first four lines state the principle in metaphorical language: To insure a fruitful harvest, one must clear the ground before he sows his seed (1–4). The next six lines offer three illustrations of the effectiveness of contrast in allowing one to discern and appreciate: the tongue after tasting bitter food finds honey all the sweeter; the stars after rain stand out all the brighter; and day after darkness appears all the more striking (5–10). In like manner, the mind after recognizing false goods is more receptive to true ones (11–13).

Book 3, the central and longest book of the *Consolation,* functions initially as an analysis of these false goods, defined here as "riches, honour, power, glory, pleasure" (pr.2). Although discussed in Book 2 as wealth, power, and fame, there they were analyzed specifically as false gifts of Fortune. Now in Book 3 the perspective is different, and they are judged according to their ability to bring man "sufficiency, respect, power, fame, delight, and joy."[15] The third book may be said to develop "in positive form the reasoning which the second has negatively suggested." Viewing the goods for which men strive as actually facets of a single good, it shows them to be worthy of desire only inasmuch as they are aspects of the *summum bonum,* the highest good, for which man by nature searches.[16]

As m.2 shows, all of nature instinctively knows and responds to this good (1–6). The several examples that follow range from the chained lion which at any moment may revert to its natural ferocity; the caged bird which if given the opportunity will return to the woods; and the bent tree which when released will raise itself toward the sky (7–30). The culminating example extends to the cosmos, specifically to the sun, which, though descending at night beneath the waves, proceeds through secret ways until it rises the next morning in its accustomed place (31–33). Although this final illustration may seem out of place, it serves to lead to the final point of the poem: not only does everything seek its proper place—to be understood as its *summum bonum*—but the only stable order is that which "doth within itself embrace / The births and ends of all things in a round" (37–38). In that endings are connected to beginnings, forming a circle, the orbit of the sun acts to illustrate this principle.

The principle may also be applied to man, who, as in a dream, acknowledges his beginning and has some vague sense of the "true end of happiness" (pr.3). But man thinks to obtain happiness from false goods, and sections three through seven of Book 3 examine, respectively, the inadequacies of wealth, high office, power, fame, and pleasure. The poems of these sections, the shortest in the entire *Consolation,* seem more like appendages to the prose sections than like parallel presentations or commentaries. The poem in the third section restates through a particular illustration the final point of pr.3, that riches not only fail to eliminate human needs, they even create new demands. In spite of the rich man's wealth, "yet biting cares will never leave his head, / Nor will his wealth attend him being dead" (5–6).

The discrepancy between the apparent worth and the real inadequacy of these false goods is emphasized in the next section, where high office is actually opposed to worthiness. And to make this point meaningful, m.4 focuses again on Nero as a type of the wicked man and asks who could think honors good when they may be given by such as he. Nero also provides a transition to pr.5, which associates power with tyranny and vulnerability; and m.5 makes clear that power will not keep man from being full of cares. Real power comes only when man is free of passion and unconquered by desire.

In like manner, fame is no prize, for "deceitful it is oftentimes, and dishonest" in that it extols the unworthy and makes one value worth according to popularity (pr.6). True nobility has nothing to do with fame but is the original condition of man, as m.6 makes clear. As God gave rays to the sun, horns to the moon, men to the earth, and stars to the sky, so he gave bodies to souls brought down from high. Since all men have the same noble origin, no one should boast of his family and no one should be thought of as base except "he that with foul vice doth his own birth deface" (9). In a sense, the Golden Age of 2:m.5 is extended in this poem to the noble origins of mankind; and as man degenerated through his concern for wealth, so he is responsible for deserting his birthright and for lowering himself through vice. This point leads to pr.7, concerning bodily pleasures, which are treated only briefly since, as Philosophy says, "the desire for them is full of anxiety, and the enjoying of them breeds repentance." Not only does pleasure not fulfill, it even causes pain, as m.7 makes clear when it compares pleasure to the bee which, while giving honey, also leaves its sting in its victim.

After summarizing these wrong roads toward happiness, Philosophy admonishes man to cease admiring base and worthless things and to turn toward the heavens and toward the reason which governs them (pr.8). Man's false search for true goods is the subject of the eighth poem, the initial two lines of which function as a topic sentence: "Alas, how ignorance makes wretches stray / Out of the way!" (1–2). Man would not look for gold on trees or for jewels on vines; nor would he fish on mountain tops or hunt goats in the sea (3–8). Though men are skillful in searching out the ocean's depths, in knowing where to find pearls and precious dyes, and in ascertaining the various fish to be found on the different coasts (9–14), when it comes to locating their chief good, "then are they blind, / And search for that under the earth, which lies / Above the skies" (15–18). Only after painfully acquiring false goods may foolish men come to recognize the true ones (19–22).

Having analyzed false happiness and its causes, Philosophy turns to true happiness, the real subject of Book 3. And here in pr.9, as in pr.3, where he introduced the ways of false happiness, Boethius begins a new subject by creating a dialogue between Philosophy and the narrator. The particular point of this dialogue—comprising the longest section of Book 3—is to define "true and perfect happiness," which men in their depravity have fragmented and made imperfect, and then confused with the whole. To find true happiness, says Philosophy citing Plato, men should invoke God for help; and m.9, perhaps the most famous of all the poems in the *Consolation,* is this prayer. [17]

In its first twenty-one lines, a hymn celebrating God as creator of the universe, Philosophy emphasizes what might be termed the all-encompassing philosophical principle of the work: everything has its source in the perfection of God, and while away from Him in this world, everything seeks to effect its return. The first nine lines reveal God as the unmoved mover, as the principle of life, fashioning the universe from Himself into a perfect whole. The next twelve lines move from a general picture of creation to the particular acts of ordering the elements, animating everything through the world soul, and filling heaven and earth with individual souls, all of which return to God (10–21). In the last part of the poem (22–28), the principle of return is extended to man; and the hymn celebrating God changes to a personal prayer for God to help man participate in this circular movement. Constructed according to the classical form of a hymn to a divinity, this poem "most adroitly" transfers Boethius's frame of reference "from the mundane to the celestial, from a world of false goals to a universe ultimately good in its divine ordinance."[18] Notwithstanding the fact that the poem is spoken by Philosophy, the voice here is more that of one finally aware of the highest good and yearning after it. The end of the journey, the sight of God, offers rest and peace to man, for God is man's beginning and end, his guide, lord, path, and goal (*principium, uector, dux, semita, terminus,* 28).

This concluding list of nouns, representing attributes of divinity that blend ostensible dichotomies, may be compared to the list at the end of the *De fide Catholica*—the fourth theological tractate, which may be by Boethius—of what man will find when he contemplates God at the end of this world. Here, however, the journey to God has to do with the journey of the soul to its real home. A meaningful contrast may be made between this prayer and that found earlier in *Consolation* 1:m.5, where the narrator prays to God to make the earth stable and to hold in check the mutability that controls this world. Notwithstanding the similarities in the view of deity, the two poems are quite different in their actual prayers. Whereas the first, asking God to change the nature of this world, shows both error and presumption on the part of the narrator, the second demonstrates the correct view, that man should be concerned with returning to God and with asking God to help him with this journey. Although it is Philosophy who actually states the prayer, the sense now is that she is speaking as much for the narrator as to him, that the narrator is in full agreement with the need to turn not only from the false goods of this world but also to the true good found in God alone.

The last three sections of Book 3 make clear the point of this poem: the *summum bonum* and happiness—which are the same thing—are found in God and, further, are God; and, moreover, goodness is the reason for man's ascent to God. Boethius's vision of the *summum bonum* offers "a way of viewing life in a totality from which all other action and thought may evolve." In the *Consolation,* as in Plato's *Republic,* "the ideal vision becomes the maker and measure of derivative realities."[19] In pr. 10, where he again employs the terms and methods of logic—in fact, more so than in any previous section of the *Consolation*—Boethius shows that the essence of God consists of goodness and nothing else. And m. 10, continuing the subject of m. 9, makes more immediate the need for the soul's ascent to God. Man, depicted as bound to earth by the chains of his desire, is urged to come to God, who offers "a port of pleasant rest" and a "refuge from his pains" (5–6). The eighteen lines of this poem, differentiating between the true light of God and the false lights of this world, are divided into three sections of six lines each: The first section urges man to make the journey to God; the second analyzes the goods of this world that cloud man's thoughts (7–12); and the third contrasts the charms that man finds in the deep caves of earth with the light of heaven (13–18). The images of bondage and darkness—seen in the poems of the *Consolation* as early as 1:m. 1—here give way to those of freedom and light; but it is necessary for man to realize that this release and this brightness are to be found only beyond this world, in God.

The discussion in pr. 11, that unity and goodness are identical and are found only in God, again takes the form of a dialogue, and may be meaningfully compared to the discussion in Boethius's third theological tractate, *Quomodo substantiae*. After this, m. 11 extends m. 10 in showing that knowledge of the truth lies within man, and that for him to understand it, he should turn within, bringing his wandering thoughts back to himself. Thus man the microcosm will reaffirm the circular movement of creation out from and then back to God. But here the emphasis is on man's recollection of the truth, and Boethius—citing Plato's views, as found in the *Meno* and *Phaedo,* that when man learns something, he is merely remembering it anew (15–16)—stresses that man already knows where truth, goodness, and happiness lie, and where his new life should be. Though life in this world may blind him, man does not have to remain blind; by turning within, he sees the need to turn away from the created world to its creator.

In pr. 12, the narrator states explicitly that he agrees with Philosophy's teaching; he acknowledges that he has been over-whelmed by his grief, and admits the folly of his depression. Now, as Philosophy makes clear, little more needs to be done before the narrator can find happiness and return safely to his own country. What follows on the existence of evil in this world is an extension of the acknowledgement of God as the equivalent and only source of goodness; and the argument that evil is noth-ing, since God—who can do everything—cannot do evil, will be a major point in the next book of the *Consolation*.

The concluding poem of Book 3 focuses not on the need for man to leave this world but on the dangers of his looking back after he has left it. This twelfth poem—the longest poem in Book 3—is in the form of an exemplum from classical mythology with a frame that gives it explicit significance. The first four lines state the point of the poem: Happiness comes to him who perceives the source of goodness and breaks the chains which bind him to earth (1–4). What follows, from lines 5 to 51, recounts the story of Orpheus's attempt to rescue Eurydice from the Un-derworld. Although through his music Orpheus could control nature, he could not control the passions within himself; and although through music he could effect the release of his wife from hell, his inability to refrain from looking back caused him to lose all that he had gained. The application of the story is made in the last seven lines of the poem: Should man, seeking to raise his mind from darkness, turn back to what he has left behind, he will lose all that he has gained (52–58).

This poem, emphasizing at its outset the man who is happy (*felix*, 1, 3), itself looks backward to the concluding poem of Book 2, which ends with an assertion of how happy (*felix*) men would be if their minds were ruled by the love that guides the heavens (2:m.8, 28–30). But whereas in the earlier poem happiness lay in man's being guided by divine love, here it rests in man's raising himself to God (3:m.12, 1–2), or again, in man's loosing the chains that bind him to the earth (3–4). While both poems express love, that seen in the story of Orpheus, ruled by no law other than itself (47–48), does not reflect the divine love celebrated in 2:m.8. The "ephemeral law of lovers" is the love which binds man to this earth and darkness; it does not lift him to "the divine love ruling the universe."[20]

At the same time, 3:m.12 functions as a transition between the teachings of Books 3 and 4 of the *Consolation*. And although we may think that the subsequent books will represent the narrator's turnabout and reflect the concerns of the mind that has been lifted above this earth, actually, while profiting greatly from Philosophy's teachings, the narrator is still not free of his grief.

Universal Goodness

The concerns of the first half of Book 4 are with understanding the place of evil in the world. The narrator's sorrow is "that since the governor of all things is so good, there can either be any evil at all, or that it pass unpunished" (pr. 1). Philosophy's response is an affirmation that with God's help the narrator will learn "that the good are always powerful, and the evil always abject and weak, and that vices are never without punishment, nor virtue without reward, and that the good are always prosperous, and the evil unfortunate"—in effect the restatement of a position that goes back to Plato's assertion in the *Apology* that evil cannot befall a good man either in life or in death. Since the narrator has understood the essence of true happiness and the place where it resides, all he needs to know, says Philosophy, is the way to his heavenly home and the means. What she offers him here are the wings with which he may make the journey.

The flight of the soul back to God is the subject of m.1, which, after a four-line statement, details the progress of the soul from earth through the spheres and beyond the farthest star (5–16) to the realm of "glorious light," where the lord of the universe reigns, holding everything in order (17–22). Once there, the soul will recognize its own country where it properly belongs. Should the soul look again at earth—referring back to the prohibition of 3:m.12—it will see that the supposedly powerful tyrants are actually the exiles (23–30). While stemming from the last several poems of Book 3, which focused on the need for man to turn back to his heavenly home, this poem goes beyond these in that the narrator no longer needs to be convinced to make the journey. Now the rhetoric is less persuasive than celebratory, and the impression is that the poem acts as a promise of the journey itself. More accurately, it sketches the outline of the journey, to be filled in by the subsequent discussion on will and power.

In pr.2, the instruction is presented as though it were a step on a ladder to truth or, in terms of the more dominant image, a component of the wings which the narrator will use to fly from his earthly prison. He must recognize the validity of the apparent paradox that the good are necessarily strong and happy, and the wicked necessarily weak and unhappy, as m.2 illustrates. Only ten lines long, this poem is comparable to those of Book 3 that act as little more than verse reaffirmations of main points in the prose. Also, in showing that the tyrant is himself enslaved, it may be seen developing the last lines of m.1. The initial lines of m.2 assert the reality hidden by the surface: beneath the bright garb of the kings are tight chains that bind them. Although the kings may seem to be rulers, they are themselves enslaved by lust, wrath, and the contradictory passions of sorrow and hope (6–10).

While representing a paraphrase of Plato's *Gorgias,* Boethius's discussion here—as well as that in pr.3, which extends the contrast between the good and the wicked to their respective rewards and punishments—expresses a commonplace of Neoplatonic and Christian thought. Inasmuch as they possess goodness, the "common reward for all human actions and that which makes man divine, the good are always rewarded (pr.3). In like manner, the wicked are always punished since they possess not goodness but wickedness, which leads to their being less than human, even bestial, as Boethius interprets the mythology of Plato's *Phaedrus*. The metamorphosis of man caused by wickedness is more insidious than mere physical transformation. The familiar episode from Homer's *Odyssey*, of Ulysses with the sorceress Circe, which Boethius recounts in m.3, involved only the change of human into animal form (1–26). Although the men of Ulysses were physically transformed, their minds remained human. Commenting on this story, Philosophy notes the weakness of Circe's potions, which could change only the outward appearance (27–34). More deadly are those poisons which, affecting not the body but the mind, transform the inner man (35–39).

The unhappiness of the wicked is detailed in pr.4. Incredible as it may seem, the wicked are far more unhappy when they escape punishment than when they are justly punished; the man who does evil is more miserable than the man to whom the evil is done; and in general, wickedness by its very nature makes men unhappy: It is like weakness, though it is a sickness of the mind, not of the body; and those who are evil deserve pity more than hate. In m.4, Philosophy stresses the irony of man's seeking to destroy himself when death is already so near at hand. Continuing the animal imagery of the previous poem by depicting man as prey of serpent, lion, tiger, bear, and boar, it wonders at man's preying on man. The point is to externalize both man's self-destruction and his destruction of his fellow men whose lives and manners are different. Rather than seek death, man should love the good and pity the evil (12).

The narrator's response to these teachings is to wonder why God sometimes seems to reward the wicked with happiness and the good with misery (pr.5). Feeling that such confusion must be due to the workings of chance, not to the ordering by God, he questions how one can distinguish between God's governance and accidental chance. Philosophy's answer, which begins here and continues into m.5, is that man thinks that events are unplanned and confused only because he cannot discern God's principle of order. If man did not comprehend the laws governing heavenly bodies, he would be amazed at the movements of the stars (1–6). As it is, unusual events, like eclipses of the moon, upset many people, though more common natural phenomena, like waves beating on the shore or snow drifts melting in the sun, do not bother anyone (7–16). The point of these illustrations is that when man cannot readily discern the cause of something beyond him, he is confused (17–22).

Having established the need for man to see clearly, Philosophy moves in the second part of Book 4 to what she calls the greatest of all mysteries, which may be expressed as five distinct problems: the simplicity of Providence, the course of Fate, the unforeseeable nature of chance, divine cognition and predestination, and freedom of the will. Complex as these matters are, Philosophy realizes that understanding them is necessary if the narrator is to be cured. But, she says, verse must be replaced for a while at least by well-ordered arguments. The discussion of these points is best viewed as the heart of the *Consolation,* that to which the fiction constructed by Boethius has been leading. Now that the narrator— and the audience in general—has been properly prepared, Boethius can deal with these major questions concerning the relationship between man and God; and the rest of Book 4, along with Book 5, offers succinct but effective discussions of these main questions. It is noteworthy that Boethius's words on these great and deep matters represent by and large the definitive view of the Western world for at least the next eight hundred years.

The first clarification concerns the relationship between Providence and Fate, and in pr.6 Boethius harmonizes the Stoic concept of Fate—especially as found in Seneca—with the Christian concept of God as an active and constantly present force in the governance of the universe.[21] Whereas both Providence and Fate are concerned with order in the universe, the former properly refers to order as it emanates from God: "Providence is the very Divine reason itself " which governs all things. The order considered in reference to that which is controlled by it is called Fate: "Fate is a disposition inherent in changeable things," by which Providence connects all things in their proper order. Providence includes all things at the same time; Fate controls the movement of various individual things over a period of time. Although the two terms are different, they are related and depend on one another: The simple, unified whole that is Providence leads to the unfolding complex order that is Fate. Providence is "the simple and unchanging plan of events," whereas Fate is "the ever-changing web." To make the point as meaningful as possible, Boethius uses analogous relationships in the mind and in nature: Moveable Fate is to stable Providence as reason is to pure understanding, as becoming is to being, as time is to eternity, as the moving circle is to the still point at the center.[22]

Although the world may seem confused and disordered to man, who cannot properly discern the order—who thinks, for instance, that the evil prosper while the good are punished—everything is directed by its own proper order toward the good. Instead of attempting to comprehend the workings of Providence, man should be content with recognizing that God the creator of all things directs everything to goodness. Also, just as the closer one is to the center of a moving wheel the less he feels the motion, so the more man participates in divine harmony the less subject he is to the workings of Fate, the moving image of Providence.

After the lengthy arguments of pr.6, representing in fact the longest prose section in the *Consolation,* Philosophy offers again "the delight of verses," a song that may refresh the narrator so that he may proceed with his understanding. In m.6, the longest poem in Book 4, focusing on the order of the universe as it is apparent in the heavens (1–15), Philosophy restates the concluding point of pr.6 in terms of "mutual love," which removes discord from the heavens (16–18). This *concordia oppositorum*—which controls the balance of elements, the succession of seasons, and even the movement from life to death (19–33)—is an expression of God, who as unmoved mover keeps everything from flying apart (34–43). This stabilizing order is seen in the final lines as love, through which everything is created and ordered, and through which everything returns to its source (44–48). [23]

Instead of being the pawn of Fortune, man may make of his fortune what he wishes (pr.7); and m.7, the concluding poem of Book 4, provides illustrations of how man may overcome adverse fortune and effect his desired end. In the form of accounts of unequal length concerning figures from classical mythology—Agamemnon, Ulysses, and Hercules—figures who all prevailed, it urges man to follow these examples. Instead of yielding, he should strive to overcome the earth; and when he has done so, he will have gained the stars (32–35). Representing a culmination of the earlier ideas that man must free himself from the earth and look to the heavens, his place of origin, this poem makes clear that if he is to attain his proper place, man must rise above concerns with Fortune.

Man and Providential Order

The fifth and final book is, after Book 1, the shortest in the *Consolation,* but, at the same time, it is concerned with more, as well as with more difficult, questions than any other book. For all the length of Book 3, the bulk of it merely offers different particular applications of the inadequacy of the gifts of Fortune. Although Book 5 may be regarded as extending the understanding of Providence reached in Book 4, it focuses on issues that may not seem to be either immediately connected to Providence or easily comprehended. The first section reassesses the meaning of chance, which, if defined as an event produced by random motion, must be a meaningless term, since in an ordered universe random events are impossible (pr. 1). Chance is more properly understood as the unexpected outcome of actions done with different purposes in mind—a definition stemming from Aristotle's *Physics*—and is unexpected only because man cannot see the entire picture and the working out of events that have come from the fount of Providence. In m. 1 this point is illustrated by means of the Tigris and Euphrates, which, although flowing from the same source, soon part into two rivers and go their separate ways. Should they, however, come together again and form one river, the new path would be controlled by such forces as the fall of the land and the flow of the current (3–8). As the last lines make clear, chance too is actually controlled and ruled by an order beyond it.

From chance the discussion turns to free will, which Philosophy immediately affirms must exist in every rational entity (pr.2). Man is most free when he is least bound by the desires of the flesh. A complicating factor, however, is God's foreknowledge, which, as Philosophy asserts in m.2, is an expression of God's seeing everything at once. The impetus for the poem is a line from Homer stating how, although the sun views everything, its rays cannot pierce far beneath the surface of the earth (1–6). In contrast, God sees everything, even within dense matter and in darkest night (7–10). Moreover, He who is the true Sun sees at once, in a single glance, everything: "What are, and what have been, / And what shall after be" (11–14).

Far from being enlightened, the narrator is now additionally perplexed, and asks how God's foreknowledge can be reconciled with man's free will. Since, according to him, foreknowledge means necessity, divine foreknowledge is incompatible with human free will. The conclusion of his argument is that "there is no freedom in human counsels and actions" (pr.3), and its implication is that if man's good and wicked acts do not result from his free choice, it is both pointless and unjust for rewards and punishments to be assigned to these acts. Moreover, continues the narrator, since everything is determined unalterably, hope and prayer are pointless; and mankind, necessarily "separated and severed from its source," must "fail and fall away."

It is significant that here for the first time since 1:pr.4, where the narrator revealed his personal misfortunes, he, instead of Philosophy, is the speaker. But rather than think that Boethius is using the narrator's voice as he did earlier to show his state of confusion, we should realize that he means to vent a position that is both obvious and compelling. In m.3, also uttered by the narrator, man's helplessness and uncertainty provide the basis for a series of paradoxes. This poem takes the form of an internal dialogue, a psychomachia of sorts, based on several questions. The initial puzzle stems from the possibility that divine foreknowledge and human free will, both of which seem certain when viewed separately, are irreconcilable when put together (1–7). In musing on this apparent paradox, the narrator becomes increasingly uncertain of both the nature of truth and the ability of the mind, overcome by the body, to discern "the secret laws which things do bind" (8–10). He wonders further what to make of the mind's desire to discover truth (11–19). Rather than conclude that the mind is ignorant of truth or that it already knows it, the narrator decides that although the mind is unable to perceive many of the particulars it knew when it was with God, it still retains general truth and uses this to help recall particulars (20–31).

This point, that real knowledge is recollection, should be related to what was seen earlier in 3:m.11; but here it is the narrator's insight, not the teaching of Philosophy. Although the several questions that fill the first twenty-one verses here may reflect the confusion existing within the narrator's mind, the poem does not end in confusion or despair. The narrator could easily have become again the sorrowful, bewildered creature he was at the beginning of the *Consolation*. But now he shows himself capable of moving beyond ambiguity and apparent paradox to reaffirm not only the order of Providence but man's responsibility to use his mind to recall the truth he once perceived clearly. Along with venting an obvious argument about the incompatibility of foreknowledge and free will, the third section also offers an opportunity for the narrator to demonstrate how far he has indeed progressed in his understanding. Though his arguments are proved to be inadequate and erroneous, the conclusion of m.3 indicates his ability to receive Philosophy's correction.

Philosophy's answer, which occupies the remaining sections of the *Consolation,* is not to scorn him or his view, but rather to say that his difficulty is an old one. Not only had Cicero raised it, Boethius himself had investigated it in detail in his earlier works. So far, she says, "none of you"—that is, apparently, no philosopher—has used sufficient care and rigor to examine the issue (pr.4). What follows is thus a corrective to all the older views on the subject of the interrelationship of divine foreknowledge and human free will. It does not treat either the pagan problem of divination, brought up by Cicero, or the Christian problem of free will and grace, discussed by Augustine. Rather it is concerned with the purely logical problems raised by the Neoplatonic commentators on Chapter 9 of Aristotle's *On Interpretation*.[24]

The discussion does not take the form of a single monologue by Philosophy but rather that of a dialectic in which the narrator participates in the logical demonstration. The first point emphasizes the difference between divine and human ways of knowing: The operations of human reasoning cannot approach the immediacy of divine understanding (pr. 4). In particular, Philosophy distinguishes among sensory perception, which examines forms contained in matter; imagination, which discerns form alone without matter; reason, which investigates the species which is inherent in the particulars; and *intellegentia* ("intelligence" or understanding), which beholds pure form itself. The higher powers of learning include the lower ones, but the lower do not include the higher. Here, in making it clear that the reality which corresponds to universals is that of the Idea, Boethius offers what may be seen as his own solution to the problem of universals, which he had dealt with in his early commentaries on Porphyry's *Isagoge*.[25]

In m. 4, the longest poem in Book 5, Boethius examines further the workings of the mind and its ways of knowing. The forty lines may be viewed as divided into three segments. The first states as a premise the Stoic notion of the mind as a passive receiver of external impressions (1–9). The second examines the implications of this premise in the form of a series of questions: How, if the mind has no power of its own, is it able to perceive and distinguish at all (10–19); how does it both analyze and synthesize (20–25)? Since such movement would seem to belie the premise of the mind's passive nature, the third part of the poem offers a conclusion affirming the mind's active nature and its ability to relate the form it holds within itself to those forms it perceives outside (26–40).

The various kinds of knowledge are discussed again in pr.5: Sensory perception is proper to unmoving creatures like shellfish; imagination is proper to all other animals; reason to man; and pure intelligence, or immediate understanding, to divinity alone. The "most excellent" knowledge is that which knows what is proper to itself and also to all lower kinds of knowledge. The hierarchy of knowing is such that though man can comprehend the workings of reason as well as those of the imagination and the senses, he cannot easily comprehend how divine foreknowledge sees even those occurrences which man judges to be uncertain; for this foreknowledge is "the boundless immediacy of the highest form of knowing."[26] Rather than extend this argument, m.5 shows the need for man to turn from what is below him to what is above. The first nine lines survey the various forms of life on earth, moving from those which crawl and fly and swim to those which walk, culminating in man who, unlike the others, does not need to focus downward to the earth: "Men only with more stately shape to higher objects rise, / Who with erected bodies stand and do the earth despise" (10–11). As man raises his eyes to heaven—this condition is now the given for the narrator—so must he raise up his mind as well (12–15). This poem, the last in the *Consolation,* when juxtaposed against that at the beginning of the work which shows man, overcome by his grief, contemplating the lowly earth (1:m.2), functions as a dramatic statement of the progress of the narrator.

Philosophy's final words occupy pr.6, the longest prose section in Book 5. In accord with the movement to divine intelligence, the initial subject is the contrast between time and eternity. As divine intelligence is the immediate comprehension of everything, so eternity is "the complete, simultaneous and perfect possession of everlasting life," and is distinct from endless life, which is a movement from past to future. Though having its roots in Plato's doctrine of Forms, this distinction—which Boethius expressed earlier in Book 4 of his *De Trinitate*—was immensely influential in the Middle Ages, in particular in the writings of Thomas Aquinas.[27] As Philosophy makes clear, only God lives in the eternal present, and divine foreknowledge is best understood as "knowledge of a never fading instant." Rather than think of foreknowledge as prevision, or "seeing beforehand," we should understand it as "providence," or "looking forth," as from a lofty peak. As C. S. Lewis explains this point, God "sees (not remembers) your yesterday's acts because yesterday is still 'there' for Him; he sees (not foresees) your tomorrow's acts because He is already in tomorrow."[28] This seeing does not necessitate the occurrence of events, and Philosophy notes that while a future event may be considered necessary in relation to divine foreknowledge, it is free and unrestricted when considered in terms of itself.

Philosophy also makes the significant distinction between simple and conditional necessity: simple being that which is absolute and not dependent on any particular condition, like the statements "all men are mortal" and "the sun rises"; conditional being that which may or may not be true at any given moment, like the statement "the man is walking." The man who is voluntarily walking is walking of his own free will; the fact that Providence sees his walking in the present means only that the walking necessarily occurs, not that it is caused by being seen.[29]

The conclusion to this section, as well as to the *Consolation* itself, is an affirmation of the existence of both man's free will and divine Providence, which—unchanging, ever-present, and all-encompassing—comprehends all of man's actions, "distributing rewards to the good and punishments to the evil." In response to the narrator's earlier conclusion, Philosophy makes clear that man's hopes and prayers are not at all in vain. Indeed, as she asserts in her final address, man should "fly vices, embrace virtues," lift up his mind "with worthy hopes," and "offer up humble prayers" to heaven. Since man lives in the sight of the judge who sees all, a "great necessity of doing well" is laid on man.

These final words serve not only to justify virtuous actions but to reaffirm the presence of divine and universal justice. As an ending it is, as Lewis says, "a stroke of calculated and wholly successful art. We are made to feel as if we had seen a heap of common materials so completely burnt up that there remains neither ash nor smoke nor even flame, only a quivering of invisible heat."[30] In terms of this final and all-encompassing lesson, Boethius moves beyond the affirmation that all that happens is for the best and makes it man's "responsibility" to act well in accord with his nature. The better a man uses his reason, the freer he is; the more a man patterns his soul on divine thought, the freer it is. To will what the body desires is the highest degree of slavery; to will what God wills and to love what He loves is the highest form of liberty, and therefore happiness.[31]

As this journey of the mind to God is brought to a close, so is the theodicy and the full consolation offered by Boethius. The ending shows clearly that the *Consolation of Philosophy* represents not only the spiritual testimony left to mankind by Boethius but the moral program of his entire life and works.[32]

Chapter Six

Form and Method
in the *Consolation*

Structural Patterns

Whereas linear progression is the most obvious structural pattern
of the *Consolation,* this progression involves much more than a
simple movement from a beginning to an ending, or a simple
change of the narrator from despair to hope and from ignorance
to understanding. As the work develops and consolation yields
to instruction and to an awareness of truth, so simplicity yields
to complexity—of thought, language, and structure. The five-
book structure of the *Consolation,* where the subject of one book
overlaps to that of the next, reveals a movement beyond the
overall one that extends from Book 1, with its statement of the
problem in terms of its effect on the narrator, to Book 5, with
its detachment from the personal and its discussion of man's
responsibility in a world governed by providential order. The
fiction with which the work begins gives way to the presentation
of truth itself. And though this process may be regarded as, on
the one hand, an objectifying of that which had been presented
subjectively, it may also be described as a moving from superficial
appearance to essential truth, reflected by the narrator's looking
into himself, a turning from external concerns to those at the
heart of one's being.

It is not accidental that the so-called autobiographical parts
of the *Consolation* are limited to the first two books. Similarly,
the movement from emotion to reflection is mirrored by the
movement from the initial emotional passage in verse to the final
philosophical statement in prose. And beyond this, the alterna-

tion from verse to prose to verse and so on to the final prose passage necessarily entails a two-fold movement: on the one hand, the movement of the discrete forms, the narrative in the denotative language of prose and the songs in the connotative language of verse; and, on the other hand, the necessary interrelationship of these forms, the way the particular poem, for instance, stems from and leads to the prose passages around it. [1]

The five-book structure of the work may also be seen revealing the traditional five-part division of oration that Boethius would have known from the *Institutio oratoria* of Quintillian. The structure first appears in the *Consolation* in microcosm, as Kurt Reichenberger recognized, as the controlling device of 1:pr.4, where the narrator delivers what amounts to an apologia for his life. Using the *exordium* (or *prooemium*), in which the speaker prepares the audience to be well disposed to his argument, Boethius has his narrator make the point that he has not deserved his misfortune; in the *narratio,* or recounting of the facts, he shows how he has always opposed injustice and worked for the common good; in the *probatio,* or proof, he states how he has been falsely accused; in the *refutatio* he rebukes his accusers and reaffirms his innocence; and in the *peroratio,* using eloquence and emotion, he relates his particular case to what he takes to be the state of the world: the innocent being overcome by the wicked. [2] In terms of the rhetoric, the so-called personal details in this section of the first book—including the references to Basilius, Opilio, and Gaudentius, Boethius's false accusers—function essentially as *topoi,* or, as they were termed in Latin rhetorical tradition, *loci communes,* devices to develop the oration at hand.

Applying this five-part division to the *Consolation* as a whole, we may regard each book as equivalent to one part of a discourse, though we should realize that the discourse is finally that of neither the narrator nor Philosophy, but of Boethius the author. Book 1, the *exordium,* uses the narrator's particular condition to make the problem meaningful; Book 2, the *narratio,* states the facts of the narrator's good and bad fortune to examine the gifts of Fortune; Book 3, the *probatio,* demonstrates the nature of true happiness; Book 4, the *refutatio,* clarifies the nature of evil and the state of the wicked; and Book 5, the *peroratio,* makes clear man's responsibility in a world governed by Providence. The *Consolation* may be regarded in one sense as Boethius's demonstration of the uses of rhetoric and grammar, as well as a meaningful part of his educational program, coming after his study of the sciences of the *quadrivium* and the language of logic, and perhaps stemming from his treatises dealing with rhetoric, *In topica Ciceronis* and *De topicis differentiis.*

At the same time, not only is the dialogue that Boethius creates between the narrator and Philosophy itself a form of drama, especially in Book 1, but the five-book structure of the *Consolation* may reflect the five-act structure of Roman drama. This structure may be found in the plays of Seneca, which are cited several times in the *Consolation;* and the basis for the structure is spelled out by Horace in his *Ars poetica.* Moreover, the change of the narrator from grief to serenity, seen in Book 3, the middle of the *Consolation,* may be understood to correspond to the *peripeteia,* or turning point, which, according to Aristotle in his *Poetics,* is central to the drama.[3]

Beyond their relationship to oratory and drama, the five books of the *Consolation,* divided unevenly into thirty-nine sections of alternating verse and prose, are organized so that the third book is the longest of all, the second and fourth the next longest, and the first and fifth the shortest. Book 1, with seven verse and six prose sections, is shorter than Book 2, composed of eight sections of each form, which is shorter in turn than Book 3, the central book, having twelve sections of verse and of prose. Book 4, composed of eight sections of each form, is likewise shorter than Book 3; and Book 5, with five verse and six prose parts, is shorter than Book 4.[4] Such variations in length indicate a structure which may be described as X XX XXX XX X, and suggest that, along with the linear structure of the *Consolation,* there exists a ring structure emphasizing the dramatic center, Book 3, where the narrator changes from the despairing figure seen at the beginning and begins to pursue the *summum bonum.*[5]

Ring structure also seems to be an especially pertinent way of describing how the thirty-nine poems are organized, though with

these the organizing principle is not a quantitative, but a thematic
or verbal, linking of parts. In this the first element is related to
the last, the second to the penultimate, the third to the ante-
penultimate and so forth, resulting in a structure which may be
described as ABCCBA. In the *Consolation,* though the actual
arrangement of poems in each of the five books is more complex—
and imprecise—than this simple statement would suggest, the
arrangement itself may nevertheless be meaningfully described
as ring structure.

In Book 1, the organization of the seven poems may be understood as follows. Poem 1, the introductory soliloquy showing the
narrator's sorrow, stands apart from the other poems. Poem 2,
which at the end tells of the mind's losing its light and man's
being in chains, has as its counterpart m.7, which likewise shows
the mind clouded and in chains. Similarly, m.3, relating the
coming of light to man's eyes to the shining of the sun over all,
may be linked to m.6, which, beginning with the rays of the
sun—both poems refer to the *radiis Phoebi*—reexpresses the light-
theme of the previous poem as the principle of order. And m.4,
which celebrates the unmoved man, may be related to m.5, which
invokes God as unmoved mover to make the earth stable.

In Book 2, the poems again seem to be organized into four
pairs. Poem 1, on Fortune's ruling the world in disharmony, may
be related to m.8, which emphasizes Love's ruling the world in
harmony. Poem 2, on man's greed as boundless, contrasts with
m.7, where man is seen as nothing in regard to the immensity
of the universe and the fact of death. Poem 3, on change as a
principle of the world, leads to m.6, on the instability of earthly
empire. And m.4, on the need for man to lead a serene life, is
generalized in m.5, on the need for man to return to the Golden
Age. Here the emphasis on happiness *(felix)* at the end of m.4
is repeated at the beginning of m.5.

The ring structure of the poems in Book 3 is more complex
because of Boethius's fragmentation of the false desires of man.
Poem 1, which ends with man's finding truth, may be seen
leading to m.12, which begins with man's seeking truth—now
reexpressed as love. Moreover, as m.1 ends with man's shaking

off his yokes, so m. 12 begins with man's shaking off his chains. Poem 2, asserting the principle that everything desires to return to its home, may be joined to m. 11, which calls for man to return to his home; here m. 2 ends with the image of the circle *(orbem)*, and m. 11 begins with this image. The five poems represented by the short verses 3 through 7 may be understood to form a single unit in that they present man's false desires—wealth, high office, power, fame, and pleasure—and correspond to m. 10, which shows man's release from these false desires. And m. 8, detailing the blindness of man in pursuing false goals, leads to m. 9, the prayer to God to reveal the *summum bonum* to man.

A similar joining of the separate parts would seem to be revealed in Book 4, but instead of being organized in terms of four groups of poems, it employs two groups. Poem 1, on ascending to the skies with the wings of Philosophy, has as its correlative m. 7, on overcoming fortune and the earth, and on reaching to the stars. The four poems, from 2 through 5, are joined in showing man as an inadequate ruler, brought down by his vices to the level of beasts, perversely seeking to destroy himself in his ignorance of the proper order of things. The corrective to this group is m. 6, where God the high king rules all, where man is brought up by God, where love banishes dissension, and where man understands the laws of God.

In Book 5, m. 1, which presents the river guided by a higher law, may be related to m. 5, that details the variety of life forms in the world, each likewise guided. Poem 2, citing Homer's picture of the sun shining on but not into the earth, may be echoed in m. 4, with its statement of the Stoic view of images implanting the mind. In this book m. 3, on man's being assured in his search for truth in God, stands in isolation, though at the same time, it may be regarded as coupled with the likewise-isolated first poem of Book 1, with its emphasis on the narrator's fall through his unsure foothold in this world.

The point of this ring structure is to provide an additional pattern of meaning to the *Consolation*. Not accidentally, the climaxing poem of each book is in most instances the longest and / or most significant poem in the book, and the one that emphasizes

love and harmony as principles of the universe which should be
extended to man. The prayer to God of 1:m.5 emphasizes God's
joining everything in harmony; the picture of the Golden Age
in 2:m.5 stresses peace and harmony; the prayer to God the
Creator in 3:m.9 amounts to a celebration of universal *concordia;*
the hymn of praise of 4:m.6 emphasizes the mutual love *(alternus
amor)* that holds everything in order, the *concordia oppositorum;* and
the questions of 5:m.3 function as an assertion that man must
discern the *connexio rerum,* the connections among all things, and,
rather than break the bond of things through discord, should
extend this bond to himself.[6]

If these five key poems are likewise examined in terms of ring
structure, 1:m.5, which shows the narrator's improper prayer to
God to provide for man the laws guiding the universe, and which
reveals, as Philosophy says, the extent of his illness, easily leads
to 5:m.3, the narrator's last speech, where he comes to a proper
understanding of Truth, and in effect shows that he has been
healed. Similarly, the harmony expressed in the picture of the
Golden Age in 2:m.5 may be seen leading to the full statement
of universal harmony in 4:m.6. The culminating, or central,
poem, of the *Consolation* is then 3:m.9, the prayer to "the Father
of all things" that celebrates and joins all of creation. More than
a Platonic hymn to God, this important poem expresses, perhaps
not accidentally, such basic Christian elements as the Lord's
Prayer and liturgical *Gloria.*[7]

Along with linear and ring structure, we should also note the
use of the circle as a structuring principle of the *Consolation.*
Expressed spatially as the celestial spheres suggesting cosmic order, the circle is also the thematic principle of return itself, man's
turning back to God after his descent into the world of matter,
parodied in the circling of the Wheel of Fortune, as seen in
2:m.1. In the final poem of the *Consolation,* 5:m.5, the image
of man's raising his eyes to heaven not only refers back to man's
looking downward to the earth, the image at the beginning of
the work (1:m.2), it provides its corrective. Similarly, Philosophy's final admonition to man to lift up his mind in hope (5:pr.6)
counteracts the despair pervading the initial poem of Book 1 and

illustrates the change from complaint to affirmation seen in the course of the *Consolation*.

Such relationships depend on our awareness of an earlier given. The affirmation of life and human dignity at the end of the *Consolation*, while contrasting with the emphasis on death and despair at the beginning, necessitates our reassessing this earlier position. Our being taken back to the beginning functions to transform the initial point. Moreover, just as Philosophy leads the narrator to God, so her final point in Book 5, that man lives in the sight of a judge who beholds all, gives meaning to her initial appearance, as the divine emissary who sees all and who provides for man.

Forms of Dialogue

This return, this completion of a circle, is actually effected through the dialogue between the narrator and Philosophy, the two characters in Boethius's drama. Although Boethius had employed the dialogue as a structuring form as early as his *Dialogue* on Porphyry's *Isagoge*, he here uses a complex blend of several kinds of discourses, including monologue, Socratic dialogue, and apocalyptic dialogue. From beginning to end, however, the *Consolation* is also a conversation, in which we are aware of the interacting of voices. Even when one voice is extended or dominant, as Lady Philosophy's voice so often is, the other frequently punctuates it. Didactic as the work is, it retains throughout a sense of voice as though what is at hand has a living presence. And even when the dramatic and personal are least present, the work gives the impression of being something other than an essay or even a lecture. Though at times the statement may be so extensive that we may tend to forget that it is speech, the lapse is but for a moment. In the last book, for instance, where the narrator's lengthy arguments about the necessary opposition of divine foreknowledge and human free will (5:3) are followed by an even longer reply by Philosophy, which offers a corrective to the narrator's position (5:4–6), we have little sense of conversation. But at the same time, Boethius insists that we differentiate the particular speakers and be aware that the first argument is but a jumping-off point for the second.

Boethius takes us from an awareness of the silent musing of the narrator at the beginning of the *Consolation* to speech and then back again at the end to an awareness of silence—there is no answer to Philosophy's last words. The initial and final speeches function as monologues that frame the entire work. The narrator's report at the beginning of his visit by Philosophy is balanced by Philosophy's final affirmation of universal justice. What happens is that the silent musing leads to a single voice which yields to two voices as the dialogue begins; then at the end this gives way to one voice again, which in turn leads to silence. Unlike the initial silence, the final silence suggests fulfillment. Now that speech has led to understanding and agreement, the need for words no longer exists.[8]

As dialogue, the *Consolation* is obviously artificial: We recognize that it is actually the externalizing of an internal conflict. What Boethius does at the outset of this work may be meaningfully compared to what Augustine does at the beginning of his *Soliloquies*. There, after the narrator notes how for many days he has been seeking to know himself and the highest good, he suddenly hears someone speak: "whether it was myself or someone else from without or within I know not."[9] When Augustine's narrator answers this voice, which he calls Reason *(Ratio)*, the dialogue begins. So in the *Consolation,* the dialogue is a voicing of the feelings and thoughts existing within the narrator. Although Boethius externalizes these into contrasting positions represented by two characters, and creates two contrasting forms of language—the prose, denotative and analytic; and the verse, connotative and celebratory—the whole dialogue is less dialectic than didactic. Even though at the end, on the matter of reconciling God's foreknowledge and man's free will, we see something of an exchange of ideas, throughout most of the *Consolation* Philosophy is in the position of correcting the obviously erroneous views of the narrator, and of reaffirming accepted truth.

Although the kind of dialogue employed by Socrates in Plato's dialogues was well known in Latin literature, both in classical

writings in the dialogues of Cicero and in Christian writings as
early as the *Octavius* of Minucius Felix, Boethius's actual application of this kind of dialectic is only sporadic. [10] The *Consolation*
is more obviously a work of instruction and, more apparently,
a protreptic, or *exhortatio,* to proper understanding. While perhaps to be understood in terms of Boethius's earlier protreptics,
it leads to the study not of the preparatory *quadrivium* or of logic,
but of philosophy itself, that which is at the end of the earlier
studies. While as a protreptic the *Consolation* may be related to
several Neoplatonic treatises, including those by Plutarch and
Iamblichus, and while it may have had its impetus in the now-
lost *Protrepticus* of Aristotle and the *Hortensius* of Cicero, it is
finally quite different from all these works. As an *exhortatio* to
philosophy, the *Consolation* is really an *exhortatio* to God, in which
man is urged to seek the highest good. [11]

Both monologue and Socratic dialogue should be viewed as
part of a larger overall structure, that may be termed the sacred,
or apocalyptic, dialogue. This is less the kind of discourse found
at the end of the Book of Job, when God finally speaks to man,
than that found in the apocryphal 2 Esdras, where a divine spirit
reveals hidden wisdom to man. This kind of revelation became
a genre at the end of the second century and was favored by both
Christians and pagans, as may be seen in the extremely popular
Shepherd of Hermas, as well as the Neoplatonic *Poimandres* of
Hermes Trismegistes, where, as in the *Consolation,* a narrator
numbed and immersed in his reflections is visited by a being of
immeasurable height, signifying the highest Intelligence, who
shows him a vision and then discusses with him various metaphysical issues. Closer to Boethius's lifetime are such other rel-
evant examples of this genre as the *Soliloquies* of Augustine and
the *Mitologiae* of Fulgentius, a Neoplatonic work more or less
contemporaneous with the *Consolation,* that is likewise concerned
with revealing the nature of divinity. [12]

At the same time, we should note the significance of Boethius's
making his instructor an allegorical personification and not a
human figure, say Symmachus, thereby projecting a relationship
of the sort he had created with Fabius in his early *Dialogue* on

the *Isagoge;* or even Plato, thereby creating a human representative of philosophy. It is also significant that Boethius calls his instructor Philosophy and not Reason, or Intelligence, or Wisdom. Though containing reason, she is more than this way to truth; and similarly, she is not truth or wisdom itself; for in Boethius's view the personification of wisdom would have indicated God alone. Rather, the name Philosophy suggests both the way to truth and the end of the journey, in a sense as logic in Boethius's earlier writings was considered to be both a tool and a part of philosophy. And Boethius's understanding of philosophy in the *Consolation* is wholly in accord with his earlier definitions of it, as in the *Arithmetic,* when he writes that "philosophy is the love of wisdom," and as in his first commentary on the *Isagoge,* when he calls philosophy "the love and pursuit of wisdom and in some way the friendship with it." Philosophy should thus be understood as both the inclination toward wisdom and the expression of what is to be learned. [13]

The Allegorical Principle

As an apocalyptic dialogue, the *Consolation* is necessarily an allegory. However, its allegory is "not a mere device" but rather a narrative principle. [14] We are in fact aware of allegory from the beginning of the work with the mysterious appearance and description of Philosophy. Although we do not know whether or not her strange and contradictory appearance—both old and young, both of average height and higher than the heavens—is the product of the narrator's dulled perception, we soon realize that such details reveal the nature, scope, and purpose of philosophy itself. The point of her varying height, for instance, is obviously to show that philosophy pertains both to ordinary human existence and to the truth that is so far beyond man's ordinary understanding that he cannot hope to know it fully. Similarly, her dress further reveals her nature. The *pi* at the bottom of her dress and the *theta* at the top—probably indicating the first letters of the Greek terms for the two divisions of philosophy, *practica* and *theoretica*—make even clearer that Boethius means for his character to be understood as encompassing all of philosophy, while the link between the letters shows that it is possible to move from one to the other. [15]

The unity of philosophy is reinforced, moreover, by the detail of the tear in her dress. All that is stated at first is that marauders had carried off pieces of the material, but we are told a bit later that after the death of Socrates, the various philosophical schools—what are called the "mob" of Epicureans, Stoics, and others—tried to seize philosophy for themselves. Though they succeeded in obtaining pieces of her garb, they foolishly thought these to be the whole thing (1:pr.3). Beyond representing a criticism of the ancient schools of thought after Plato, this allegory makes clear a major point of Boethius—that philosophy naturally battles the rash forces of folly. The narrator, the character Boethius, who has been one of Philosophy's staunchest supporters, should not be surprised at his predicament since wicked men have always tried to hurl down those who are concerned with truth. The unity of philosophy extends to the final detail in the description of the lady, the books and scepter she carries. These go beyond the different spheres of philosophy and focus on its twin roles. Through studying philosophy, man may reach wisdom; and through following its precepts, he may properly rule himself and his society.

The details of this description have been carefully emphasized by Boethius to achieve a certain purpose and to give a certain view of philosophy. But regardless of how vivid some of these details may seem, we should recognize their essentially traditional nature. For all of her individuality, Lady Philosophy is in a long line of allegorical personifications who instruct man, including the female instructors in the *Shepherd of Hermas*, Reason in Augustine's *Soliloquies*, and Nature—who is also both old and young—in Claudian's panegyric *On the Consulship of Stilicho* (early fifth century). Moreover, the depiction of wisdom as a female figure in general and as a beautiful, radiant goddess in particular expresses a convention which may be traced back to Plato's *Phaedrus* and which was well known in Latin literature from Cicero on. [16]

Notwithstanding all of these analogous figures, the most likely source of Boethius's Philosophy is the nameless figure in Plato's *Crito* who, as Socrates reports, appears to him in a vision. Doubtless representing philosophy, this figure—like Boethius's character—is fair and comely and clothed in bright dress. While apparently making clear to the imprisoned Socrates the imminence of his death, she also seems to provide that which allows him to accept his death resolutely, just as Boethius's Philosophy teaches the narrator to accept his fall and to look beyond his personal misfortune. Moreover, it hardly seems coincidental that when noting how wisdom has always been threatened by the forces of evil, Philosophy focuses on the death of Socrates, which, while unjust, nevertheless represents a victory for her who, she says, was at his side (1:pr.3).[17]

Not only does the description of Philosophy in the *Consolation* represent a way of regarding philosophy that would probably have been familiar to Boethius's audience, it seems likely that Boethius was relying on familiarity with the tradition. His allegory is not creating meaning; it is, rather, a way of referring to preexisting meaning. The fact that the narrator is unable at first to use the traditional and obvious details offered to recognize his visitor shows clearly how dulled he has become. Moreover, the initial contrast between the two figures is purposeful: Whereas Philosophy is calm and tranquil, the narrator is agitated and distraught; whereas her eyes are clear, his are full of tears; whereas she is ageless, he has moved from youth to old age; whereas she stands above him, he is fallen. In contrast with her brightness and vitality, his countenance is "sad with mourning, and cast upon the ground with grief " (1:pr.1). Her words, as may be seen in 1:m.2 in particular, concern the "perturbation" of the narrator's mind, which is "headlong cast/In depths of woe" and which has lost its light (1–2).

As Wolfgang Schmid first noticed, the condition of the narrator here is that of someone overcome by lethargy. According to a long tradition in which man's physical appearance is taken to be a sign of his spiritual condition, we may see that the narrator has fallen victim to lethargy, or sloth, which is the cause of the despair and mourning that occupy him totally. Regardless of whether or not the sickness detailed here represents the actual condition of Boethius after his fall, it functions in the *Consolation* as a symbolic expression of his spiritual condition. [18]

The contrast between the narrator and Philosophy is but the first instance in the work of a blending of ordinarily disparate elements. Although we might think it incongruous that a figure from the familiar world of man should appear on the same plane as an allegorical personification, we should understand that this procedure is not unusual either in late classical writings or in the *Consolation*. In fact, simultaneous linking and juxtaposing may even be regarded as the dominant method, if not the overall literary and philosophical principle, of the work, involving language, narrative details, literary structures, and philosophical ideas. It extends to the blending of the legendary and the historical, the fictional and the factual, and the personal and the traditional, and reflects Boethius's concern throughout the *Consolation* with relating the particular to the general and the individual to the typical. It is also the basis for the unusual mixture of prose and verse continued systematically throughout the entire work.

Prose and Verse

The prosimetric form of the *Consolation* necessarily relates the work to the Menippean satire—after the work of Menippus of Gadara (third century B.C.)—which had been Latinized as early as Varro's *Satyrae Menippeae* in the first century B.C. While *satura,* or satire, originally meant nothing more than a mixture or medley, in particular one of alternating prose and verse passages, in Roman literature it typically appeared in such works as the *Apocolocyntosis divi Claudii,* a lampoon of the dead emperor Claudius attributed to Seneca the Younger, and the bawdy and likewise comic *Satyricon* of Petronius—an author alluded to by Boethius at the end of his *Dialogue* on the *Isagoge.* Closer in spirit to the *Consolation,* and perhaps Boethius's actual source for the form, is the *De nuptiis Philologiae et Mercurii* of Martianus Capella. But notwithstanding the similarity in form of the *Consolation* and these antecedents, the "grave impressiveness" with which Boethius's work treats its passages of prose and verse removes it from these other instances of Menippean satire and raises the form to a position in literature it had never before attained.[19]

Both the prose and the verse of the *Consolation* may be properly and meaningfully judged as literary language. While recognizing that Boethius's prose is hardly "the classical Latin of the Ciceronian age," we should recognize that it still offers "a simplicity, a restraint, a clarity of diction which are in very marked contrast to the over-ornate, diffuse and excessively rhetorical style" prevalent in the literature of the time. Indeed, Boethius's style may be regarded as "well nigh a miracle" in view of the tendency of contemporary writing toward "distorted ornateness." And it is hardly an exaggeration to say that Boethius in his prose is not only nearer than any of his contemporaries to the great age of Cicero, but "nearer than any of his predecessors had been for centuries."[20]

The thirty-nine poems have not been so consistently praised over the centuries as the prose. Although offered by and large by Philosophy—and not by the narrator—to give a pleasant and welcome rest from the strain of following the arguments developed in the prose passages, they are more than diversions or decorations. Their function is to do more than intersperse the prose passages or enliven the instruction the narrator is receiving. Sometimes they summarize the argument of the prose; at other times they carry the discussion forward; and at still other times they comment on what is at hand, functioning, like the chorus in a Greek tragedy, to provide perspective for assessing the progress of the dialogue at hand. When the narrator is too weak to take the strong medicine of Philosophy, the poems provide relief; but as he becomes increasingly receptive to her words, they in turn become more complex. Although it has been suggested that as the argument becomes increasingly difficult, the verses occur less often, we should recognize that their connotative language is frequently more demanding than the relatively straightforward denotative language of the prose passages.[21]

Widely different evaluations have been made of this poetry. An anonymous ninth-century critic felt that just as Boethius's prose was not inferior to Cicero's, so his verse was the equal of Virgil's; and in the Renaissance, Julius Caesar Scaliger spoke of these verses as "divine." In the nineteenth century, however, Hermann Usener was quite critical of them. Although he saw in the prose "a thinker of a greater time," he regarded the verse as the voice of "a child of the sixth century," an evaluation that led twentieth-century readers to affirm anew the power and poetic skill of the poems. Probably the most accurate view of the verses is still that of Rand: "Some are exceedingly good, some are only moderate, and a few are insignificant—that being the only way, according to the poet Martial, in which one can write a book."[22]

The thirty-nine meters themselves are so varied that they not only provide representatives of almost every meter known in the sixth century, they include two or three meters apparently invented by Boethius. But while they may represent a tour de force of prosody, we should realize that for Boethius the poems must be viewed in conjunction with the prose. The final poem in each book would seem to provide a transition to the next book. And the fact that all the books except the last end with a poem suggests that Boethius intended to move from verse to prose, and, moreover, to include in the *Consolation* precisely thirty-nine examples of each form—whatever the significance of this number may be.[23]

Whereas the rational dialectic of the prose takes the form of catechism, syllogism, and dialogue, the verses, linguistically and functionally distinct, may be said "to constitute modes of knowing and discoursing alternative to those central to speculative philosophy."[24] As Boethius makes clear, the operation of human reasoning has its limitations. Though higher than animal sensation, it is lower than divine understanding (5:pr.4), and rational discourse as the expression of this is likewise limited. Besides knowing through reasoning, man knows through remembering. Emphasizing the Platonic doctrine of reminiscence, where learning is viewed as a matter of recollection (3:m.11), Boethius points out that although man cannot foresee the future, he can remember the past. By doing so, he not only knows truth, thus becoming godlike, but he may also come to understand the perplexing disorder of the world. The recall of truth shares some meaningful similarities with the discovery of it by syllogistic argument: As the conclusion of a syllogism is implicit in its premise, so the object of reminiscence is contained in the memory. But Boethius emphasizes the differences by using prose as the language of rational discourse and verse as the language of recall, that which is appropriate for expressing history and myth.

To make this point is not to say that allusions to the past are absent from the prose sections of the *Consolation*. Not only does Boethius cite classical authorities throughout the entire work, he also alludes to historical and mythological figures.[25] In the prose, however, these allusions function mainly as points of reference in Philosophy's argument, whereas in the verse they are in effect expressions of the movement through time and space demanded of the narrator and Boethius's audience. The verses refer in particular to great figures from history and myth who provide models and warnings for man. From Roman history, Boethius singles out such figures as Nero (2:m.6; 3:m.4), Fabricius, Cato, and Brutus (2:m.7); and from myth he uses the story of Orpheus (2:m.12), as well as episodes from the stories of such heroes as Ulysses (4:m.3, m.7), Agamemnon, and Hercules (m.7).

The poems take the mind on journeys across time and space, insisting that it see what is beyond its immediate concerns, recall the past, and finally leave the earth behind and look to God. The verses are full of spatial references—equivalents, as it were, to the figures from history and myth—often based on the four elements—earth, air, fire, and water—and the four points of the compass (1:m.3–5; 2:m.4). Also they look to far off lands— Thrace (1:m.3), India, Thulé (3:m.5), Armenia (5:m.1)—and to the spectacular and exotic features of this world: to the mountains Vesuvius (1:m.4) and Etna (2:m.5), and to the rivers Tagus, Hermus, Indus (3:m.10), Tigris and Euphrates (5:m.1). And they even look beyond this world to the underworld (3:m.12) and to the heavens (4:m.1). In making the mind move back in time and across the earth and the universe, Boethius offers exercises of a sort that, on the one hand, make the torpid narrator come alive and cease musing on his personal troubles and, on the other hand, "set the memory going, turning over its riches until the desired truth is reclaimed."[26]

The Philosophical Synthesis

While uniting such apparent alternatives as space and time, recollection and dialectic, and verse and prose, Boethius also extends the principle of synthesis to the philosophical content of the *Consolation*. Although the work may well be described as remarkably heterogeneous, it, like Boethius's earlier writings, represents an amalgamation of classical thought. But rather than postulate different sources for different sections of the work—for instance, a Stoic section, an Aristotelian section, a Platonic section—we should recognize that regardless of where the seed of Boethius's thought originated, the "inspiring and sustaining spirit" of the *Consolation* is Plato, and the real unifying factor is late Neoplatonism.[27]

To affirm the essential Neoplatonism of the work is not to deny the obvious Aristotelian influence. Not only does Philosophy once refer to "my Aristotle" (5:pr. 1), she cites his ideas again and again. Besides showing the influence of treatises comprising the *Organon*, notably *On Interpretation*, the *Consolation* reveals that Boethius obviously knew well such other works by Aristotle as the *Nicomachean Ethics*, with its definition of happiness (3:pr. 10); the *Physics*, with its definition of chance (5:pr. 1); and *On the Heavens*, with its distinction between eternity and temporal duration (5:pr. 6). But since Boethius had devoted the greater part of his work before the *Consolation* to translating and interpreting Aristotle, "it would be surprising"—as Helen Barrett realizes—if the *Consolation* did not show the influence of Aristotelian thought.[28]

We must likewise acknowledge the general sense of Stoic resolution that permeates the *Consolation*. It is hardly accidental that Philosophy, when identifying her martyrs, should single out Stoics (1:pr. 3); and it may be significant that the Stoic thinker Seneca is, along with Cicero, the main Latin authority cited in the work. Moreover, Stoic ethical teachings, "strong and bracing" as they were, may well have had a special appeal to Boethius after his fall. But Stoicism was a major part of Boethius's cultural heritage, and the *Consolation* shows little Stoic influence on its particular ideas. In fact, Boethius is explicitly unsympathetic to the Stoic theory of the mind as a passive receiver of impressions (5:m.4), and he has little use for the Stoic theories of materialism, pantheism, and fatalism.[29]

By far the greatest influences on the *Consolation* come from Platonic and Neoplatonic sources. Plato himself is at the heart of the work, and the *Timaeus* and *Gorgias* are notably significant. The *Timaeus* is the basis of the significant prayer to God in 3:m.9; and the *Gorgias* is the source of Boethius's solution to the problem of evil in 4:pr.2–3. But the bulk of Boethius's relationships to Plato are due to the influence of Neoplatonic intermediaries. Although it has been suggested that Boethius actually translated the *Timaeus,* he most likely knew the work as it existed in the commentary of Proclus; similarly, whether or not he knew the *Gorgias* itself, he certainly knew the commentaries of the Alexandrian Neoplatonists Ammonius Hermiae and Olympiodorus. Moreover, the *Enneads* of Plotinus may have provided Boethius with the framing principle of Philosophy's drawing up the mind of the narrator from earthly things, as well as with the identification of God as the highest good; Proclus certainly influenced Boethius's view of Providence and Fate; and Ammonius Hermiae influenced his distinction between the eternity of God and the perpetuity of the world, as well as his statement of the relationship between foreknowledge and free will.[30]

To note these influences is not at all to suggest that the *Consolation* is a pastiche of earlier thought, or that, because Boethius does not produce a new philosophical system as such, he is "a mere collector" of the ideas of others.[31] Rather, we must recognize that as with such earlier work as the *Principles of Music,* where he synthesizes several earlier views and authorities, Boethius uses the material in the *Consolation* to construct a new and autonomous work. And while it is most in harmony with the fundamentals of Neoplatonic thought, it is also in accord with the tenets of Christianity.

At the same time, the nature and extent of the influence on the *Consolation* of Christian doctrine in general and Augustinian thought in particular are not clear. In part, the problem stems from the accommodation by Christianity—and especially by Augustine—of Neoplatonism, and from the difficulty of isolating peculiarly Christian elements within this philosophical work. But it is not sufficient to say that whereas Boethius often echoes the Neoplatonists, "he studiously avoids any attempt to blend Christ with Plato."[32] Whereas this evaluation may be correct in its recognition that the *Consolation* contains no overtly Christian doctrine, it is misleading in its implication that Boethius is not at all concerned here with the overlapping of Neoplatonism and Christianity. It is likewise misleading to say that both Christianity and Augustine "would of course be in the background of his mind and could not have been without influence on what he wrote in the *Consolation*."[33] The implication of this statement is that Christianity—like Stoicism—was merely part of the cultural heritage of the time and represented nothing special for Boethius.

Just as the affinity between Philosophy and Christ as healers— what Wolfgang Schmid calls *philosophia medicans* and *Christus medicans*—may be more than coincidental, so the similarity between certain issues of the *Consolation* and concerns of Christianity—for instance, the problem of evil—may not be accidental. And Augustine—who was very much troubled by the question of evil—may well have exerted a particular influence on the *Consolation,* not only on Boethius's method of allegory and dialogue but also on his thought.[34] At times, as Antonio Crocco recognizes, "we sense clearly the presence of Augustine." And inasmuch as Boethius at the beginning of his *De Trinitate* openly cites Augustine as his authority, we may feel with Etienne Gilson that "one hardly risks being mistaken in saying that where the doctrine of the *De consolatione philosophiae* coincides with that of Augustine, the coincidence is not fortuitous. Even when he is speaking only as a philosopher Boethius thinks as a Christian."[35]

But though cases have been made for a pervasive Augustinian influence, though the *Consolation* has even been presented as a sequel to Augustine's *Soliloquies,* and though the work has been thought to have its nucleus in Augustine's early dialogues, mainly the *Contra Academicos,* the arguments supporting this relationship are too frequently neither sufficiently clear nor persuasive.[36] At the same time, however, arguments concerned with negating the possible Augustinian influence or with differentiating the thought of the two men have likewise been less than convincing.[37] While on the one hand we may be left with a sense that, as Rand expresses it, "there is nothing in this work for which a good case might not have been made by any contemporary Christian theologian, who knew his Augustine," on the other hand we should also recognize that Boethius's accomplishment is finally rather different from Augustine's. We may get a sense of this difference by noting that Fortune and Fate, two terms in fact proscribed by Augustine, are fundamental to Boethius's argument.[38]

The problem of establishing an Augustinian basis for the *Consolation* may be related to that of understanding Boethius's citation of authorities. Inasmuch as all of these are figures who lived before the first century A.D., the implication is that Boethius systematically omitted all references to later authorities, even though he clearly knew and used such writers as Plotinus, Porphyry, Proclus, and Augustine. Pierre Courcelle feels that this strange omission is due to Boethius's purposely citing only pagan authorities who lived before Christ. Having chosen as his fictional guide a figure representing Philosophy, Boethius could hardly have had her allude to Scripture or Christian theology, for such inconsistency would have amounted to "a fault of logic and of taste." Thus, when the narrator asks about the punishment of the soul after the death of the body, Philosophy acknowledges such punishment but says, "I purpose not now to treat of those" (4:pr.4). Moreover, argues Courcelle, Boethius purposely refrained from citing any of the Neoplatonists who lived after Christ—and who clearly influenced his thought in the *Consolation*—because the figure of Philosophy he created is, in effect, the representative of Neoplatonic thought: "she is their own philosophy," that which they all have in common.[39]

If this is indeed an accurate statement of Boethius's procedure, we should realize that it does not mean that the *Consolation* is thereby a celebration of Neoplatonic thought. Rather, Boethius may well have used philosophy in general and Neoplatonism in particular as a means of justifying the ways of God to man and of making man understand the need to return to God. The *Consolation* is without doubt "a theodicy of great power and scope." To assert divine justice in the face of obvious evil, Boethius had to face not only the helplessness and inadequate understanding of man but "the mysteries of divine unity and goodness, of fate and human freedom." Whether or not Boethius sets forth "all that he can see of life and time and eternity," we should recognize that these are indeed the concerns of his discourse.[40]

What is important for Boethius is not to prove the existence of God or to define God. Rather, he intends, first, to show "the existence of a perfect Good which must be identical with God," and, second, to stress the workings of divine order in the universe—the term *ordo,* which describes the same reality as Providence and Fate, permeates the *Consolation*—and the need for man to participate in this order by returning to God.[41] This return, which is at the heart of both Neoplatonism and Christianity, is not only a major structuring principle of the *Consolation,* it is also a major theme. Representing the journey of the mind away from the world and back to God, it may be meaningfully described as a "conversion," in the literal sense of a turning around—here effected by means of philosophy; and the *Consolation* itself may be regarded as what Courcelle calls "a dual conversion in three stages," overseen by Plato. First comes knowledge of the self (Book 2); second, knowledge of the purpose of things (Book 3 to 4:pr.5); and third, knowledge of the laws that govern the universe (end of Book 4 and Book 5).[42] The need for this conversion provides the *Consolation* with its subject which, though described as "human happiness and the possibility of achieving it in the midst of the suffering and disappointment which play so large a part in every man's experience," may more accurately be considered as the reaffirmation of the point and purpose of the universe and of man's place in God's creation: man's "loving participation in God's divine ordinance of the universe, informed by philosophical study."[43]

The journey that comprises this "loving participation" involves understanding such distractions as Fortune and Fate. Fortune, though appearing in the first three books of the *Consolation* as above all harmful and detrimental to man, comes to be seen in the last two books as a principle related to Providence. Fortune—which Boethius distinguishes, initially at least, from Fate—is "merely an instrument in God's hand for the correction and education of man, and however harmful and capricious she may appear to his limited intelligence, she is really good in whatever guise she comes."[44] Although Boethius's words may be thought to "constitute a polemical treatise against Fortune," it is clear that Fortune changes in the course of the *Consolation* from a mythological and allegorical figure to a philosophical concept. In making this revision of Fortune, Boethius is unique. Although Christian authorities had forbidden belief in the goddess Fortune and had even hesitated to employ the name itself, the *Consolation* not only addresses the issues of the nature of Fortune and its role in creation, it provides for the Western world the definitive way of regarding Fortune.[45] In a similar demythologizing of Fate, a familiar figure in Greek myth and a popular folk deity, Boethius transforms this figure into a philosophical concept. And, following such Neoplatonists as Proclus, he links Fate with Providence and shows it to be subject to God.[46]

Boethius's conception of God in the *Consolation* may likewise stem from various manifestations of deity in classical metaphysics. This God resembles Plato's Demiurge, Aristotle's Unmoved Mover, and Plotinus's One; He is the Supreme Orderer and the Highest Good, as well as Reality itself. While this conception is by and large Neoplatonic, it is also decidedly Christian inasmuch as it identifies God with Love.[47] Perhaps, since God was not his subject any more than theology was, Boethius purposely refrained from limiting his principle of deity to that of any one religion or philosophical system. But at the same time it is clear that the God of the *Consolation* evades all of man's categories. As Gilson writes about Boethius's view, "when man has said all he can about God, he has not yet attained what God is."[48]

For Boethius, what one can say about God applies less to God Himself than to His manner of administering the world. And God is finally best referred to as Love *(Amor)*, the creative force and principle of harmony in the universe. This is the Love celebrated in at least five key poems as that which rules the sun and the other stars.[49] While the notion of Love as a cosmic principle and a natural force may simply represent "that amalgamation of Greek and Christian thought which is so familiar to any reader of patristic texts," in identifying God as Love and Providential order as an expression of Love, Boethius "was probably inspired by the Christian faith and the spiritual climate of Christian reflection about the love of God."[50] Moreover, in framing his discussion of the *summum bonum,* the central argument of the *Consolation,* with two poems on love—2:m.8 and 3:m.12—Boethius emphasizes that the highest good is not "an abstract cosmological force" but "an active outgoing love, descending from heaven to earth."[51] This love is ideally common and mutual, embracing both God and man, who must recognize his need and responsibility to respond to it and participate in it. Man's desire for the good and his expression of this desire, his return to that which gave him being, are thus to be understood as manifestations of love, as well as of the search for truth.

Chapter Seven

The Boethian Legacy

The Impact of the *Consolation*

Had Boethius lived longer, he might well have followed his *Consolation of Philosophy* with a *Consolation of Theology*. It is not surprising that among the many imitations and adaptations of Boethius's work in subsequent centuries at least two important works, by John of Dambach (fourteenth century) and Jean Gerson (fifteenth century), both having the title *Consolatio Theologiae*, suggest this obvious continuation.[1] Moreover, had Boethius completed his educational program and reconciled Plato and Aristotle, it would have been natural for him to go on to harmonize Greek philosophy with Christian thought.[2] As it is, the *Consolation* exerted a greater influence on Western thought and literature than any other book except the Bible. Not only did it make Boethius's name "precious to educated men for centuries," it has been said to be "the source of all that is best in the literature of western Europe."[3] The work offered the Christian Middle Ages a blending of history and legend, as well as a glimpse of the strange notions of pagan Neoplatonism: knowledge as reminiscence, the preexistence of the soul, the world soul. And it provided the solution to such pressing problems as how to view the gifts of Fortune and how to reconcile evil with providential order, as well as the definitive answer to questions concerning the relationship between foreknowledge and free will and between eternity and time. The central problems of the *Consolation* were those that occupied the attention of philosophers for the next thousand years, and the answers Boethius gave came to be the answers of the Middle Ages and of Christianity.[4]

From the time that the *Consolation* was rediscovered by Alcuin in the late ninth century, it was copied continually throughout the Latin West.[5] More than four hundred medieval manuscripts of the work have come down to us, and it was printed as early as 1471. Between this date and the end of the fifteenth century some thirty different editions of it were made in almost sixty different printings. Moreover, the *Consolation* was the source of hundreds of illustrations, and its influence on subsequent iconographic tradition has only recently begun to be appreciated.[6] Between the late ninth and the fifteenth century it was translated into English—both Old and Middle English—German, Provençal, French, Catalan, Spanish, Italian, Norse, Flemish, Dutch, Greek, Hebrew, Hungarian, and Polish; and it was the basis of nearly three dozen known commentaries.[7] Such significant commentaries as those by Remigius of Auxerre (turn of the tenth century), William of Conches (twelfth century), and Nicholas Trevet (fourteenth century)—frequently included in both manuscripts and printings of the original text—not only reveal how important the *Consolation* was to Christian thought of the Middle Ages, in effect justifying Boethius's appellation as father of scholasticism, they also act as a short course in methods of exegesis, the development of allegory, and even the history of medieval Platonism and Aristotelianism.[8]

Similarly, the different ways the *Consolation* was used by translators and adapters provide a course in the history and nature of medieval translation. King Alfred, rendering the work into late ninth-century English, used it as the basis for what amounted to a new treatise. He not only made the *Consolation* overtly Christian, but, by inserting familiar Germanic terms and lore and by altering several doctrinal points, he adapted it to his Anglo-Saxon audience. Notker Labeo (late tenth century), on the other hand, in rendering the *Consolation* into Old High German, intended to write not a substitute for Boethius's work but a version that would take his audience to Boethius's Latin original. The fragmentary eleventh-century Provençal verse *Boecis*—the earliest extant composition in the Provençal language—apparently used what is found in the *Consolation* to tell the story of Boethius the

Christian martyr. Simund de Freine, in his twelfth-century An-
glo-Norman verse *Romance of Philosophy*, used the *Consolation*,
especially its treatment of the gifts of Fortune, as part of his
philosophical romance. Jean de Meun (late thirteenth century)
translated Boethius's work into French, expanding it in accord
with points brought out in the commentaries. And Geoffrey
Chaucer, relying also on a French version of the work as well as
on Trevet's commentary, translated the *Consolation* into Middle
English in the second half of the fourteenth century. Such extensive translating, adapting, and commenting would seem to
indicate that, although the learned and cultured during the Middle Ages knew enough Latin to read the *Consolation* without
assistance, men wanted real intimacy with the book and not just
a reasonable knowledge of it.[9]

Throughout the Middle Ages the *Consolation* was quoted ver-
batim thousands of times in almost every context and paraphrased
scores of thousands of times. As the nineteenth-century English-
man flavored his speech with Horace, so the cultivated man of
the Middle Ages found it decorous or illuminating to cite a phrase
or two from the *Consolation*.[10] Far from indicating a trivializing
of the work, this tendency shows that the *Consolation* was more
than an esoteric treatise available only to the scholarly world. It
was in fact a standard reference work and next to the Bible the
basic authority for the Western world for at least six hundred
years. Boethius himself was everywhere recognized as an *auctoritas*
as eminent as the most important Church Fathers, and it is not
at all surprising that Dante, referring to him as "the holy soul
who makes plain the world's deceitfulness," should have placed
him in Paradise in the circle of the Sun along with the greatest
Christian sages.[11] The *Consolation* itself was recognized as a major
work of literature, and its poems were particularly prized. Not
only were they set to music, they were continually commented
on and translated, from the early famous work of Lupus of Fer-
rières in the ninth century to the rendition of 3:m.9 attributed
to Samuel Johnson in the eighteenth century.[12]

If one were to list all the medieval authors who show an indebtedness to the *Consolation*, one would have to call the roll of

practically everyone of any account in the period; and the influence
of Boethius on the Renaissance, though less definite or precise,
may be no less dominant than that on the Middle Ages. Not only
were such important thinkers as Peter Abelard, Albert the Great,
Thomas Aquinas, and Thomas More inspired by the *Consolation*,
so were the greatest poets, in the vernacular as well as in Latin.
Besides translating the work, Jean de Meun used it as a basis for
his ideas and methods in the *Romance of the Rose*, and Geoffrey
Chaucer showed its influence from his early dream visions and
Troilus and Criseyde through his *Canterbury Tales*. Moreover,
Dante, who knew the *Consolation* thoroughly, used it as the basis
of his *Divine Comedy;* and Boccaccio relied heavily on it in both
his Italian and his Latin works. [13]

When a medieval or Renaissance writer discusses a topic like
true nobility, free will, or the workings of Fortune, it is most
often impossible to tell whether his particular thoughts derive
directly from Boethius or from Boethius via the *Romance of the
Rose*, Dante, or Chaucer. We should realize that Boethius's work
had become so pervasive and so much the common property of
the age that the full extent of the influence enjoyed by the *Consolation* is beyond our power today to estimate. [14] Moreover, its
prosimetric form was imitated in such philosophical works as the
Complaint of Nature of Alan of Lille (twelfth century) and the *New
Life* of Dante; and it seems to have influenced the medieval
chantefable, as in the early French romance *Aucassin and Nicolette*.
The *Consolation* also insured the popularity of allegory: Fortune
and her wheel enjoyed a long life, and Lady Philosophy had such
worthy successors as Nature in Alan's *Complaint*, Reason in the
Romance of the Rose, Holy Church in *Piers Plowman*, and even
Beatrice in the *Divine Comedy* and the maiden in the Middle
English *Pearl*. The dialogue method of the *Consolation* was more
immediately influential on medieval dialogues than were the dialogues of either Plato or Cicero. And the work became the model
for all sorts of literary and philosophical consolations, as well as
the inspiration for a host of writings concerned with the gifts of
Fortune. [15]

Assessing the Influence

What took place after the rediscovery of Boethius's writings in the ninth century was ironically the renaissance of learning Boethius had fully expected to occur at the time he was writing. But for many reasons the early sixth century in Italy was clearly not propitious for such a renaissance. Along with the debilitating effects of Gothic rule and the confusions in a world marked by political and ecclesiastical schisms, it seems clear that Boethius's Roman contemporaries were simply not capable of grasping his remarkable accomplishment. Although Pierre Riché may seem to be too severe when he writes that during his lifetime Boethius's work "interested no one but a few intimate friends," his view is doubtless more accurate than that of Pierre Courcelle, who feels that the Hellenic culture brought to the West by Boethius produced "a veritable literary renaissance in Italy during the reign of Theodoric."[16] The praise Boethius received led to little understanding and even less change. When Cassiodorus praised Boethius as translator but ignored him as philosopher, he reflected the common notion that philosophy was something strange. For many of Boethius's contemporaries it was confused with the occult sciences condemned by both church and state. And even learned men like Cassiodorus and Ennodius thought of it in the main as natural science, physics, and medicine.[17] Although Boethius revived the Hellenic view of philosophy as the crown of the Liberal Arts, this revival took almost four hundred years to come to fruition; and it was only with the renewal of learning in Carolingian times that the Western world was capable of receiving what he had to offer. Had the political and cultural split between the Latin and the Greek worlds in the sixth century not been so complete, had Gothic Italy been peacefully amalgamated into the Empire, had Boethius lived to complete his work, the Dark Ages might not have engulfed the West. At the same time, we should recognize that it is in large measure because of Boethius that the Latin world was able to leave the darkness and come into the light.

The *Consolation* offered to the world of the Latin Middle Ages not only something of Aristotle's metaphysics but a good deal of Plato's cosmology and epistemology. By bringing medieval man into touch with classical philosophy, it, along with Boethius's works on arithmetic and music, kept his name alive between the sixth and the late tenth century, when Boethius's translations and commentaries on Aristotle began to be influential. Not only did Boethius introduce the Middle Ages to logic and to Aristotelian thought, but the part he played in the history of dialectic can hardly be overstated. As his work on arithmetic and music continued to provide the definitive word on these subjects for the Western world well into modern times, and as his conception of the *quadrivium* led to the medieval classification of the sciences and to the standard course of studies in medieval universities, so from the late tenth century when Gerbert of Aurillac lectured on Boethius's logical work, logic came to have an importance it had never previously attained in the Latin world.

Before the mid-twelfth century, Boethius was the sole transmitter of Aristotle to the West. For almost two hundred years logic for the Latin Middle Ages meant largely Boethius's work on Porphyry's *Isagoge* and his versions of and commentaries on Aristotle's *Categories* and *On Interpretation*—the so-called Old Logic. The rest of the *Organon*—the New Logic—was merely glimpsed through Boethius's commentaries and original logical treatises. And even after the mid-twelfth century, when knowledge of Aristotle began to pour into the West from the Arab world, and when new Latin translations were made, Boethius still provided the way for those making their first acquaintance with Aristotle, and his commentaries were the basis of all subsequent interpretations. While Boethius's work gave familiarity with the scope, organization, and method of Aristotelian logic, it did not satiate but rather served to whet the appetite for more. As R. W. Southern writes, "If Aristotle, in Dante's famous phrase was the 'master of those who know,' Boethius was the master of those who wanted to know. He was the schoolmaster of medieval Europe."[18]

Explaining the attraction of logic to the medieval mind, Southern points out that in a disordered world, where politics, law, and rhetoric did not satisfy, logic "opened a window on to an

orderly and systematic view of the world and of man's mind."
The more the other arts and sciences declined, "the more pre-
eminent appeared the orderliness of Aristotle's comprehensive
picture of the workings of the human mind."[19] In studying Aristotle's *Organon* and Boethius's writings, the student began to
analyze the workings of the mind and learned to classify the types
of valid argument so as to detect the cause of error and to avoid
deceptions. The whole process of simplification and arrangement
that Boethius's work offered to the Middle Ages not only revealed
what the mind was capable of but it made meaningful "the
orderliness which lay behind a bewildering complexity of apparently unrelated facts." What Boethius dramatized in the *Consolation* he had in effect documented in his logical writings. Largely
because of his work logic became "the touchstone of truth" and
"the foundation of all discussion," and particulars of his logical
analyses, such as the nature of universals, came to be at the heart
of medieval philosophy.[20]

Similarly, the applications of logic to theology that Boethius
made in his *opuscula sacra* were very influential in the Middle
Ages. These theological tractates were the basis of interpretations
attributed to such major early medieval thinkers as John Scotus
Erigena and Alcuin; as the impetus for notable commentaries by
Thierry of Chartres and Gilbert of Poitiers, they were central to
the theological concerns of the important twelfth-century School
of Chartres; and they were significant to the developing theology
of the most important thinker of the Middle Ages, Thomas
Aquinas.[21]

While he may have been the first of the scholastics, Boethius
should also be considered as the first of the humanists. But
ironically, with the triumph of humanism in the Renaissance,
Boethius was no longer the stimulus he had been throughout the
Middle Ages. For those who acquired once again an ability to
read Greek and could turn to Boethius's sources, his work, including the *Consolation,* became something of "a superannuated
trot."[22] At the same time, because of printing and increased
literacy, the *Consolation* enjoyed a larger audience than ever, and
the work continued to be translated and imitated. Following in

the steps of King Alfred were later British rulers, who found a special attraction in the work. In the fifteenth century, James I of Scotland, held prisoner at the English court, apparently found solace in it and used it as the basis of his *Kingis Quair;* and at the end of the sixteenth century, Queen Elizabeth I translated it in a period of not much more than twenty-four hours, though whether for amusement or for consolation is not clear.[23] Moreover, it was in the Renaissance that Boethius received some of his most effusive praise. Not only did Scaliger put Boethius's poetry and Virgil's on the same level, but Politian asked rhetorically, "Who is keener in dialectic than Boethius, or subtler in mathematics, or more satisfying in philosophy, or more sublime in theology?"[24]

This praise should be understood as looking backward to recognition given Boethius throughout the Middle Ages, such as that of John of Salisbury in the twelfth century—"Without difficulty he is profound in doctrine, without levity striking in expression, fervent in speech, effective in demonstration"—and forward to tributes by such twentieth-century readers as H. R. Patch: "Of his works men shall say, here is wisdom; and his words run to and fro like sparks among the stubble."[25] Although other individuals might excel in particulars, Boethius has few rivals when one considers the extent of his accomplishment or the degree of his influence. Boethius deserves to be remembered and indeed to be better known than he is, not only because he is one of the most important philosophers of the Western world but also because he is one of its most accomplished men of letters and poets. The *Consolation of Philosophy* is without a doubt one of the greatest books ever written. It possesses that certain timeless quality which marks all great works of literature, and it gives the impression that it can never be used up. The more one reads the work, the more one finds in it, and the more one comes to admire the artistry and genius of the public administrator-scientist-philosopher-theologian-poet who was its author.

Notes and References

Chapter One

1. See *Anonymous Valesii,* sect. 61, 79; ed. Roberto Cessi, *Fragmenta historica ab Henrico et Hadriano Valesio,* Rerum Italicarum Scriptores, 24.4 (Città di Castello: Lapi, 1913), pp. 16, 19. On Theodoric's learning, see Pierre Riché, *Education and Culture in the Barbarian West, Sixth through Eighth Centuries,* tr. J. Contreni (Columbia: University of South Carolina Press, 1976), pp. 56–59.

2. For a sense of Theodoric's achievements, see Maurice Dumoulin, "The Kingdom of Italy under Odovacar and Theodoric," *The Cambridge Medieval History,* 2nd ed. (New York: Macmillan, 1924), 1:432–55; also the still-useful study by Thomas Hodgkin, *Theodoric the Goth, The Barbarian Champion of Civilisation* (New York: Putnam's Sons, 1894), esp. pp. 126–73.

3. See *Anonymous Valesii,* sect. 59–61 (Cessi, 16); also Helen M. Barrett, *Boethius. Some Aspects of His Times and Works* (Cambridge, Eng., 1940; reprinted., New York, 1965), pp. 26–30.

4. See *Anonymous Valesii,* sect. 59–61; also Barrett, *Boethius,* p. 29.

5. See Cesare Foligno, *Latin Thought during the Middle Ages* (Oxford: Clarendon, 1929), p. 49.

6. Pierre Courcelle, *Late Latin Writers and Their Greek Sources,* tr. H. E. Wedeck (Cambridge, Mass., 1969), p. 148.

7. Ibid., pp. 148, 274. See the correction to this view in Riché, *Education,* p. 44.

8. See H.-I. Marrou, *History of Education in Antiquity,* tr. G. Lamb (New York: Sheed and Ward, 1956), p. 459.

9. On the culture of the time, see especially M. L. W. Laistner, *Thought and Letters in Western Europe, A.D. 500 to 900,* rev. ed. (Ithaca: Cornell University Press, 1957), pp. 85–103; and Arnaldo Momigliano, "Cassiodorus and Italian Culture of His Time," *Proceedings of the British Academy* 41 (1956):207–45.

10. For a recent argument that Boethius's birth may have been a few years earlier, most likely sometime between 475 and 477, see Luca Obertello, *Severino Boezio* (Genoa, 1974), 1:18–20.

11. It is possible that the greatest figure of the late sixth century, Pope Gregory the Great, was also a member of this family. On the Anicii, see Obertello, *Severino Boezio,* pp. 5–15.

12. The possibility that Boethius may have been named after Saint Severinus, who died in 482, is unlikely; but a connection between Boethius and this saint may have been made after Boethius's death. In the Renaissance the name Torquatus was introduced before Severinus as part of Boethius's name; see Obertello, *Severino Boezio,* p. 16.

13. This circle doubtless included the Cassiodorus family.

14. According to tradition, Boethius also had another guardian named Festus, perhaps a senator, and supposedly first married Festus's daughter Helpes, who wrote Christian hymns. As Hugh F. Stewart states, this tradition would seem to be the result of a desire to give symmetry to the details of Boethius's life (*Boethius: An Essay* [Edinburgh, 1891], p. 24).

15. See Riché, *Education,* pp. 7, 26; also Marrou, *History,* pp. 369–80.

16. See Courcelle, *Late Latin Writers,* pp. 331–32; Riché, *Education,* pp. 63–64.

17. See, e.g., Ennodius, *Epistola* 7.13; *Opera,* ed. Fridericus Vogel, Monumenta Germaniae Historica, Auctorum Antiquissimorum, 7 (Berlin: Weidmann, 1885), p. 236.

18. See Marrou, *History,* pp. 353–54; Riché, *Education,* p. 28.

19. See especially C. J. de Vogel, "Boethiana," *Vivarium* 9 (1971):49–51.

20. See, e.g., Courcelle, *Late Latin Writers,* pp. 275–76; also Cassiodorus, *Variae,* 1:45; ed. Theodorus Mommsen, Monumenta Germaniae Historica, Auctorum Antiquissimorum, 12 (Berlin: Weidmann, 1894), p. 40; see *The Letters of Cassiodorus,* ed. Thomas Hodgkin (London: Froude, 1886), p. 169. For the misreading of apparent evidence in Ennodius, *Epistola* 7.13, see de Vogel, "Boethiana," *Vivarium* 10 (1972):37, 51–52.

21. See Courcelle, *Late Latin Writers,* pp. 284 ff., also 275 ff., which develops Courcelle's earlier argument for Boethius's study in Alexandria, "Boèce et l'école d'Alexandrie," *Mélange d'Archéologie et d'Histoire de L'Ecole Française de Rome* 52 (1935):185–223.

22. See Obertello, *Severino Boezio,* pp. 28–29; also the view by James Shiel that these writings were in an annotated edition of Aristotle's *Organon,* which Boethius worked with in his library in Rome ("Boethius' Commentaries on Aristotle," *Mediaeval and Renaissance Studies* 4 [1958]: esp. 242–44).

23. De Vogel, *Vivarium* 9 (1971):65; though cf. Jan Satorowicz, "De Boethii in Graeciam itinere," *Divus Thomas* 72 (1969):430–40.

24. Cassiodorus, *Variae,* 2:40 (Mommsen, pp. 70–72; Hodgkin, *Letters,* pp. 193–94).

25. Ibid., 1:10 (Mommsen, pp. 18–20; Hodgkin, *Letters,* pp. 150–51).

26. Ibid., 1:45 (Mommsen, pp. 39–41; Hodgkin, *Letters,* pp. 168–70); see also *Variae,* 1:46.

27. Ibid. (Mommsen, p. 40); tr. in Howard R. Patch, *The Tradition of Boethius. A Study of His Importance in Medieval Culture* (New York, 1935), p. 2.

28. *De institutione arithmetica,* 1. praefatio; ed. Godredus Friedlein, *Anicii Manlii Torquati Severini Boetii de institutione arithmetica libri duo, de institutione musica libri quinque, accedit geometria quae fertur Boetii* (Leipzig, 1867; Frankfurt, 1966), pp. 3 ff; summarized in Courcelle, *Late Latin Writers,* p. 276.

29. See Courcelle, *Late Latin Writers,* pp. 327–28.

30. See *De inst. arith.,* 1:1 (Friedlein, pp. 7–12). Cf. L. M. de Rijk, who feels that Theodoric's letter cannot be dated before 515 ("On the Chronology of Boethius' Works on Logic," *Vivarium* 2 [1964]:143).

31. See Cassiodorus, *Variae,* 9:24 (Mommsen, pp. 289–91; Hodgkin, *Letters,* 410–11); also Riché, *Education,* p. 58.

32. See Plato, *Republic,* 7:523–24; also H.-I. Marrou, *Saint Augustin et la fin de la culture antique* (Paris: Boccard, 1950), pp. 222–23; and William H. Stahl, *Martianus Capella and the Seven Liberal Arts. I: The Quadrivium of Martianus Capella* (New York: Columbia University Press, 1971), p. 91.

33. Augustine excluded Varro's medicine and architecture; see Foligno, *Latin Thought,* pp. 46–47.

34. See *De inst. arith.,* 1:1 (Friedlein, p. 9). Actually Boethius's term is *quadruvium,* which was later corrupted to *quadrivium,* apparently on the basis of the term *trivium,* which, dating from Carolingian times, came to describe the other three subjects. See Pio Rajna, "Le denominazioni *Trivium* e *Quadrivium,*" *Studi Medievali* 1 (1928):4–36; Laistner, *Thought and Letters,* p. 41; and Etienne Gilson, *History of Christian Philosophy in the Middle Ages* (London: Sheed and Ward, 1955), pp. 97–98.

35. *De inst. arith.,* 1. praefatio and 1 (Friedlein, pp. 5, 7–12, esp. 9). See Hans M. Klinkenberg, "Der Verfall des Quadriviums im frühen Mittelalter," *Artes Liberales von der antiken Bildung zur Wissenschaft des Mittelalters* (Leiden: Brill, 1959), p. 2; Stahl, *Martianus Capella,* pp.

92 ff.; and Michael Masi, "Boethius and the Iconography of the Liberal Arts," *Latomus* 33 (1974):58–59.

36. *De inst. arith.*, 1:1 (Friedlein, p.9).

37. Nicomachus's work may be part of the scholarly commentary on Plato, especially on the *Timaeus*, the most mathematical of all his works. On Greek arithmetical tradition, see *Nicomachus of Gerasa, Introduction to Arithmetic*, tr. Martin L. D'Ooge (Ann Arbor: University of Michigan Press, 1938), esp. chs. 2 and 9 by Frank E. Robbins, pp. 16 ff., 124 ff.

38. The older view is expressed in Martianus Capella, *De nuptiis*, where Geometry is the first of the arts of the *quadrivium* to come forward, followed by Arithmetic. See Marrou, *History of Education*, p. 247; and Stahl, *Martianus Capella*, pp. 154–55.

39. *De inst. arith.*, 1. praefatio (Friedlein, pp. 4–5).

40. See Robbins, in D'Ooge, *Nichomachus*, p. 133; also Henry O. Taylor, *The Mediaeval Mind. A History of the Development of Thought and Emotion in the Middle Ages*, 4th ed. (Cambridge, Mass.: Harvard University Press, 1959), 1:90; and Gregor Maurach, "Boethiusinterpretationen," *Antike und Abendland* 14 (1968): 129–32; repr. *Römische Philosophie*, Wege der Forschung, 193 (Darmstadt: Wissenschaftliche Buchgesellschaft, 1976), pp. 391–95.

41. Courcelle suggests that he did so (*Late Latin Writers*, p. 278).

42. Cassiodorus, *Institutiones*, 2:4:7; ed. R. A. B. Mynors (Oxford: Clarendon Press, 1937), p. 140; tr. L. W. Jones, *An Introduction to Divine and Human Readings* (New York: Columbia University Press, 1946), p. 187.

43. See Patch, *Tradition*, pp. 36 ff., 116; and the illustrations of Boethius as Arithmetic in Pierre Courcelle, *La Consolation de Philosophie dans la tradition littéraire. Antécédents et postérité de Boèce* (Paris: Etudes Augustiniennes, 1967), pls. 1–3, and pp. 67–69.

44. See Obertello, *Severino Boezio*, p. 173; Courcelle, *Late Latin Writers*, pp. 278–79; Ubaldo Pizzani, "Studi sulle fonti del De institutione musica di Boezio," *Sacris Eruditi* 16 (1965):7–10; and on the unity of Books 1–4, Calvin Bower, "Boethius and Nicomachus: An Essay Concerning the Sources of *De institutione musica*," *Vivarium* 16 (1978):4–11, 38–41. On the problems of the fourth book, see Pizzani, pp. 87 ff., though Bower makes a good case for Nicomachus's sole authorship (11 ff., esp. 40–41).

45. See *De institutione musica*, 1:2 (Friedlein, pp. 187–89); tr. Calvin Bower, "Boethius' *The Principles of Music*. An Introduction, Translation, and Commentary" (Ph.D. dissertation, George Peabody College,

1976), pp. 44–48. On Book 5 and its possible relationship to the first four books, see Bower, *Vivarium* 16 (1978):43–45.

46. This would have been the case regardless of the source of Book 4. See Henri Potiron, *Boèce. Théoricien de la musique grecque.* Travaux de l'Institut Catholique de Paris, 9 (Paris, 1961), p. 15.

47. Obertello feels that the *Music*—which cites the *Arithmetic*—followed it "more or less immediately" (*Severino Boezio,* p. 308). See also Samuel Brandt, "Die Entstehungszeit und zeitliche Folge der Werke von Boethius," *Philologus* 62 (1903):152–54. Cf. Arthur P. McKinlay, "Stylistic Tests and the Chronology of the Works of Boethius," *Harvard Studies in Classical Philology* 18 (1907):esp. 146–48. McKinlay's procedure of dating has been criticized as "based on nothing but adverbs and particles" (de Rijk, *Vivarium* 2 [1964]:2).

48. See Pizzani, "Studi," p. 155; and, on the relationship of Book 1 to Nicomachus, Gualtherus Miekley, *De Boethii libri de musica primi fontibus* (Iena: Nevehahn, 1898).

49. See Potiron, *Boèce,* p. 15. Cf. *De inst. arith.,* 1:1; *De inst. musica,* 2:3.

50. See David Chamberlain, "Philosophy of music in the *Consolatio* of Boethius," *Speculum* 45 (1970):81–84, esp. 84; also Roger Bragard, "L'harmonie des sphères selon Boèce," *Speculum* 4 (1929):206–13; and Luca Obertello, "Motivi dell'estetica di Boezio," *Rivista di Estetica* 12 (1967):360–87. Also on moral music, see Potiron, *Boèce,* pp. 35–36.

51. *De inst. musica,* 1:34 (Friedlein, pp. 224–25); see Edward K. Rand, "Boethius, the First of the Scholastics," *Founders of the Middle Ages* (Cambridge, Mass., 1928; repr. New York, 1957), pp. 147–48. On the matter of Boethius's originality in this three-fold concept of music, see Bower, *Vivarium* 16 (1978):44.

52. See Leo Schrade, "Music in the Philosophy of Boethius," *Musical Quarterly* 33 (1947):198 ff.; also two earlier essays by Schrade, "Das Propädeutische Ethos in der Musikanschauung des Boethius," *Zeitschrift für Geschichte der Erziehungs und des Unterrichts* 20 (1930):179–215; and "Die Stellung der Musik in der Philosophie des Boethius als Grundlage der ontologischen Musikerziehung," *Archiv für Geschichte der Philosophie* 41 (1932):368–400.

53. See the discussion in James Collins, "Progress and Problems in the Reassessment of Boethius," *Modern Schoolman* 23 (1945):12.

54. See the discussion in de Vogel, *Vivarium* 9 (1971):53; also Potiron, *Boèce,* pp. 13 ff. Bower calls him "primarily a moderator" between Nicomachus and Ptolemy (*Vivarium* 16 [1978]:45).

55. See Pizzani, "Studi," esp. pp. 122–23, 164.

56. Cassiodorus, *Institutiones*, 2:5:10 (Mynors, p. 149; Jones, *Introduction*, p. 196). Four such references exist in the *Institutiones*. See also Pizzani, "Studi," pp. 89–91.

57. De Vogel, *Vivarium* 9 (1971):53.

58. On the musical works of Augustine and Boethius, see, e.g., Marrou, *Saint Augustin*, pp. 209–10. For Chaucer see *Nun's Priest's Tale*, B² 4483–84. For illustrations of Boethius as patron of Arithmetic, see Courcelle, *Consolation*, pls. 4–6, and pp. 69–71. See also Roger Bragard, "Boethiana: Etudes sur le *De institutione musica* de Boèce," *Hommage à Charles van den Borren, Mélanges* (Anvers: Nederlandsche Boekhandel, 1945), esp. pp. 84–101; and Lucas Kunz, "Die Tonartenlehre des Boethius," *Kirchenmusikalisches Jahrbuch* 31 (1936):5–24.

59. Cassiodorus, *Institutiones*, 2:6:3 (Mynors, p. 152; Jones, *Introduction*, p. 198). On the four-part division of Euclid, see 2:6:2; also Courcelle, *Late Latin Writers*, p. 351; and Stahl, *Martianus Capella*, p. 128. The text edited by Friedlein (pp. 372–428) is probably not Boethius's; cf. the edition and study by Menso Folkerts (*'Boethius' Geometrie II. Ein mathematisches Lehrbuch des Mittelalters*, Boethius, Texte und Abhandlungen zur Geschichte der Exakten Wissenschaften, 9 [Wiesbaden: Franz Steiner, 1970]), especially the reconstructed text, pp. 173–217.

60. Cassiodorus, *Institutiones*, 2:7 (Mynors, pp. 153 ff., Jones, *Introduction*, pp. 199 ff.) See Courcelle, *Late Latin Writers*, p. 353; and Stahl, *Martianus Capella*, pp. 173–74, n.6.

61. See, e.g., Courcelle, *Late Latin Writers*, p. 279, n.8.

62. See Obertello, *Severino Boezio*, pp. 471–73.

63. See Stahl, *Martianus Capella*, pp. 57–58.

64. On what remains of Augustine's work on the Liberal Arts, see Marrou, *Saint Augustin*, pp. 570–79; also Stahl, *Martianus Capella*, p. 7.

65. Cassiodorus, *Variae*, 1:10 (Mommsen, p. 19; Hodgkin, *Letters*, p. 150).

Chapter Two

1. See *In Aristotelis de interpretatione, editio secunda*, 2:3; *Anicii Manlii Severini Boetii commentarii in librum Aristotelis Peri Hermeneias*, ed. Carolus Meiser, Pars Posterior, (Leipzig, 1880), pp. 79–80. On the improbability that Boethius translated other works of Aristotle, see Obertello, *Severino Boezio*, p. 201; although a case has been recently made for the *Metaphysics* by Lozano Millán Bravo, "El Códice Sa. 2706 y la presunta

versión boeciana de la Metafísica de Aristoteles," *Helmantica* 17 (1966):3–48.

2. On the history of the *Organon*, see William and Martha Kneale, *The Development of Logic* (Oxford: Clarendon Press, 1962), pp. 23 ff. On Boethius's plan, see esp. Alfred Kappelmacher, "Der schriftstellerische Plan des Boethius," *Wiener Studien* 46 (1928):215–25. On the *Organon* as it was known to Boethius, see Friedrich Solmsen, "Boethius and the History of the *Organon*," *American Journal of Philology* 65 (1944):69–74.

3. Pierre Courcelle says that "there can be no doubt" that Boethius's philosophical program derives from the School of Porphyry (*Late Latin Writers,* p. 282).

4. *Anicii Manlii Severini Boethii in Isagogen Porphyrii commenta, editio prima,* 1:1; ed. Georg Schepss, rev. Samuel Brandt, Corpus Scriptorum Ecclesiasticorum Latinorum, 48 (Leipzig, 1906), pp. 3–4. See Rand, *Founders,* p. 143; and Obertello, *Severino Boezio,* p. 306.

5. For the text see Paul Monceaux, "L'Isagoge latine de Marius Victorinus," *Philologie et linguistique. Mélanges offerts à Louis Havet* (Paris, 1909; repr. Geneva: Slatkine, 1972), pp. 291–310; and, more recently, Laurentius Minio-Paluello, *Aristoteles Latinus,* 1:6–7 (Bruges, Paris: Desclée de Brouwer, 1966), pp. 63–68; and Pierre Hadot, *Marius Victorinus. Recherches sur sa vie et ses oeuvres* (Paris: Etudes Augustiniennes, 1971), pp. 366–80 and also pp. 184–85; and Courcelle, *Late Latin Writers,* pp. 280–81.

6. See Hadot, *Marius Victorinus,* p. 183; also *In Isag. ed. prima,* 1:1 (Brandt, p. 4).

7. *In Isag., ed. prima,* 1:3 (Brandt, p. 7). See Luigi Adamo, "Boezio e Mario Vittorino traduttori e interpreti dell'*Isagoge* di Porfirio," *Rivista Critica di Storia della Filosofia* 22 (1967):esp. 160; and Obertello, *Severino Boezio,* pp. 548–50.

8. The old view, that it is Boethius's first work, has recently been argued again, though not well, by Obertello (*Severino Boezio,* p. 306). For the manuscripts, see Brandt, *In Isag.,* pp. xxxvi ff.; though none is earlier than the tenth century.

9. *In Isag., ed. prima,* 1:3 (Brandt, pp. 8–9). See Antonio Crocco, *Introduzione a Boezio,* 2nd ed. (Naples, 1975), p. 43; also Gilson, *History,* pp. 68, 97. Boethius goes on to divide practical philosophy as well, but the terminology is not esoteric.

10. Porphyry alters Aristotle's predicables, adding species and difference and deleting definition.

11. *In Isag., ed. secunda,* 1:1 (Brandt, p. 135); cf. tr. Richard McKeon, in *Selections from Medieval Philosophers, I: Augustine to Albert*

the Great (New York: Scribner's Sons, 1929), p. 70. For Boethius's translation of Porphyry, see *Aristoteles Latinus*, 1:6–7, ed. Minio-Paluello, with B. G. Dod, pp. 1 ff.; and for the titles *Dialogue* and *Commentarius*, see p. xiv.

12. Whereas both of Boethius's commentaries seem to show the influence of Ammonius, the second reveals it more strikingly than the first. It has also been suggested that along with the strong resemblances are equally strong divergencies, perhaps indicating that Boethius and Ammonius followed a common source. See Brandt, *In Isag.*, pp. xxiii–xxiv; and Courcelle, *Late Latin Writers*, pp. 285–88.

13. *In Isag.*, ed. *secunda*, 1:1 (Brandt, p. 135; cf. McKeon, *Selections*, p. 70). For Boethius's work in relation to Victorinus's, see Adamo, *Rivista Critica* 22 (1967):160–64; Obertello, *Severino Boezio*, pp. 549–50; and Hadot, *Marius Victorinus*, p. 185. Some scholars think that Boethius's second commentary is as elementary as the first and that the two should be regarded as a twin exposition; see, e.g., Shiel, *Mediaeval and Renaissance Studies* 4 (1958):235–37.

14. See, e.g., the criticism in Joseph Bidez, "Boèce et Porphyre," *Revue Belge de Philologie et d'Histoire* 2 (1923):195.

15. *In Isag.*, ed. *secunda*, 1:1 (Brandt, p. 135; cf. McKeon, *Selections*, p. 70).

16. *In Isag.*, ed. *prima*, 1:10; ed. *secunda*, 1:11 (Brandt, pp. 24–30, 166). On the association with Plato, see, e.g., Barrett, *Boethius*, p. 42; and Rand, *Founders*, p. 314, n.20.

17. *In Isag.*, ed. *secunda*, 1:11 (Brandt, p. 167; cf. McKeon, *Selections*, p. 98). See also the discussion and translation—which is followed here—in Gilson, *History*, pp. 99–100.

18. See, e.g., the discussion in McKeon, *Selections*, p. 68. See also Augusto Guzzo, "Boezio e il prologo dell'*Isagoge* di Porfirio," *Concetto e saggi di storia della filosofia* (Florence: Le Monnier, 1940), pp. 67–91.

19. *In Isag.*, ed. *secunda*, 1:3 (Brandt, pp. 142–43; cf. McKeon, *Selections*, 77). On the possible indebtedness to Ammonius, see Courcelle, *Late Latin Writers*, pp. 288–89.

20. *In Isag.*, ed. *prima*, 2:32 (Brandt, pp. 131–32). The line of Petronius cited here is not found in the extant work of this first-century-A.D. writer.

21. R. W. Southern, *The Making of the Middle Ages* (New Haven: Yale University Press, 1953), p. 179.

22. Ibid., p. 180; also Kneale, *Development*, p. 174.

23. See Lorenzo Minio-Paluello, e.g., "Les traductions et les commentaires aristotéliciens de Boèce," *Studia Patristica*, 2:2, Texte und

Untersuchungen, 64 (Berlin: Akademie-Verlag, 1957), pp. 361–63; also "The Genuine Text of Boethius' Translation of Aristotle's Categorics," *Mediaeval and Renaissance Studies* 1 (1943):151–77. On Minio-Paluello's views, see Obertello, *Severino Boezio,* p. 203 ff. The bulk of the manuscripts of the Latin *Categories,* though attributed to Boethius, are not of his translations; see the editions of translations offered by Minio-Paluello in *Aristoteles Latinus,* 1:1–5 (1961), pp. 1 ff. and 43 ff. Minio-Paluello also feels that Boethius's work is valuable for understanding the nature of his Greek original ("The Text of the *Categoriae:* The Latin Tradition," *Classical Quarterly* 39 [1945]:68–70).

24. See Minio-Paluello, *Classical Quarterly* 39 (1945):65–68.

25. *In Categorias Aristotelis,* 1, ed. J.-P. Migne, Patrologia Latina, 64:160.

26. See Courcelle, *Late Latin Writers,* p. 289; Shiel, *Mediaeval and Renaissance Studies* 4 (1958):226–27, 242; and de Vogel, *Vivarium* 9 (1971):57, 59.

27. *In Categ.,* 1 (PL, 64: 160). See Minio-Paluello, *Studia Patristica,* 2:2, pp. 361–62. Obertello sees no justification for thinking that Boethius wrote a second commentary (*Severino Boezio,* pp. 224, 226).

28. See Pierre Hadot, "Un fragment du commentaire perdu de Boèce sur les *Catégories* d'Aristote dans le Codex Bernensis 363," *Archives d'Histoire Doctrinale et Littéraire du Moyen Age* 26 (1959):11–27.

29. Obertello, *Severino Boezio,* pp. 226–28, 479–80.

30. See de Rijk, who argues that if Boethius ever did write a second commentary on the *Categories,* it would have had to be after his first commentary on Aristotle's *On Interpretation;* but apparently, by the time he wrote his second commentary on this treatise, he still had not written the second one on the *Categories.* De Rijk also feels that Hadot's fragment is so small as to preclude any certainty (*Vivarium* 2 [1964]:132 ff., esp. 139).

31. Cassiodorus, *Institutiones,* 2:3:11 (Mynors, p. 114; Jones, p. 163). For Boethius's statement of the work's difficulty, see *In Aristotelis de interpretatione, editio secunda,* 4:10 (Meiser, pp. 250–51).

32. The edition of this translation by Minio-Paluello (*Aristoteles Latinus,* 2:1–2 [1965], 1 ff.) has superseded that in Meiser, pp. 3 ff.

33. See Crocco, *Introduzione,* pp. 55–56; and *In De interp., ed. ecunda,* 2:8; 4:10; 6:13 (Meiser, pp. 185, 251, 421).

34. On this Apuleian work, see the discussion in Georg Pfligersdorffer, "Zu Boëthius, *De Interpr. Ed. Sec.* I. p. 4, 4 sq. Meiser nebst Beobachtungen zur Geschichte der Dialektik bei den Römern," *Wiener Studien* 66 (1953):131–35; also Obertello, *Severino Boezio,* pp. 553–54;

and Hadot, *Victorinus,* pp. 188–89. This work is not only cited by Cassiodorus (*Inst.* 2:3:18), but it would also seem to be the basis of his initial discussion of syllogisms (2:3:12). Cassiodorus also refers to Victorinus's lost translation, as well as to Boethius's second commentary, "in six books, which contain most minute reasoning" (2:3:18; tr. Jones, p. 177).

35. Although Courcelle feels that Boethius's commentaries show "still more clearly" his "entire indebtedness" to Ammonius Hermiae (*Late Latin Writers,* pp. 291–92), Shiel argues that the numerous parallels with Ammonius's work, which is the only extant Greek commentary to offer material useful for comparison, prove merely that Boethius was translating from the Greek, not that he was following Ammonius, whose commentary seems to him to be completely different in structure and nature from either of Boethius's (*Mediaeval and Renaissance Studies* 4 [1958]:228). For Shiel, the only "basic certainty" is that most of Boethius's material, including allusions to older Greek commentaries, comes from Porphyry. Other post-Porphyrian material, such as quotations from Syrianus (d. 430), the teacher of Proclus, shows once again Boethius's indebtedness to the school of Proclus (pp. 230–31). See also de Vogel, *Vivarium* 9 (1971):57.

36. Albinus's work is still lost. Minio-Paluello identifies it as the Pseudo-Augustinian *Decem Categoriae* (*Classical Quarterly* 39 [1945]:67 ff.).

37. See, e.g., Minio-Paluello, *Studia Patristica,* 2:2, pp. 362–63; also the discussion in Obertello, *Severino Boezio,*, pp. 210–12, 327–28.

38. For the *Prior Analytics,* see Minio-Paluello, *Aristoteles Latinus* 3:1–4 (1962):1 ff., 141 ff., xi ff.; also Minio-Paluello, "Note sull'Aristotele latino medievale," *Rivista di Filosofia Neo-Scolastica* 50 (1958):212–18.

39. For this scholia, see Minio-Paluello, *Aristoteles Latinus,* 3:1–4, pp. lxxix ff. 293 ff.; also Minio-Paluello, "A Latin Commentary (? Translated by Boethius) on the *Prior Analytics,* and Its Greek Sources," *Journal of Hellenic Studies* 77 (1957):93–102. Cf. de Rijk, who expresses "serious doubts" that Boethius ever completed this commentary (*Vivarium* 2 [1964]:156); also Obertello, *Severino Boezio,* pp. 230–33. The commentary included in the Patrologia Latina (64:639 ff.) is not by Boethius.

40. See Minio-Paluello and Bernardus G. Dod, *Aristoteles Latinus,* 4:1–4 (1968):xii ff.; Minio-Paluello, "Note sull'Aristotele latino medievale," *Rivista di Filosofia Neo-Scolastica* 43 (1951):97–124; and Obertello, *Severino Boezio,*, pp. 212–13.

41. See de Rijk, *Vivarium* 2 (1964):156; but cf. Sten Ebbesen, "Manlius Boethius on Aristotle's *Analytica Posteriora,*" *Cahiers de l'Institut du Moyen-Age Grec et Latin* (Copenhagen) 9 (1973):68–73. Again, the text of the commentary in the Patrologia Latina (64:712 ff.) is spurious.

42. The reference in Cassiodorus (*Inst.* 2:3:18) to Boethius's translation in eight books is found in manuscripts of two recensions; see Mynors, p. 129n; Jones, *Introduction,* p. 177n. See the edition of the translation in Minio-Paluello, *Aristoteles Latinus* 5:1–3 (1969):1 ff., 181 ff., x ff.; also Minio-Paluello, *Rivista di Filosofia Neo-Scolastica* 50 (1958):97–116; and Obertello, *Severino Boezio,* pp. 213–15. The commentary on the *Topics* in the Patrologia Latina (64:909 ff.) is spurious.

43. Bernardus G. Dod, *Aristoteles Latinus,* 6:1–3 (Leiden: Brill; Brussels: Desclée de Brouwer, 1975), pp. 1 ff; see also Minio-Paluello, "The Text of Aristotle's Topics and Elenchi: The Latin Tradition," *Classical Quarterly* 49 (1955):108–18. The commentary on the *Sophistical Refutations* in the Patrologia Latina (64:1007 ff.) is spurious.

44. See Shiel, *Mediaeval and Renaissance Studies* 4 (1958):237–38. This connection is rejected by de Rijk, *Vivarium* 2 (1964):37–38; see also Obertello, *Severino Boezio,* pp. 228–30; and Boethius, *In De interp., ed. secunda,* 4:10 (Meiser, p. 251). For editions of these two treatises on categorical syllogisms, see Migne, Patrologia Latina, 64:761 ff., 793 ff.

45. See McKinlay, *Harvard Studies in Classical Philology* 18 (1907):140–44; also Brandt, *Philologus* 62 (1903):243–45; de Rijk, *Vivarium* 2 (1964):23; and Obertello, *Severino Boezio,* pp. 234–48.

46. See McKinlay, "The *De Syllogismis Categoricis* and *Introductio ad Syllogismos Categoricos* of Boethius," *Classical and Mediaeval Studies in Honor of Edward Kennard Rand* (New York, privately printed, 1938), pp. 211–12; also Obertello, *Severino Boezio,* p. 243.

47. See McKinlay, *Classical and Mediaeval Studies,* p. 217; also de Rijk, *Vivarium* 2 (1964):39–42, 161–62. *Antepraedicamenta,* a manuscript term for the *Introduction,* may indicate that it was designed to be "before" Boethius's work on the *Praedicamentae,* or *Categories;* see Obertello, *Severino Boezio,* pp. 247–48.

48. *De hypotheticis syllogismis,* 1:1:3; ed. and tr. Luca Obertello (Brescia: Paideia, 1969), p. 206.

49. See Cassiodorus, *Institutiones,* 2:3:13; and *Commentary on the Psalms,* 7; also the discussion of classical work on hypothetical syllogisms in Karl Dürr, *The Propositional Logic of Boethius* (Amsterdam: North-Holland, 1951), pp. 12–13; and Obertello, *De hyp. syll.,* pp. 61 ff.,

194–96. Shiel feels that Boethius's work on these syllogisms has its source in the school of Proclus (*Mediaeval and Renaissance Studies* 4 [1958]:239). See also René van den Driessche, "Sur le *De syllogismo hypothetico* de Boèce," *Methodos* 1 (1949):293–307.

50. This friend has also been identified as Patricius, to whom Boethius addressed his commentary on Cicero's *Topica* and, perhaps, his treatise on geometry; see de Rijk, *Vivarium* 2 (1964):147; and Obertello, *De hyp. syll.*, pp. 134–35. It should also be noted that this proemium differs considerably from the epistle at the beginning of the *Arithmetic,* where Boethius sets forth his educational program.

51. *De divisione,* 1:31; ed. Migne, Patrologia Latina, 64:875. See also *Boezio, Trattato sulla divisione,* tr. Lorenzo Pozzi (Padua, 1969), pp. 7–8.

52. See Pozzi, *Boezio,* pp. 9–11. Boethius also cites a treatise by Andronicus of Rhodes, which he probably knew only indirectly (*De divisione,* 1:1; PL, 64:877).

53. See esp. the discussion in Eleonore Stump, *Boethius's De topicis differentiis* (Ithaca: Cornell University Press, 1978), pp. 16, 159–78.

54. On differences between Aristotle's and Cicero's treatments of topics, see ibid., pp. 22–23.

55. See Cassiodorus, *Institutiones,* 2:3:18. On Cicero's work, see Stump, *Boethius's . . . ,* pp. 20–22.

56. See Crocco, *Introduzione,* pp. 63–64. De Rijk thinks on the basis of *In topica Ciceronis,* 1 (PL, 64:1041) that Boethius "undertook to complete Victorinus' commentary" (p. 51). See the collected vestiges of Victorinus's commentary in Hadot, *Victorinus,* pp. 313–21. This work is mentioned by Cassiodorus (*Inst.* 2:3:18), although some recensions cite Boethius's commentary in its place; see above, n. 42. For the text of Boethius's commentary, see Migne, Patrologia Latina, 64:1040 ff.

57. See also Michael C. Leff, "Boethius' *De differentiis topicis,* Book IV," *Medieval Eloquence. Studies in the Theory and Practice of Medieval Rhetoric* (Berkeley: University of California Press, 1978), p. 3. For text see Migne, Patrologia Latina, 64:1173 ff.; for translation see Stump, *Boethius's . . . ,* pp. 29 ff.

58. See Stump, *Boethius's . . . ,* pp. 180, 205; Leff, *Medieval Eloquence,* pp. 6–7.

59. See Stump, *Boethius's . . . ,* pp. 179, 214; also Stump, "Boethius's Works on the Topics," *Vivarium* 12 (1974):77.

60. Rand, *Founders,* p. 167; *In Isag., ed. prima,* 1:3 (Brandt, p. 7).

61. Gilson, *History,* p. 98; see also Rand, *Founders,* p. 149.

62. *In De interp.*, ed. *secunda*, 2:2 (Meiser, p. 79); tr. Taylor, *The Mediaeval Mind*, 1:91–92.

63. Cassiodorus, *Variae*, 1:45. De Rijk thinks that these terms stem from the above passage of Boethius's second commentary on Aristotle's *On Interpretation* (*Vivarium* 2 [1964]:143).

Chapter Three

1. On the chronology, see especially the views of Brandt, *Philologus* 62 (1903):141–54, 234–75; McKinlay, *Harvard Studies in Classical Philology* 18 (1907):123–56; de Rijk, *Vivarium* 2 (1964):1–49, 125–61; and Obertello, *Severino Boezio*, pp. 297–342.

2. *In Categ.*, 2 (PL, 64:201); tr. Rand, *Founders*, p. 158.

3. Rand, *Founders*, p. 158; cf. Plato, *Republic*, 6:487.

4. See Ennodius, *Epistola* 8.1 (Vogel, p. 268); and Stewart, *Boethius*, pp. 27–28.

5. See Barrett, *Boethius*, pp. 44–46. On the office of *Magister Officiorum*, see Cassiodorus, *Variae*, 6:6; and Hodgkin, *Letters*, pp. 36–37.

6. Hermann Usener, *Anecdoton Holderi, Ein Beitrag zur Geschichte Roms in ostgothischer Zeit* (Bonn, 1877; repr. Hildesheim: Georg Olms, 1969), p. 4; see also Barrett, *Boethius*, p. 143. Cassiodorus also cites a *carmen bucolicum* that is now unknown. William Bark feels that the "dogmatic chapters" must refer to Boethius's affirmation of faith ("Boethius' Fourth Tractate, the So-Called *De fide catholica*," *Harvard Theological Review* 39 [1946]:59).

7. See Laistner, *Thought and Letters*, pp. 54–55.

8. Rand, *Founders*, p. 51. See, e.g., Konrad Bruder, *Die philosophischen Elemente in den Opuscula Sacra des Boethius: Ein Beitrag zur Quellengeschichte der Philosophie der Scholastik*, Forschungen zur Geschichte der Philosophie und der Pädagogik, 3.2 (Leipzig: Meiner, 1928); Hermann J. Brosch, *Der Seinsbegriff bei Boethius, mit besonderer Berücksichtigung der Beziehung von Sosein und Dasein*, Philosophie und Grenzwissenschaften, 4.1 (Innsbruck: Rauch, 1931).

9. *De Trinitate*, 6; *Utrum Pater*; in *Boethius, The Theological Tractates* ed. and tr. H. F. Stewart and E. K. Rand, Loeb Classical Library, 74 (Cambridge, Mass., 1918), pp. 31, 37.

10. See Stewart, *Boethius*, p. 126. Stewart also feels that these works are juvenilia, and betray "many faults of youth and inexperience" (p. 108).

11. *De Trinitate*, 2 (Loeb, p. 9). See also Gilson, *Christian Philosophy*, p. 97.

12. *De Trinitate,* 4, 6 (Loeb, pp. 17, 29).

13. *Utrum Pater* (Loeb, p. 33); *Quomodo substantiae* (Loeb, esp. pp. 39, 41).

14. See Rand, *Founders,* pp. 152–53.

15. Augustine, *Confessionum,* 4:16. For Boethius's application of the categories, see esp. *De Trinitate,* 4 (Loeb, pp. 16 ff.).

16. See the account in William Bark, "The Legend of Boethius' Martyrdom," *Speculum* 21 (1946):316–17.

17. See, e.g., Laistner, *Thought and Letters,* pp. 57–63; also Bark, "Theodoric vs. Boethius. Vindication and Apology," *American Historical Review* 49 (1944):411 ff.; and Barrett, *Boethius,* pp. 49–50.

18. See Viktor Schurr, *Die Trinitätslehre des Boethius im Lichte der 'Skythischen Kontroversen,'* Forschungen zur Christlichen Literatur- und Dogmengeschichte, 18.1 (Paderborn, 1935), pp. 127 ff.; and Obertello, *Severino Boezio,* pp. 44–49.

19. See Schurr, *Trinitätslehre,* pp. 127 ff.; and Obertello, *Severino Boezio,* pp. 49–54. Bark points to the similarity between Boethius's arguments in the *Contra Eutychen* concerning the divine nature of Christ and the position of the Scythian monks (*American Historical Review* 49 [1944]:413).

20. *Quomodo substantiae,* ed. Loeb, p. 39. See Barrett, *Boethius,* p. 160; also Bark, *American Historical Review* 49 (1944):416–19; and Emanuele Rapisarda, *La crisi spirituale di Boezio* (Florence, 1947), pp. 69–70.

21. *Contra Eutychen,* proemium (Loeb, pp. 75, 77).

22. *Quomodo substantiae* (Loeb, p. 39); *De Trinitate,* proemium (Loeb, p. 3).

23. See Bark, *American Historical Review* 49 (1944):412. On the *sermo humilis,* see Erich Auerbach, *Literary Language and Its Public in Late Latin Antiquity and in the Middle Ages,* tr. Ralph Mannheim (London: Routledge & Kegan Paul, 1965), esp. pp. 50–51. Auerbach, however, feels that in the sixth century numerous Christian writers, "principally Boethius," show only the barest suggestion of *sermo humilis* (p. 195).

24. *De Trinitate,* proemium (Loeb, p. 5); *Quomodo substantiae* (Loeb, pp. 39, 41). I alter slightly the translation of the last passage quoted.

25. Matthew 13:10 ff.; see also Mark 4:10 ff.; Luke 8:10. Isaiah 6:9–10, e.g., is cited in Matthew 13:14–15.

26. *De Trinitate,* proemium (Loeb, p. 5); *Quomodo substantiae* (Loeb, p. 39).

27. See Riché, *Education and Culture,* p. 45. Speaking of the *De Trinitate* in particular, Crocco writes that in his sour and bitter prologue

Boethius is probably referring to the negative and distorted responses to his *Contra Eutychen (Introduzione,* p. 70).

28. *Contra Eutychen,* proemium (Loeb, pp. 75, 77). See *In Isag., ed. secunda,* 1:1 (Brandt, p. 135).

29. Bark, *Harvard Theological Review* 39 (1946):67. Cf. Obertello, *Severino Boezio,* pp. 259 ff.; and earlier, E. K. Rand, "Der dem Boethius zugeschriebene Traktat *De fide catholica," Jahrbuch für Klassische Philologie,* Supplementband 26 (1901):407–61; and *Founders,* pp. 156–57.

30. Rand, *Founders,* p. 156; see also Bark, *Harvard Theological Review* 39 (1946):57.

31. Bark, Ibid., pp. 68–69. Its particular phrases have been seen to link it to Boethius's Trinitarian tractates, written in the early 520s. See also Bark, *Speculum* 21 (1946):316. Schurr considers it an affirmation of faith elaborated in a manner singularly accurate and eminently theological (*Trinitätslehre,* pp. 8–9).

32. Rand, *Founders,* p. 157. Cf. Bark, *Harvard Theological Review* 39 (1946):68; and Obertello, *Severino Boezio,* p. 258.

33. See Obertello, *Severino Boezio,* pp. 271, 280. Gratian (twelfth century) even thought that the *De fide* was by Augustine; see Obertello, *Severino Boezio,* p. 274.

34. See, e.g., Barrett, *Boethius,* pp. 151–52.

35. Ibid., p. 150. Boethius's view in *Contra Eutychen,* 3 (Loeb, p. 85) is used by Aquinas in *Summa Theologica,* 1:q.29. esp. a.1. See also Maurice Nédoncelle, "Les variations de Boèce sur la personne," *Revue des Sciences Religieuses* 29 (1955):201–38; and Enrique Dussel, "La doctrina de la persona en Boecio: solución cristológica," *Sapientia* 22 (1967):101–26.

36. See, e.g., Rapisarda, *Crisi,* p. 85; and Crocco, *Introduzione,* pp. 71–72; Boethius, *De Trinitate,* proemium (Loeb, p. 5).

37. *De Trinitate,* 4 (Loeb, pp. 17, 19); see Crocco, *Introduzione,* p. 80.

38. See Schurr, *Trinitätslehre,* pp. 97–104; also Obertello, *Severino Boezio,* pp. 335–36. Boethius's full title is "Utrum Pater et Filius et Spiritus Sanctus de Divinitate substantialiter praedicentur."

39. *Quomodo substantiae* (Loeb, p. 39); see *De Trinitate,* 6; also Rapisarda, *Crisi,* p. 73.

40. Although the Middle Ages referred to Tractate 3 as *De Hebdomadibus,* it is clear that Boethius's reference is to another work.

41. See Rapisarda, *Crisi,* p. 73. At the same time, the important distinction made here between being *(esse)* and that which is *(id quod est)* should not be ignored. See *Quomodo substantiae* (Loeb, p. 40) and

the discussion in Gilson, *History,* pp. 104–105. Also Brosch, *Der Seinsbegriff,* e.g., pp. 5–10; and Pierre Hadot, "La distinction de l'être et de l'étant dans le *De Hebdomadibus* de Boèce," *Die Metaphysik im Mittelalter,* Miscellanea Mediaevalia, 2 (Berlin: De Gruyter, 1963), pp. 147–53; and Hadot, *"Forma essendi.* Interprétation philologique et interprétation philosophique d'une formule de Boèce," *Les Etudes Classiques* 38 (1970):143–56.

42. Obertello, *Severino Boezio,* p. 336. It has also been suggested that the *Hebdomads* refer to works designed to be read at a society of that name, which met weekly to discuss theological and philosophical questions; see, e.g., August Hildebrand, *Boethius und seine Stellung zum Christentume* (Regensburg: Manz, 1885), pp. 289 ff.; and Barrett, *Boethius,* pp. 145 ff. Rapisarda, among others, feels that it cannot possibly refer to a work by Boethius (*Crisi,* pp. 71–72).

43. Cf. Momigliano, *Proceedings of the British Academy* 41 (1956):211. Although Victorinus became a Christian late in life, Boethius cites only his earlier work.

44. Augustine, *De civitate Dei,* 1:33; tr. Marcus Dods (New York: Modern Library, 1950), p. 37.

45. *De fide catholica* (Loeb, pp. 68–69).

46. See esp. the account in Bark, *American Historical Review* 49 (1944):412–13.

47. See Riché, *Education,* p. 44; also Charles H. Coster, *The Iudicium Quinquevirale* (Cambridge, Mass.: Mediaeval Academy of America, 1935), p. 40.

48. Boethius, *De Trinitate,* 6 (Loeb, p. 31).

Chapter Four

1. This is the point of C. H. Coster, "The Fall of Boethius: His Character," *Annuaire de l'Institut de Philologie et d'Histoire Orientales et Slaves* 12 (1952); *Mélanges Henri Grégoire* 4 (Brussels, 1953):45. See also Barrett, *Boethius,* pp. 49–51; and W. Schooneman, "Boethius martelaar des Katholieke Orthodoxie?" *Studia Catholica* 25 (1950):286–309. Much of the content of this chapter appears in a somewhat different form in Edmund Reiss, "The Fall of Boethius and the Fiction of the *Consolatio Philosophiae,*" *Classical Journal* 76 (1981):37–47.

2. On Italy under Theodoric in the early sixth century, see, e.g., Bark, *American Historical Review* 49 (1944):410–26; also Friedrich Klingner, "Boethius," *Römische Geisteswelt,* 4th ed. (Munich, 1961), pp. 565–99.

3. *De consolatione Philosophiae,* 1, prose 4; tr. V. E. Watts (Baltimore, 1969), p. 44; cf. ed. with tr. by "I. T." (1609), rev. H. F. Stewart, Loeb Classical Library, 74 (Cambridge, Mass., 1918), p. 151. Except when the translation in Loeb is annoyingly archaic or imprecise, I cite it simply because the original Latin text is available on facing pages. Of the recent English translations, I generally prefer that of Watts in Penguin to that of Richard Green in Library of Liberal Arts (Indianapolis, 1962) only because Watts renders the poems as verse. The most recent critical edition of the *Consolation* is by Ludwig Bieler, in *Opera,* 1, Corpus Christianorum, Series Latina, 94 (Turnholt: Brepols, 1957). Prose and verse sections of the *Consolation* will hereafter be cited as pr. (for *prosa*) and m. (for *metrum*).

4. *Consolation,* 1:pr.4 (Loeb, pp. 147, 149).

5. Ibid. (Loeb, p. 147; Watts, pp. 42–43).

6. This account tends to follow the order of events as given by Coster, *Iudicium Quinquevirale,* pp. 53–55; "Fall," *Annuaire,* pp. 53–55. Coster accepts the revised chronology of the *Anonymous Valesii* suggested by Cessi, *Fragmenta historica,* pp. cxxvi ff. Though Boethius is generally thought to have been put to death in 524, before the Pope's return, Coster suggests that he may not have been executed until later, perhaps 526 ("Fall," *Annuaire,* p. 59). Coster's dating has been supported by de Vogel, *Vivarium* 9 (1971):66; for the evidence in favor of 524, see Obertello, *Severino Boezio,* pp. 125 ff. For further points, see G. B. Picotti, "Il Senato romano e il processo di Boezio," *Archivio Storico Italiano* 89 (1931):205–28.

7. Bark, *American Historical Review* 49 (1944):425–28.

8. Procopius, *History of the Gothic Wars,* 5:1 *Procopius,* ed. and tr. H. B. Dewing (London: Heinemann, 1919), pp. 12–15. I follow here the translation in Barrett, *Boethius,* pp. 59–60.

9. *Anonymous Valesii,* sect. 83–87 (Cessi, *Fragmenta historica,* pp. 19–20). In her translation, which I follow here, Barrett omits most of 83 and all of 84, thereby minimizing the marvelous (pp. 58–59).

10. It is hardly adequate to say, as Barrett does, that "in spite of a certain legendary and mythical element in the work, a narrative so nearly contemporary is of great interest and considerable value" (p. 6).

11. See Coster, "Fall," *Annuaire,* esp. pp. 65–67; and Cassiodorus, *Variae,* 5:40, 41; 8:16, 17, 21, 22; 4:22, 23.

12. See Moorhead, "Boethius and Romans in Ostragothic Service," *Historia* 27 (1978):esp. pp. 609 ff.

13. See Hodgkin, *Letters,* p. 246n; also Watts, *Consolation,* p. 180. While acknowledging that "no surviving evidence" for identifying

Gaudentius exists, Moorhead feels that the name of one "Fl[avius] Gaudentius v[ir] c[larissimus]" in a mutilated piece of papyrus "probably refers to him" *Historia* 27 (1978):609–10 and n. 34).

14. See also the reference to "the excellent Patrician Paulinus" in Cassiodorus, *Variae,* 2:3; Hodgkin, *Letters,* p. 173. See the analysis of evidence in Barrett, *Boethius,* pp. 67–69.

15. See C. S. Lewis, *The Discarded Image. An Introduction to Medieval and Renaissance Literature* (Cambridge, Eng., 1964), p. 80.

16. *Consolation,* 1:m.1; I follow the literal translation of these lines given in Loeb, p. 128n.

17. See Aristotle, *Nicomachean Ethics,* 1:5 (1095b–1096a); and Plato, *Republic,* 8:544–56. For the temptations of 1 John 2:15–16—also related to the temptations of Adam and Eve (Genesis 3) and of Christ (Matthew 4:1–11, Luke 4:1–13—see, e.g., Augustine, *Confessions,* 10:30–40. On Hellenistic and early Christian versions of the temptations and their possible relationship to the tripartite soul, see Donald R. Howard, *The Three Temptations: Medieval Man in Search of the World* (Princeton: Princeton University Press, 1966), pp. 45 ff.

18. *In De interp., ed. secunda,* 2:7 (Meiser, p. 137); see Alvin Plantinga, "The Boethian Compromise," *American Philosophical Quarterly* 15 (1978):132.

19. Plato, *Republic,* 8:553; tr. F. M. Cornford (New York: Oxford University Press 1945), p. 277.

20. See Georg Misch, *A History of Autobiography in Antiquity,* tr. E. W. Dickes (Cambridge, Mass.: Harvard University Press, 1951), 2:670 ff.

21. Although this work by Cicero has not come down to us, it is alluded to in Cicero's letter *Ad Atticum,* 12:14.3; Misch, pp. 358, 690. On the genre of the *consolatio,* see esp. Peter von Moos, *Consolatio. Studien zur mittellateinischen Trostliteratur über den Tod und zum Problem der christlichen Trauer,* Münstersche Mittelalter-Schriften, 3 (Munich: Wilhelm Fink, 1971–72), 1:59 ff.

22. See the list in Henricus Hüttinger, *Studia in Boethii carmina collata* (Stadtamhof: Mayr, 1902), pt. 2, p. 23; on Seneca in particular, see the edition of the *Consolation* by Rudolf Peiper (Leipzig, 1871), pp. 228–33.

23. See, e.g., Barrett, *Boethius,* pp. 166–67; Rand, *Founders,* p. 162.

24. Usener, *Anecdoton Holderi,* esp. pp. 51–52; see the summary in Rand, "On the Composition of Boethius' *Consolatio Philosophiae,*" *Harvard Studies in Classical Philology* 15 (1904):1–2.

25. Rand, *Founders,* p. 164; Stewart, *Boethius,* p. 106.

26. See, e.g., Hans von Campenhausen, *The Fathers of the Latin Church,* tr. M. Hoffmann (London: Adam and Charles Black, 1964), p. 308.

27. *Wisdom* 8:1; cf. *Consolation,* 3:pr. 12 (Watts, p. 112). See the work by Adrian Fortescue in George D. Smith's edition of the *Consolation* (London: Burns, Oates & Washbourne, 1925).

28. See de Vogel, *Vivarium* 10 (1972):4–17; and Watts, *Consolation,* p. 98. See also the recognition that expressions of piety having their source in the liturgy show through the philosophical dialogue, in Christine Mohrmann, "Some Remarks on the Language of Boethius, *Consolatio Philosophiae,*" *Latin Script and Letters, A.D. 400–900. Festschrift Presented to Ludwig Bieler* (Leiden: Brill, 1976), p. 61.

29. Lewis, *Discarded Image,* p. 78.

30. C. J. de Vogel, "The Problem of Philosophy and Christian Faith in Boethius' *Consolatio,*" *Romanitas et Christianitas. Studia Iano Henrico Waszink* (Amsterdam, 1973), pp. 363–64; Courcelle, *Late Latin Writers,* pp. 319–20.

31. See de Vogel, *Romanitas,* pp. 358–59.

32. Ibid., pp. 359–60; and Rand, *Founders,* p. 178.

33. Though this third explanation is an old view, see its recent restatement in Philip Merlan, "Ammonius Hermiae, Zacharias Scholasticus and Boethius," *Greek, Roman and Byzantine Studies* 9 (1968):202–3.

34. Lewis, *Discarded Image,* p. 77.

35. See Rand, *Founders,* pp. 160, 201–2; also Pierre Courcelle, "Tradition platonicienne et traditions chrétiennes du corps-prison," *Revue des Etudes Latines* 43 (1965):406–43; "L'âme en cage," *Parusia. Studien zur Philosophie Platons und zur Problemgeschichte des Platonismus. Festgabe für Johannes Hirschberger* (Frankfurt: Minerva, 1965), pp. 103–16; and "Le corps-tombeau," *Revues des Etudes Anciennes* 68 (1966):101–22.

36. Campenhausen, *Fathers,* p. 306.

37. For the *vitae,* see Peiper's edition of the *Consolation,* p. xxxv. See Bark, *Speculum* 21 (1946):312–17; H. R. Patch, "The Beginnings of the Legend of Boethius," *Speculum* 22 (1947):443–45; and C. H. Coster, "Procopius and Boethius," *Speculum* 23 (1948):284–87; also Patch, *Tradition,* p. 15; and Arturo Graf, "Severino Boezio," *Roma nella memoria e nelle immaginazioni del Medio Evo,* rev. ed. (Turin: Chiantore, 1923), pp. 624–49. See also the modern saint's life of Boethius by Gerolomo Vanzini, *Vita di San Severino Boezio console-filosofo-martire* (Pavia: Artigianelli, 1939).

38. E. M. Young, "Boethius," *A Dictionary of Christian Biography* (London: J. M. Murray, 1877), 1:320–23. It is to St. Severinus that one twelfth-century manuscript of *De fide catholica* is ascribed; see Stewart, *Boethius*, pp. 140–41. See Eugippius, *Vita S. Severini*, 7, 32, 44; and, on Boethius's being named after the saint, the discussion in Obertello, *Severino Boezio*, p. 17.

Chapter Five

1. Barrett, *Boethius*, pp. 119, 123; see Gibbon, *The Decline and Fall of the Roman Empire*, 4, ch. 39.

2. See Rand, *Founders*, p. 168.

3. On the relationship of Boethius's elegies to traditional Latin elegies, see Kurt Reichenberger, *Untersuchungen zur literarischen Stellung der Consolatio Philosophiae*, Romanistische Arbeiten, 3 (Cologne, 1954), pp. 8—10; and Luigi Alfonsi, "De Boethio elegiarum auctore," *Atti del Reale Istituto Veneto di Scienze, Lettere ed Arti*, Classe di Scienze Morali 102.2 (1942–43):723–27. On 1:m.1, see also Arnold Meese, "Zur Funktion der Carmina in der *Consolatio philosophiae* des Boethius," *Vergleichen und Verändern. Festschrift für Helmut Motekat* (Munich: Max Hueber, 1970), pp. 338–39; and Helga Scheible, *Die Gedichte in der Consolatio Philosophiae des Boethius*, Bibliothek der Klassischen Altertumswissenschaften, 46 (Heidelberg, 1972), pp. 12–16.

4. Rand, *Founders*, p. 177; and especially Augustine, *De civitate Dei*, 2:14.

5. On these motifs, see Scheible, *Gedichte*, pp. 26–27; Reichenberger sees the poem in the tradition of classical poetry of instruction (*Untersuchungen*, pp. 11–16).

6. See Reichenberger, *Untersuchungen*, pp. 16–19.

7. I follow Watts's translation of m.5 (pp. 46–48). On the relationship of pr.4 to forensic discourse, see Reichenberger (*Untersuchungen*, pp. 19–22), who also discusses the prayer style of m.4 and its unusual use of clauses, as well as its possible relationship to a song from Seneca's drama *Phaedra* (pp. 22–26).

8. As Reichenberger notes, these teachings are in the form of *suasoria*, according to the rhetorical principles of the *genus deliberativa* (*Untersuchungen*, pp. 27–30).

9. Examining pr.6 in terms of Platonic dialogue, Reichenberger suggests that Boethius may have had in mind the dialogue in the *Symposium* between the youthful Socrates and his teacher Diotima (*Untersuchungen*, pp. 30–31).

10. Watts, *Consolation,* p. 53. On the meter of this poem as suggesting that used for celebrations, and on its possible relationship to the greeting of Philology in Martianus Capella's *De nuptiis,* see Reichenberger, *Untersuchungen,* pp. 32–33.

11. See Rand, *Founders,* p. 168; and Crocco, *Introduzione,* p. 93.

12. On the tradition of Fortune, along with her wheel, see Howard R. Patch, *The Goddess Fortuna in Mediaeval Literature* (Cambridge, Mass.: Harvard University Press, 1927), esp. pp. 10 ff.; and Courcelle, *Consolation,* pp. 103–58.

13. Boethius presents Fortune here and in Book 3, as well as at the beginning of Book 1, as something harmful and generally noxious; and although the discussion of Fate in Books 4 and 5 refers implicitly to Fortune, the *Consolation* may be said to represent on the whole "a polemical treatise against Fortune"; see Obertello, *Severino Boezio,* p. 707.

14. Cf. the discussion in C. J. de Vogel, "Amor quo coelum regitur," *Vivarium* 1 (1963):2 ff.; and Marco Galdi, "Il canto dell'amore universale in Boezio," *Saggi boeziani* (Pisa: Giardini, 1938), pp. 114–30.

15. The false goods are termed here "opes, honores, potentiam, gloriam, uoluptates," although later in this section they are referred to as "diuitias, dignitates, regna, gloriam, uoluptates" (Loeb, pp. 230, 232).

16. See Rand, *Founders,* pp. 170–71; also Karl Büchner, "Bemerkungen zum dritten Buche von des Boethius Trost der Philosophie," *Historisches Jahrbuch* 62 (1949):31–42; repr. as "Bemerkungen zum dritten Buche der Consolatio Philosophiae des Boethius," *Studien zur römischen Literatur, IV: Tacitus und Ausklang* (Wiesbaden: Steiner, 1964), pp. 122–33; and Susan F. Wiltshire, "Boethius and the *Summum Bonum,*" *Classical Journal* 67 (1972):216–20.

17. The reference is to *Timaeus,* 27, a work "evidently much in Boethius's thoughts" while he was writing the *Consolation* (Barrett, *Boethius,* p. 118). M.9, besides being a summary of part of the *Timaeus,* is also full of Neoplatonic thought, especially that of Proclus. See, e.g., Crocco, *Introduzione,* pp. 107 ff; and Gilson, *History,* who calls it "nothing but a résumé . . . of the *Timaeus* annotated by Chalcidius" (p. 103).

18. Wiltshire, *Classical Journal* 67 (1972): 219.

19. Ibid., p. 217. Courcelle notes that Boethius's point in Book 3 is to probe the existence not of God but rather of the *summum bonum,* which is to be identified with God (*Consolation,* p. 163). On the relationship of Boethius's view of the *summum bonum* to various philo-

sophical traditions, see G. Capone Braga, "La soluzione cristiana del problema del *Summum Bonum* in *De philosophiae consolatione libri quinque* di Boezio," *Archivio di Storia della Filosofia Italiana* 3 (1934):101–16.

20. Wiltshire, *Classical Journal* 67 (1972):218.

21. See Crocco, *Introduzione,* pp. 125–26; also the full discussion of the history of these ideas in Obertello, *Severino Boezio,* pp. 700–34.

22. Watts, *Consolation,* p. 136; cf. Loeb, pp. 342–43. This last image would seem to come from Proclus's *De providentia et fato,* perhaps via Ammonius Hermiae. See H. R. Patch, "Fate in Boethius and the Neoplatonists," *Speculum* 4 (1929):64 ff., who senses also the influence of Plotinus; cf. Courcelle, *Late Latin Writers,* pp. 305–7.

23. See H. R. Patch, "*Consolatio philosophiae,* IV, m.vi, 23–24," *Speculum* 8 (1933):41–51.

24. It is not clear what works Boethius has in mind here, but the relationship between divine foreknowledge and human free will was the subject of "numberless treatises" from Cicero to Augustine. See Courcelle, who also points out that Boethius uses "sometimes word for word" the phrasing of his own commentary on Aristotle's *On Interpretation (Late Latin Writers,* p. 308); and N. W. Gilbert, "The Concept of Will in Early Latin Philosophy," *Journal of the History of Philosophy* 1 (1963):17–35.

25. See Gilson, *History,* p. 100.

26. Watts, *Consolation,* p. 162; cf. Loeb, p. 397.

27. Watts, *Consolation,* p. 163; cf. Loeb, p. 401. On the notion of eternity and its philosophical tradition, see Romano Amerio, "Probabile fonte della nozione boeziana di eternità," *Filosofia* 1 (1950):365–73; K. J. Popma, "De eeuwigheid Gods volgens Boëthius," *Philosophia Reformata* 22 (1957):21–51; and Obertello, *Severino Boezio,* pp. 673–99.

28. Lewis, *Discarded Image,* p. 89. As Gilson notes, God "does not *foresee,* he *provides;* his name is not 'foresight' but 'providence' " (*History,* p. 103). I follow Watts's translation here (*Consolation,* p. 165); cf. Loeb, p. 405.

29. On the relationship of Boethius's explanation to traditional views of necessity, see H. R. Patch, "Necessity in Boethius and the Neoplatonists," *Speculum* 10 (1935):393–404. See also Ernst Gegenschatz, "Die Freiheit der Entscheidung in der *consolatio philosophiae* des Boethius," *Museum Helveticum* 15 (1958):110–29; and "Die Gefährdung des Möglichen durch das Vorauswissen Gottes in der Sicht des Boethius," *Wiener Studien* 79 (1966):517–30.

30. Lewis, *Discarded Image,* p. 90.

31. See Gilson, *History*, p. 102.

32. See Rand, *Founders*, p. 177; and Crocco, *Introduzione*, pp. 144–45.

Chapter Six

1. Winthrop Wetherbee speaks of this as the "larger dialogue between rational argumentation and poetry" (*Platonism and Poetry in the Twelfth Century. The Literary Influence of the School of Chartres* [Princeton: Princeton University Press, 1972], p. 77). The discussion of structure in the present chapter is based on the premise that the *Consolation* is indeed complete as it stands. The issue has recently been reassessed by Hermann Traenkle, "Ist die *Philosophiae consolatio* des Boethius zum vorgeschenen Abschluss gelangt?" *Vigiliae Christianae* 31 (1977):148–56.

2. See Reichenberger, *Untersuchungen*, pp. 35–76; also Quintilian, *Institutio oratoria*, 3:9; and cf. Cicero, *De inventione*, 1:14:19; and *Rhetorica ad Herennium*, 1:3:4.

3. See Wiltshire, *Classical Journal* 67 (1972):216; also Horace, *Ars poetica*, 1:189; Aristotle, *Poetics*, 11:1.

4. Book 1, however, contains 178 lines of verse, and Book 2 only 172 lines.

5. On the centrality of Book 3, see esp. Büchner, *Historisches Jahrbuch* 62 (1949):31 ff.; and Wiltshire, *Classical Journal* 67 (1972):216 ff.

6. On love, which is explicitly mentioned only in the poems, see Patch, *Speculum* 8 (1933):41; and de Vogel, *Vivarium* 1 (1963):4.

7. See esp. Watts, *Consolation*, p. 98n.

8. Cf. Wetherbee, who feels that this final silence, where "reason and intuition give way to faith," represents the final dissatisfaction of the narrator (*Platonism*, p. 82).

9. Augustine, *Soliloquia*, 1:1; see also Edmund T. Silk, "Boethius's *Consolatio Philosophiae* as a Sequel to Augustine's Dialogues and *Soliloquia*," *Harvard Theological Review* 32 (1939):35 ff.

10. On the relationship to the Socratic dialogue, see Friedrich Klingner, *De Boethii Consolatione Philosophiae*, Philologische Untersuchungen, 27 (Berlin: Weidmann, 1921), pp. 74–83. If Boethius used a particular dialogue of this kind as a source, it may well have been Augustine's *De ordine*, which is likewise concerned with understanding the order of the universe and with the role of evil in the world; see Laistner, *Thought and Letters*, pp. 49–51.

11. On the influence on the *Consolation* of the protreptic tradition, see Luigi Alfonsi, "Studi boeziani," *Aevum* 25 (1951):210–22; also Courcelle, *Late Latin Writers,* p. 296; and *Consolation,* p. 18.

12. See Klingner, *De Boethii,* pp. 113–18; and Courcelle, *Consolation,* pp. 19–20.

13. Cf. King Alfred's version of the *Consolation,* which makes the speakers Wisdom and Mind. See the discussion in F. Anne Payne, *King Alfred & Boethius. An Analysis of the Old English Version of the Consolation of Philosophy* (Madison: University of Wisconsin Press, 1968), pp. 111–12.

14. Rand, *Founders,* p. 161.

15. This is the division already seen in Boethius's commentaries on the *Isagoge,* as well as in his *Arithmetic.* Vincenzo Di Giovanni has suggested that the distinction here is between *pistis* ("faith") and *Theos* ("God") in that faith is the ladder to God ("Boezio e il suo libro *De consolatione philosophiae,*" *Rivista Universale* 147 [1888]:8; see the discussion in Crocco, *Introduzione,* p. 85.

16. See Pierre Courcelle, "Le personnage de Philosophie dans la littérature latine," *Journal des Savants* (1970), pp. 209–52; also "Le visage de Philosophie," *Revue des Etudes Anciennes* 70 (1968):110–20; and Lewis, *Discarded Image,* p. 80. See also the analysis in Paul Piehler, *The Visionary Landscape. A Study in Medieval Allegory* (Montreal: McGill—Queen's University Press, 1971), esp. pp. 34–41.

17. See Vincenzo Cilento, *Medio Evo monastico e scolastico* (Milan: Ricciardi, 1961), p. 53. On the antecedents of Lady Philosophy, see also Joachim Gruber, "Die Erscheinung der Philosophie in der *Consolatio Philosophiae* des Boethius," *Rheinisches Museum für Philologie* 112 (1969):166–86; and Courcelle, *Journal des Savants* (1970), pp. 209 ff.

18. Wolfgang Schmid, "Philosophisches und Medizinisches in der *Consolatio Philosophiae* des Boethius," *Festschrift Bruno Snell* (Munich: Beck, 1956), pp. 113–44; repr. *Römische Philosophie,* Wege der Forschung, 193 (Darmstadt: Wissenschaftliche Buchgesellschaft, 1976), pp. 341–84; also Schmid, "Boethius and the Claims of Philosophy," *Studia Patristica* 2:2, Texte und Untersuchungen, 64 (Berlin: Akademie-Verlag, 1957), pp. 368–75; and the later refinement by Christine Wolf, "Untersuchungen zum Krankheitsbild in dem ersten Buch der *Consolatio Philosophiae* des Boethius," *Revista di Cultura Classica e Medievale* 6 (1964):213–23. On the symbolic use of lethargy in Augustine's sermons and *Confessions,* see Schmid, *Studia Patristica,* pp. 371 ff. Also see the recent correlation of philosophy and therapy, in which healing is seen to come with insight, by Donald F. Duclow, "Perspective and

Therapy in Boethius's *Consolation of Philosophy*," *Journal of Medicine and Philosophy* 4 (1979):334–43.

19. See, e.g., Barrett, *Boethius*, p. 76; and Crocco, *Introduzione*, pp. 81–82.

20. Rand, *Founders*, p. 161; Barrett, *Boethius*, p. 167. Barrett contrasts Boethius's prose style explicitly with that of Cassiodorus and Ennodius (pp. 166–67).

21. See the analysis in Meese, *Vergleichen*, pp. 335 ff.; and Watts, *Consolation*, p. 20; also Luigi Alfonsi, "Boezio poeta," *Antiquitas* 9 (1954):4–13; Emanuele Rapisarda, "Poetica e poesia di Boezio," *Orpheus* 3 (1956):23–40. Cf. Barrett, *Boethius*, pp. 76–77.

22. See Rand, *Founders*, p. 162; also *Harvard Studies in Classical Philology* 15 (1904):4–5; and Barrett, *Boethius*, pp. 165–66. Cf. Usener, *Anecdoton Holderi*, p. 51.

23. A convenient survey of the meters may be found in Joachim Gruber, *Kommentar zu Boethius De Consolatione Philosophiae*, Texte und Kommentare, 9 (Berlin, 1978), pp. 19–24 with chart opposite p. 16. On the relationship of these poems to Classical and later Latin poetry, see Hüttinger, *Studia in Boethii carmina collata, passim;* also Luigi Pepe, "La metrica di Boezio," *Giornale Italiano di Filologia* 7 (1954):227–43; and Scheible, *Gedichte, passim.* On the relationship of the verse to the prose, see, e.g., Alfonsi, "Studi boeziani," *Aevum* 19 (1945):148–57.

24. Richard A. Dwyer, *Boethian Fictions. Narratives in the Medieval French Versions of the Consolatio Philosophiae* (Cambridge, Mass., 1976), p. 22.

25. See, e.g., 1:pr.3; 2:pr.2, pr.6; 3:pr.5; 4:pr.6.

26. Dwyer, *Boethian Fictions*, p. 23.

27. Barrett, *Boethius*, p. 111. See also Rand, *Harvard Studies in Classical Philology* 15 (1904):1 ff.; Courcelle, *Late Latin Writers*, pp. 297–98; *Consolation*, pp. 113–14; Maurach, "Boethiusinterpretationen," *Römische Philosophie*, pp. 397 ff.; and Matthias Baltes, "Gott, Welt, Mensch in der *Consolatio Philosophiae* des Boethius. Die *Consolatio Philosophiae* als ein Dokument platonischer und neuplatonischer Philosophie," *Vigiliae Christianae* 34 (1980):313–40.

28. Barrett, *Boethius*, pp. 107–8, 112–13.

29. Ibid., pp. 103 ff. On Pythagoreanism, as well as Stoicism, in the *Consolation*, see Courcelle, *Late Latin Writers*, p. 297.

30. See Courcelle, *Consolation*, pp. 161–76, 230–31; and, for Plotinus, de Vogel, *Romanitas*, pp. 357–58. A handy guide to these sources is found in Crocco, *Introduzione*, pp. 151–52.

31. See the discussion in Barrett, *Boethius*, p. 119.

32. Stewart, *Boethius*, p. 100.

33. Barrett, *Boethius*, p. 132.

34. Schmid, *Studia Patristica*, p. 374.

35. Gilson, *History*, p. 102. Crocco is speaking in particular of Boethius's notion that happiness is to be found within the self (*Introduzione*, p. 97); see *Cons.* 2:pr. 4; and Augustine, *De vera religione*.

36. See, for instance, Raoul Carton, "Le Christianisme et l'augustinisme de Boèce," *Revue de Philosophie* 30 (1930);573–659; repr. *Mélanges Augustiniens* (Paris: Rivière, 1941), pp. 243–329; and Silk, *Harvard Theological Review* 32 (1939):19–39. On the possible relationship to the *Contra Academicos*, see Schmid, *Studia Patristica*, pp. 372–73.

37. See, e.g., de Vogel, who feels that Boethius is less interested than Augustine in "the passionate search for truth" (*Romanitas*, p. 368); also F. P. Pickering, who distinguishes the two sources of medieval historical and narrative literature, the tradition of sacred history (*Heilsgeschichte*) stemming from Augustine and that of dynastic history (*dynastische Geschichte*) stemming from Boethius (*Augustinus oder Boethius? Geschichtsschreibung und epische Dichtung im Mittelalter—und in der Neuzeit*, Philologische Studien und Quellen, 39, 80 [Berlin: Erich Schmidt, 1967, 1976], 2 vols., esp. 1:25 ff., 33 ff.).

38. Rand, *Founders*, p. 178; also Courcelle, *Consolation*, p. 340; and the discussion in Maria Teresa Antonelli, "La patristica postagostiniana. 1: Severino Boezio," *Grande Antologia Filosofica. III: Il pensiero Cristiano (La patristica)* (Milan: Marzorati, 1954), pp. 375–77.

39. Courcelle, *Consolation*, pp. 24–25. The latest writers mentioned in the *Consolation* are Cicero and Lucan.

40. Rand, *Founders*, p. 162.

41. See Stewart, *Boethius*, p. 86, who also states that "the implicit proof of God's existence is cosmological and very different from the ontological proof put forward by Augustine." *Ordo* is especially prevalent in 4:pr.6, which has been called the climax of the *Consolation* in that its discussion of Providence and Fate finally places the narrator's complaints about fortune and evil in the framework of universal order. See Payne, *King Alfred & Boethius*, pp. 31–33.

42. Courcelle, *Late Latin Writers*, p. 297. On the theme of conversion in the *Consolation*, see esp. Willy Theiler, "Antike und christliche Rückkehr zu Gott," *Mullus. Festschrift Theodor Klauser*, Jahrbuch für Antike und Christentum, Ergänzungsband, 1 (Münster: Aschendorff, 1964), esp. pp. 356–571; also Volker Schmidt-Kohl, *Die neuplatonische Seelenlehre in der Consolatio Philosophiae des Boethius*, Beiträge zur Klassischen Philologie, 16 (Meisenheim: Hain, 1965).

43. Richard Green, ed. *Consolation,* p. ix. See also Wiltshire, *Classical Journal* 67 (1972):219; and Luigi Alfonsi, "Problemi filosofici della *Consolatio* boeziana," *Rivista di Filosofia Neo-Scolastica* 35 (1943):323–28. Cf. Baltes, who finds the work finally incomplete in that it lacks the return to God (*Vigiliae Christianae* 34 [1980]:332–35).

44. Stewart, *Boethius,* p. 90.

45. Obertello, *Severino Beozio,* pp. 707–10. See such Christian works as Lactantius, *Institutiones,* 3:28:6; and Augustine, *Contra Academicos,* 1:1:1. The *Consolation* is also the source of the extremely popular image of the Wheel of Fortune (seen in 2:m.1). See Courcelle, *Consolation,* pp. 135–39; and, for a summary of Boethius's uses of Fortune, esp. pp. 103–11. On the possibility that Boethius's view of Fortune was influenced by Macrobius's Commentary on Cicero's *Dream of Scipio,* see ibid., pp. 116–24; and Alfonsi, *Aevum* 25 (1951):152, 157.

46. See Patch, *Speculum* 4 (1929):62–72; Courcelle, *Late Latin Writers,* pp. 304 ff; and Obertello, *Severino Boezio,* pp. 712–13.

47. Stewart calls Boethius's conception of God "purely Platonic" (*Boethius,* p. 81). Barrett states that in being above random chance, Boethius's God may be related to Plato's deity, as set forth in the *Laws* (pp. 82–83). Boethius's concept of God here may be linked to that in his *De Trinitate,* 3. See also Crocco, *Introduzione,* pp. 153–54; and Scheible, *Gedichte,* pp. 174 ff.

48. Gilson, *History,* pp. 101, 604, n.87.

49. 1:m.5; 2:m.8; 3:m.9; 4:m.6; 5:m.3. See Patch, *Speculum* 8 (1933):41.

50. See de Vogel, *Vivarium* 1 (1963): 10; she is speaking of 2:m.8 in particular, which she connects to the chapter on divine love (ch. 4) in the *Divine Names* of the mystical thinker known as Dionysius the Areopagite, who—like Boethius—may have attended the School of Athens during the late fifth century (p. 33).

51. Wiltshire, *Classical Journal* 67 (1972):218.

Chapter Seven

1. See Patch, *Tradition of Boethius,* pp. 92, 107–8.

2. Rand says he could thus have saved Thomas Aquinas his gigantic task (*Founders,* p. 178).

3. John Burnet, *Essays and Addresses* (New York: Macmillan, 1930), p. 268; quoted in Patch, *Tradition,* p. 44.

4. See Patch, *Tradition,* pp. 41–43; also Konrad Burdach, "Die humanistischen Wirkungen der Trostschrift des Boethius im Mittelalter

und in der Renaissance," *Deutsche Vierteljahrsschrift für Literaturwissenschaft und Geistesgeschichte* 11 (1933):530–58; and Ferdinand Sassen, "Boethius, Leermeester der Middeleeuwen," *Studia Catholica* 14 (1938):216–30.

5. See Courcelle, *Consolation,* pp. 29 ff. On various manuscript traditions of the work, see Georg Schepss, *Handschriftliche Studien zu Boethius de Consolatio philosophiae* (Würzburg: Thein, 1881); Ludwig Bieler, "Textkritische Nachlese zu Boethius' *De philosophiae consolatione,*" *Wiener Studien* 54 (1936):128–41; and Barnet Kottler, "The Vulgate Tradition of the *Consolatio Philosophiae* in the Fourteenth Century," *Mediaeval Studies* 17 (1955):209–14.

6. See esp. the iconography of the Wheel of Fortune, the Wings of the Soul, and the scenes of mythology in Courcelle, *Consolation,* pp. 380 ff. and the plates following.

7. See Patch, *Tradition,* pp. 48–66; and A. Van de Vyver, "Les traductions du *De Consolatione Philosophiae* de Boèce en littérature comparée," *Humanisme et Renaissance* 6 (1939):247–73.

8. See Courcelle, *Consolation,* pp. 239–332; and his earlier study, "Etude critique sur les commentaires de la *Consolation* de Boèce (IXe-XVe siècles)," *Archives d'Histoire Doctrinale et Littéraire du Moyen Age* 14 (1939):5–140. For work later than that noted in Courcelle, *Consolation,* see esp. N. M. Häring, "Four Commentaries on the *De Consolatione Philosophiae* in MS Heiligenkreuz 130," *Mediaeval Studies* 31 (1969):287–316.

9. See Patch, *Tradition,* pp. 46 ff., esp. p. 47.

10. Ibid., pp. 25, 87 ff.

11. Dante, *Paradiso,* 10:125–26; ed. and tr. John D. Sinclair, rev. ed. (London: The Bodley Head, 1948), p. 153.

12. See Patch, *Tradition,* pp. 25, 46.

13. Ibid., p. 24.

14. Ibid., pp. 87 ff.

15. Ibid. See also Albert Auer, *Johannes von Dambach und die Trostbücher vom 11.bis zum 16. Jahrhundert.* Beiträge zur Geschichte der Philosophie und Theologie des Mittelalters, 27. 1–2 (Münster: Aschendorff, 1928); Michael H. Means, *The Consolatio Genre in Medieval English Literature* (Gainesville: University of Florida Press, 1972); and Dwyer, *Boethian Fictions.*

16. Riché, *Education,* p. 45; Courcelle, *Late Latin Writers,* p. 273.

17. See Riché, *Education,* pp. 44–47.

18. Southern, *Making of the Middle Ages,* pp. 174, 179. See also Martin Grabmann, "Boethius, der letzte Römer—der erste Scholas-

tiker," *Die Geschichte der scholastischen Methode I: Die scholastische Methode von ihren ersten Anfängen in der Väterliteratur bis zum Beginn des 12. Jahrhunderts* (Freiburg, 1909; repr. Darmstadt: Wissenschaftliche Buchgesellschaft, 1957), pp. 148–77; Sassen, *Studia Catholica* 14 (1938):esp. 97–122; Antonio Viscardi, "Boezio e la conservazione e trasmissione dell'eredità del pensiero antico," *I Goti in Occidente. Problemi.* Settimane di Studio sull'Alto Medioevo, 3 (Spoleto: Sede del Centro, 1956), pp. 323–43; and H. Liebschütz, "Boethius and the Legacy of Antiquity," *The Cambridge History of Later Greek and Early Medieval Philosophy* (Cambridge: at the University Press, 1967), pp. 538–55.

19. Southern, *Making,* p. 180.

20. Ibid., pp. 181–82. See, e.g., J. Isaac, *Le Peri Hermeneias en Occident de Boèce à Saint Thomas. Histoire littéraire d'un traité d'Aristote,* Bibliothèque Thomiste, 29 (Paris: J. Vrin, 1953); and Lorenzo Minio-Paluello, *Rivista di Filosofia Neo-Scolastica* 42 (1950):222–26; 44 (1952):398–400, 405–11; 46 (1954):211–23; 50 (1958):97–116, 212–18; 52 (1960):29–45.

21. See Patch, *Tradition,* pp. 28–30; and Gangolf Schrimpf, *Die Axiomenschrift des Boethius (De Hebdomadibus) als philosophisches Lehrbuch des Mittelalters* (Leiden: Brill, 1966).

22. Dwyer, *Boethian Fictions,* p. 8.

23. Patch, *Tradition,* pp. 78 ff.

24. Ibid., p. 111.

25. Ibid., pp. 40, 45.

Selected Bibliography

PRIMARY SOURCES

1. Collected Works

Boethius. Annius Manlius Torquatus Severinus. Opera. Venice: Forlivio, 1491–92. *Editio princeps,* reprinted 1497–99, 1523, 1536.

Manlii Severini Boethii Opera omnia. Edited by J.-P. Migne. Patrologia cursus completus, Series Latina, 63–64. Paris: Garnier, 1882, 1891. Contains many corrupt texts and spurious works: *De unitate et uno, De diffinitione, De disciplina scholarum,* etc. Should be used only for the following works for which no critical editions yet exist: *In categorias Aristotelis* (64:159 ff.), *Introductio ad syllogismos categoricos* (64:761 ff.) *De categoricis syllogismis* (64:793 ff.), *De divisione* (64:875 ff.), *In topica Ciceronis* (64:1040 ff.), *De topicis differentiis* (64:1173 ff.).

2. Critical Editions and Translations

Anicii Manlii Torquati Severini Boetii de institutione arithmetica libri duo, de institutione musica libri quinque, accedit geometria quae fertur Boetii. Edited by Godfredus Friedlein. Leipzig, 1867; repr. Frankfurt: Minerva, 1966. Text of *Geometria* is probably spurious.

Anicii Manlii Severini Boethii in Isagogen Porphyrii commenta. Edited by Georg Schepss; revised by Samuel Brandt. Corpus Scriptorum Ecclesiasticorum Latinorum, 48. Leipzig: Freytag, 1906.

Porphyrii Isagoge translatio Boethii. Edited by Laurentius Minio-Paluello, with B. G. Dod. *Aristoteles Latinus,* 1:6–7. Bruges: De Brouwer, 1966, pp. 1–31.

Categoriae vel Praedicamenta translatio Boethii. Edited by Laurentius Minio-Paluello. *Aristoteles Latinus,* 1:1–5. Bruges: De Brouwer, 1961, pp. 1–41.

De interpretatione vel periermenias translatio Boethii. Ed. Laurentius Minio-Paluello. *Aristoteles Latinus,* 2:1–2. Bruges: De Brouwer, 1965, pp. 1–38.

Anicii Manlii Severini Boetii commentarii in librum Aristotelis Peri Hermeneias. Edited by Carolus Meiser. Leipzig: Teubner, 1877, 1880. 2 parts.

Analytica priora translatio Boethii (recensiones duae). Edited by Laurentius Minio-Paluello. *Aristoteles Latinus,* 3:1–4. Bruges: De Brouwer, 1962, pp. 1–139, 143–91.

Topica translatio Boethii. Edited by Laurentius Minio-Paluello, with B. G. Dod. *Aristoteles Latinus,* 5:1–3. Brussels: De Brouwer, 1969, pp. 1–179.

De sophisticis Elenchis translatio Boethii. Edited by Bernardus G. Dod. *Aristoteles Latinus,* 6:1–3. Brussels: De Brouwer, 1975, pp. 1–60.

A. M. Severino Boezio, De hypotheticis syllogismis. Edited and translated by Luca Obertello. Brescia: Paideia, 1969.

Boezio, Trattato sulla divisione. Translated by Lorenzo Pozzi. Studium Sapientiae. Padua: Liviana, 1969. Italian translation with Latin original of 1492 Venice edition.

Boethius's De topicis differentiis. Translated by Eleonore Stump. Ithaca: Cornell University Press, 1978. Based on text in Patrologia Latina.

Boethius. The Theological Tractates. Edited and translated by H. F. Stewart and E. K. Rand. *The Consolation of Philosophy.* Edition and translation of "I. T." (1609) revised by H. F. Stewart. Loeb Classical Library, 74. Cambridge: Harvard University Press, 1918.

Anicii Manlii Severini Boetii Philosophiae consolationis libri quinque. Edited by Rudolfus Peiper. Bibliotheca Scriptorum Graecorum et Romanorum Teubneriana. Leipzig: Teubner, 1871.

Anicii Manlii Severini Boethii philosophiae consolationis libri quinque. Edited by Guilelmus Weinberger. Corpus Scriptorum Ecclesiasticorum Latinorum, 67. Leipzig: Akademische Verlags., 1934.

Anicii Manlii Severini Boethii Philosophiae consolatio. Edited by Ludovicus Bieler. Corpus Christianorum, Series Latina, 94. *Boethius, Opera,* 1. Turnholt: Brepols. 1957.

Boethius. The Consolation of Philosophy. Translated by Richard Green. Library of Liberal Arts. Indianapolis: Bobbs-Merrill, 1962.

Boethius. The Consolation of Philosophy. Translated by V. E. Watts. Baltimore: Penguin Books, 1969.

SECONDARY SOURCES

1. General Studies

Barrett, Helen M. *Boethius. Some Aspects of His Times and Works.* Cambridge, Eng., 1940; reprint ed., New York: Russell & Russell, 1965. Largely derivative, rather outdated.

Campenhausen, Hans von. "Boethius." In *The Fathers of the Latin Church.* Translated by Manfred Hoffman. London: Adam & Charles Black, 1964, pp. 277–313. Good sketch of life, works, and influence.

Collins, James. "Progress and Problems in the Reassessment of Boethius." *Modern Schoolman* 23 (1945):1–23. Summary of Boethius's achievement in the different areas; review of various issues.

Courcelle, Pierre. "The East to the Rescue of Pagan Culture: Boethius." In *Late Latin Writers and Their Greek Sources.* Translated by H. E. Wedeck. Cambridge, Mass.: Harvard University Press, 1969, pp. 273–330. Especially on Boethius's scientific and philosophical works in relation to Greek tradition.

Crocco, Antonio. *Introduzione a Boezio.* 2d ed. Naples: Liguori, 1975. Good introduction to Boethius's thought, focusing on logical works and *Consolation.*

De Vogel, C. J. "Boethiana." *Vivarium* 9 (1971):49–66; 10 (1972):1–40. Discussion focusing on Boethius's education in Greek culture and on relationship of pagan and Christian elements in the *Consolation.*

Lewis, C. S. "Boethius." In *The Discarded Image. An Introduction to Medieval and Renaissance Literature.* Cambridge: At the University Press, 1964, pp. 75–90. Introductory sketch, mainly on Boethius's Christianity.

Obertello, Luca. *Severino Boezio, I–II.* Genoa: Accademia Ligure di Scienze e Lettere, 1974. 2 vols. Full, though verbose, analysis of issues, focusing on thought rather than on works; volume 2 contains useful annotated bibliography to 1970.

Rand, Edward K. "Boethius, the First of the Scholastics." In *Founders of the Middle Ages.* Cambridge, Mass., 1928; reprint ed., New York: Dover, 1957, pp. 135–80. Excellent introductory study of man, his ideas, and nature of his work.

Stewart, Hugh F. *Boethius: An Essay.* Edinburgh: Blackwood, 1891. By and large outdated.

2. Life and Death

Bark, William. "The Legend of Boethius' Martyrdom." *Speculum* 21 (1946):312–17. On the legend of Boethius as martyr.

————. "Theodoric vs. Boethius: Vindication and Apology." *American Historical Review* 49 (1944):410–26. On Boethius's relationship to political events and theological issues during his last years.

Coster, Charles H. "The Fall of Boethius: His Character." *Annuaire de l'Institut de Philologie et d'Histoire Orientales et Slaves* 12 (1952); *Mélanges Henri Grégoire* 4 (Brussels, 1953):45–81. Reconsideration of details of Boethius's fall and death.

3. Mathematical and Musical Writings

Bower, Calvin. "Boethius and Nicomachus: An Essay Concerning the Sources of *De institutione musica.*" *Vivarium* 16 (1978):1–45. On Boethius's use of sources in his mathematical works, especially his *Music.*

Chamberlain, David. S. "Philosophy of Music in the *Consolation* of Boethius." *Speculum* 45 (1970):80–97. On Boethius's classification of music in his *Music* and its relevance to the *Consolation.*

Pizzani, Ubaldo. "Studi sulle fonti del *De Institutione Musica* di Boezio." *Sacris Erudiri* 16 (1965):5–164. Source study with emphasis on Boethius's method of using his material.

Potiron, Henri. *Boèce, théoricien de la musique grecque.* Travaux de l'Institut Catholique de Paris, 9. Paris: Bloud & Gay, 1961. Especially concerned with Boethius's originality in using his sources to create a new work.

4. Logical and Rhetorical Writings

De Rijk, L. M. "On the Chronology of Boethius' Works of Logic." *Vivarium* 2 (1964):1–49, 125–61. Detailed examination of relationships among logical works.

Minio-Paluello, Lorenzo. "Les traductions et les commentaires aristotéliciens de Boèce." *Studia Patristica,* 2:2. Texte und Untersuchungen, 64. Berlin: Akademie-Verlag, 1957, pp. 358–67. Survey of Boethius's writings on Aristotle's logic.

Shiel, James. "Boethius' Commentaries on Aristotle." *Mediaeval and Renaissance Studies* 4 (1958):217–44. Examination of Boethius's logical works as translations of marginalia in copy of *Organon.*

Stump, Eleonore. "Boethius's Works on the Topics." *Vivarium* 12 (1974):77–93. On originality of Boethius's treatises on the topics.

5. Theological Tractates

Bark, William. "Boethius' Fourth Tractate, the So-Called *De fide catholica.*" *Harvard Theological Review* 39 (1946):55–69. On work in relation to theological controversies, and on Boethius's authorship.

Rapisarda, Emanuele. *La crisi spirituale di Boezio.* Florence: La Nuova Italia, 1947. Especially concerned with Christian doctrine as seen in *opuscula sacra* and *Consolation.*

Schurr, Viktor. *Die Trinitätslehre des Boethius im Lichte der 'Skythischen Kontroversen.'* Forschungen zur Christlichen Literatur- und Dogmengeschichte. 18.1. Paderborn: Schöningh, 1935. On relationship of *opuscula sacra* to theological controversies, especially Trinitarian, of time.

6. *Consolation of Philosophy*

De Vogel, C. J. "The Problem of Philosophy and Christian Faith in Boethius' *Consolatio.*" *Romanitas et Christianitas: Studia Iano Henrico Waszink.* Edited by W. den Boer et. al. Amsterdam: North-Holland, 1973, pp. 357–70. Examination of pagan and Christian elements and Boethius's unconscious syncretism of them.

Duclow, Donald F. "Perspective and Therapy in Boethius's *Consolation of Philosophy.*" *Journal of Medicine and Philosophy* 4 (1979):334–43. On correlation between healing of the narrator and his developing philosophical insight.

Gruber, Joachim. *Kommentar zu Boethius De Consolatione Philosophiae.* Texte und Kommentare, 9. Berlin: De Gruyter, 1978. Introductory survey, especially of literary tradition, followed by extensive textual commentary.

Patch, Howard R. "Fate in Boethius and the Neoplatonists." *Speculum* 4(1929):62–72. On relation of ideas in Book 5 to Neoplatonic concepts, especially those of Proclus.

———. "Necessity in Boethius and the Neoplatonists." *Speculum* 10 (1935):393–404. On relation of discussion in Book 5 to Neoplatonic writings.

Reichenberger, Kurt. *Untersuchungen zur literarischen Stellung der Consolatio Philosophiae.* Romanistische Arbeiten, 3. Cologne, 1954. On traditional elements, especially of rhetoric, in poems and prose.

Scarry, Elaine. "The Well-Rounded Sphere: The Metaphysical Structure of *The Consolation of Philosophy.*" In *Essays in the Numerical Criticism of Medieval Literature.* Edited by Caroline D. Eckhardt. Lewisburg, Pa.: Bucknell University Press, 1980, pp. 91–140.

Though appearing too late for me to use, this is a stimulating structural analysis.

Scheible, Helga. *Die Gedichte in der Consolatio Philosophiae des Boethius.* Bibliothek der Klassischen Altertumswissenschaften, 46. Heidelberg: Carl Winter, 1972. Full study of the poems, especially in relation to the philosophical system of the *Consolation.*

Silk, Edmund T. "Boethius' *Consolatio philosophiae* as a Sequel to Augustine's Dialogues and *Soliloquia.*" *Harvard Theological Review* 32 (1939):19–39. On resemblances between Augustine's works and the *Consolation.*

Wiltshire, Susan F. "Boethius and the *Summum Bonum.*" *Classical Journal* 67 (1972):216–20. Discussion of Boethius's idea of the highest good and its structural significance in Book 3.

7. Influence

Courcelle, Pierre. *La Consolation de Philosophie dans la tradition littéraire. Antécédents et postérité de Boèce.* Paris: Etudes Augustiniennes, 1967. Full study of traditions behind the *Consolation* and of its subsequent interpretation and influence.

Dwyer, Richard A. *Boethian Fictions. Narratives in the Medieval French Versions of the Consolatio Philosophiae.* Cambridge, Mass.: Mediaeval Academy of America, 1976. Useful for understanding medieval applications of the *Consolation.*

Patch, Howard R. *The Tradition of Boethius. A Study of His Importance in Medieval Culture.* New York: Oxford University Press, 1935. General survey of influence on the Middle Ages, including translations and imitations.

Index